MICROCOMPUTERS IN THE SCHOOLS

DATE DUE			

Microcomputers in the Schools

Edited by James L. Thomas

 ORYX PRESS
1981

The rare Arabian Oryx is believed to have inspired the myth of the unicorn. This desert antelope became virtually extinct in the early 1960s. At that time several groups of international conservationists arranged to have 9 animals sent to the Phoenix Zoo to be the nucleus of a captive breeding herd. Today the Oryx population is nearing 300 and herds have been returned to reserves in Israel, Jordan, and Oman.

Copyright © 1981 by
The Oryx Press
2214 North Central at Encanto
Phoenix, Arizona 85004

Published simultaneously in Canada

Printed and Bound in the United States of America

Library of Congress Cataloging Publication Data
Main entry under title:

Microcomputers in the schools.

    Includes bibliographies and index.
     1. Education—Data processing—Addresses, essays, lectures. 2. Computer-assisted instruction—Addresses, essays, lectures. 3. Microcomputers—Addresses, essays, lectures. I. Thomas, James L., 1945–
LB1028.43.M53   370'.28'52   81-14087
ISBN 0-89774-001-7   AACR2

For
R2-D2
and other computerized influences
of childhood

Table of Contents

Preface

During the past few years, almost every journal for educators has published articles concerning the use of microcomputers in elementary and secondary education. Readers who attempt to keep abreast of current developments in this area must find it difficult at times to sort out the flood of information. Realizing this problem, the editor has, therefore, chosen articles written by authors who have clearly identified their intent, have expressed their purpose(s) in a logical, well-developed framework, and have documented their claims either by references to authorities in the field or by showing ways practitioners are currently using this technology in the schools.

The purpose of this compilation is to show how microcomputers are being used and what their potential might be for teachers, administrators, and media specialists in the public school setting. Articles have been selected to serve the informational needs of the beginner as well as the more sophisticated reader.

The work begins with a state-of-the-art report and is followed by four main sections: considerations in selection, hardware and software development, applications in the curriculum, and trends and issues for future development. The appendices contain a glossary of terms, a resource guide, funding sources, a national report of student use of computers in schools, and a list of organizations that supply information on micros and computer literacy. An extensive bibliography provides further references.

In any compilation there is bound to be some overlap of information; however, there has been a concerted effort to keep this to a minimum. In addition to meeting with a number of experts in the field, the editor also searched ERIC (Educational Resources Information Center), ECER (Exceptional Child Education Resources), GPO *Monthly Catalog* (Monthly Catalog of United States Government Publications), INSPEC (Science Abstracts) files, *Library Literature* and *Education Index* for information directly related to the topic.

James L. Thomas

Introduction

The recent emergence of the microcomputer has removed cost as the primary obstacle to widespread use of computers for instruction. Some optimists regard the microcomputer as a panacea, while others contend it is just another fad. The cynics may be right, but this phenomenon is impossible to ignore. A recent report in *Business Week* indicates that "More computers have been installed in classrooms during the past 18 months than in the entire preceding decade. And the total continues to skyrocket."[1]

This state-of-the-art report examines current developments in the instructional use of microcomputers and presents some of the implementation considerations that should be taken into account when using them.

MICROCOMPUTER TECHNOLOGY

The use of microcomputers in education has been a rather recent development. Only since 1978 have microcomputers been extensively marketed to the business and education communities. Despite the slow start, most experts predict that use of microcomputers will increase dramatically in the next few years. The impact of the microcomputer has been called the Second Industrial Revolution—human brain power is being multiplied in the same manner that machines multiplied muscle power 100 years ago.[2]

Recent curiosity about computers has prompted some confusion about terminology. A microcomputer is a stand-alone device with binary data processing capability up to 64,000 bytes (64K). Most systems include peripherals such as disk drives, monitors, and printers. "Micro," "mini," and "mainframe" are terms that denote the relative size of the processing architecture of a computer. While some definitions are delineated on the basis of bit size, price seems to be the best defining characteristic. Most experts would agree that microcomputers are those machines which fall within the $200–$6,000 range. With present-day advances in electronics and data processing, the smallest microcomputers can easily perform most of the same instructions as the largest mainframes. The basic differences between the maxi and micro are speed of execution and the maximum amount of data that can be stored at one time.

The main advantages of microcomputers are affordability, transportability, and dedicated use. Their cost is decreasing each year while their capability is increasing. Because micros are free from a mainframe system, many communications-related problems are eliminated. With the ever-increasing costs attached to phone lines, this factor is significant. The opportunity for dedicated use is an advantage because it contributes to cost effectiveness, especially for the small user. Unlike a large computer, the micro can be used for a single purpose. Large systems that are used for a variety of data processing tasks often restrict the user's access to a mainframe system.

There is no doubt about the micro's potential for affecting educational change, but the technology is still so new that it is difficult to determine what kinds of developments will take place in the next two to five years. There are approximately 70 computer companies producing microcomputers. These companies are emerging and faltering overnight. Some predict that within a few years most of these companies will go out of business. It is possible that only five may survive. This factor alone makes the manufacturer's longevity an important consideration.

COST/TECHNOLOGY CONSIDERATIONS

Computer assisted instruction (CAI) has already proven itself effective in improving student achievement. Significant gains have been documented, particularly at the elementary and junior high levels.[3] Research has shown that CAI can be used successfully to assist learners in attaining specific instructional objectives.

Also, studies have indicated that computer use accounts for a substantial savings in time required for learning. One recent review of research reports that conventional instruction takes about 20 percent longer than computer based instruction.[4] Even though the research results are positive, most school districts have found computer instruction cost prohibitive.

Few companies have been interested in providing CAI. Computer Curriculum Corporation (CCC) has dominated the field for several years. Most of the computer mainframe manufacturers who ventured into this market (e.g., Hewlett Packard, Olivetti, IBM) have lost money. The only major company left is Control Data Corporation (CDC), which is still plunging ahead in its effort to market PLATO, a structurally sophisticated system that has proven to motivate students. Unfortunately, CDC has not been successful in promoting PLATO in the public schools. Because the cost is still extremely high, perhaps prohibitively so for most school systems, only eight school districts in the entire nation are using PLATO. After seven years of operation, the educational division of CDC is still running in the red.[5]

Despite these problems, according to a recent WICAT (World Institute for Computer Assisted Teaching) report, computers will revolutionize education. Labor costs (teachers' salaries) are going up while technology costs are decreasing at a phenomenal rate. This trend will continue, since semiconductor manufacturers are able to place more and more electronic components (transistors, resistors, capacitors, and diodes) on a small one-fourth inch piece of silicon. Every year since 1960, the number of electronic components that can be placed on a single piece of silicon has doubled. The economic implication of this doubling process is that the price remains relatively constant after the technology of a new doubling has been mastered.[6] By the mid-1980s, powerful computers, with up to a million bits of memory, will be put on one chip costing less than $100.

It seems hard to believe that the first microcomputer was made in 1975. By 1982, it is projected that one microchip will be able to remember and recall about a quarter-million bits of basic units of computer information. The number of logic, or decision-making, computer circuits on a chip climbed to roughly 25,000 by mid-1980 and will increase to 250,000 by 1987. By the year 2000, a single chip will have more computing power than systems installed today at most corporations.[7]

Similar to the cost of a calculator, the cost of the microcomputer will come down dramatically while its capabilities steadily increase. It is important to note that just a few years ago the simplest electronic calculator

sold for several hundred dollars. Today, a basic calculator can be bought for less than $10. It seems likely that the personal computer will follow the same pattern. For less than $1,000, one can now purchase a version of a computer that would have cost more than $25,000 one decade ago. This system would include a microprocessor, cathode ray tube, keyboard, cassette player, and BASIC language and floppy disk capability. Low-cost microcomputers have already profoundly affected the economics of CAI. As of 1979 Radio Shack, for example, has a computer, keyboard, cathode ray tube, and cassette tape interface available for $600.[8]

CURRENT MICROCOMPUTER DEVELOPMENTS IN EDUCATION

Many organizations are pursuing the educational market with interest and vigor, as indicated by these recent developments:

- Apple Computer, Inc. (Cupertino, California) has developed a microcomputer that is widely used in education. Apple II, noted for its color graphics, has a built-in keyboard that includes video display circuits, microprocessor, power supply, and memory integrated circuits on a single printed circuit board. The company has demonstrated its interest in the education market by donating computer equipment to a nonprofit foundation that promotes the use of computers in education.

- Bell & Howell Company (Chicago, Illinois) is distributing a special classroom version of the Apple II microcomputer. According to Richard Fowkes, president of the company's Audio-Visual Products Division, "Education is clearly moving to more self-paced instruction. The microcomputer is the audio-visual device of the 1980s." Bell & Howell has developed two courseware authoring packages (GENIS and PASS) that allow a person without programming skills to develop CAI courseware.

- Tandy Corporation/Radio Shack (Fort Worth, Texas), which markets the TRS-80 microcomputer, has sent out packets of promotional literature to every school district in the country. Free classes in computer programming for teachers are offered by many dealers. Radio Shack, unlike many other computer companies, coordinates the development of its own courseware.

- Minnesota Educational Computing Consortium (Lauderdale, Minnesota) signed a contract with Apple Computer, Inc. in January 1979. MECC has already purchased 2,000 micros for Minnesota schools. This organization leads the nation in making the transition from a mainframe to a micro delivery system for computer assisted instruction.[9] A great deal of courseware has been developed for the Apple, which MECC has been selling to other institutions.

- Control Data (Minneapolis, Minnesota) recently set up a microcomputer division. The company is investigating the possible adaptation of its PLATO courseware to microcomputers. (Rental costs for a single PLATO terminal still run about $1,100 per month. At this price, one can buy one Apple II microcomputer per month for the cost of renting a PLATO terminal for an entire year.)
- Commodore Business Machine's (Morristown, New Jersey) microcomputer was originally promoted to school people through a special "three for the price of two" sale. With this incentive, many educators bought microcomputers. The recent introduction of the VIC-20 for $299 gives Commodore a competitive edge on the cost spectrum.[10]
- Borg Warner (Arlington Heights, Illinois) has developed several comprehensive programs for the Apple II in the areas of critical reading and language arts.
- Scholastic Publishers (New York, New York) will publish the first computer technology periodical intended for classroom teachers. The first issue of *Electronic Learning* is scheduled for September 1981.
- Telesensory Systems, Inc. (Palo Alto, California) has developed some innovative computer applications for the handicapped. Telesensory's game center consists of eight micro games for the visually impaired. Oscillating tones replace the screen markings for contests such as paddle ball, and synthesized speech is used for games such as tic-tac-toe, blackjack, and skeet shoot.
- Xerox Research Center (Palo Alto, California) is presently developing a notebook-sized microcomputer. Its language (SMALLTALK—a new type of language dealing with parallel messages) will allow children and inexperienced adults to write their own computer programs.
- Region IV Education Service Center (Houston, Texas) awarded a bid to Bell & Howell for 600 Apple II microcomputers in June 1980. This service agency provides a wide array of instructional computing services to 54 school districts in Texas.
- Utah State University (Logan, Utah) is piloting the use of a videodisc microcomputer system in teaching mentally retarded children. The videodisc—a shiny, silver-colored disk that looks much like a record— has feedback response capabilities coupled with the motivational power of television.
- WICAT (Orem, Utah) has undertaken development of a reading program which will be delivered via microprocessor and is written in BASIC language.
- Prescription Learning (Chicago, Illinois) has developed software in both elementary reading and math. The programs already developed are primarily used with students who qualify for compensatory education.
- Milliken (St. Louis, Missouri) was the first company to launch full-scale production of microcomputer software. Milliken's math (K-8) and language arts (K-3) curricula operate on the Apple, PET, and TRS-80.
- Texas Instruments (Dallas, Texas) announced its new microcomputer (TI 99/4) in June 1979. TI, the only company thus far to master voice synthesis economically, has introduced devices such as the "Speak and Spell" and "Speak and Read," educational toys that feature a 200-word vocabulary stored on a solid state memory chip. Each device is currently marketed for about $75.
- Science Research Associates (Chicago, Illinois) is marketing its courseware on the Atari microcomputer. A recent promotional arrangement with Apple, Inc. provides for the inclusion of SRA's computer literacy courseware in an "Apple Seed" kit.

PRESENT MICRO USE IN PUBLIC SCHOOLS

Interest in microcomputers is steadily increasing. Educators who have had experience with timesharing systems are finding the microcomputer particularly appealing. Microcomputers are viewed as solving some of the common problems experienced with large-scale computers: (1) high cost of timesharing equipment, (2) complex installation requirements, (3) lack of local control over computing resources, and (4) escalating telecommunication costs. The microcomputer, though it lacks the sophistication of the larger systems, is perceived by many as a solution to the drawbacks of a larger timeshare system.

There is some evidence to suggest that schools are accepting the use of microcomputers before the resources are available to support their use. Many districts are purchasing the hardware with enthusiasm only to discover, after they buy their computer, that little educational software exists. At the present time, there is more educational software available for the Apple, Radio Shack, and Commodore machines. However, the available offerings for the Texas Instruments and Atari microcomputers are very limited. Also, another problem is maintenance and repair support. Service provided for the equipment is very limited. Some schools have had to return computers to the factory for repair. Lack of instructional software, however, has not been a significant deterrent. Some administrators believe that their students need exposure to computers even though the courseware offerings are limited. Only two commercial companies (Milliken and Science Research Associates) have developed any extensive programming for a computer assisted instruction curriculum. Most schools are using their microcomputers to teach computer programming (BASIC). Elementary schools are using them to provide simulations and drill and practice instruction, mostly in math. A few schools are using microcomputers for test scoring and classroom management. Computer literacy is being emphasized, but not as much as is needed for students and teachers to gain competency.

HARDWARE

The most significant advantages of the microcomputer are its color, graphics, and audio capability. The possibilities for computer based instruction are dramatically enhanced when various colors and pictures can be displayed on the screen. There remains little doubt that computer assisted instruction motivates students; the addition of color, graphics, and sound should only serve to increase the likelihood of learning.

Dependability is one of the biggest considerations to be made when procuring hardware. If there is a breakdown, prompt service must be readily available. Currently, schools must depend on their retail dealers, not all of whom provide maintenance and repair service. Service requirements also vary. Dealing with various service companies for maintenance of the machines can be a time-consuming ordeal for the school administrator.

The need for peripheral devices varies with the application. Some vendors provide for many additional hardware features while others do not. Printers are more likely to be used as adjuncts than as sole output devices, because of their high cost.

Standardization is important because the software programs available for the various microcomputers are not transportable. This means that programs written for the TI 99/4 will not operate on an Apple II and vice versa. Many districts are purchasing micros from different vendors without realizing that their hardware assortment limits flexibility in using the machines. Peripherals can be added to most personal microcomputers, but there is very little compatibility between products made by different companies.

Memory capacity is one of the more important hardware considerations for computer assisted instruction. Random access memory (RAM) is not adequate for mass program storage. This memory limitation means that most CAI programs require one or more disk drives, which usually cost about $500 each. Cartridges are even more expensive, but impossible to modify. Tape, although less expensive, is slow and unreliable. With the increasing cost of semiconductor RAMs, there will probably be less need for disk drives in the next two to three years. Fortunately, this development will reduce the need for saving memory space through painstaking programming methods.

The new bubble memory, a high-storage chip with tiny areas of magnetization, will dramatically increase the micro's capacity to a million or more bits. Bubbles will be much cheaper and smaller than disk memories. And, unlike RAMs, they will retain information permanently without requiring a continuous flow of electrical current.

Since distributing and sharing microcomputer software can be handled through a centralized computer system, it is important that microcomputers be able to communicate through standard modems to a host machine. A California-based company, NESTAR, has conducted pioneer work in this kind of networking.[11] The compatibility of various types of hardware is particularly critical to a computing consortium, since networking can facilitate the sharing of programs between different types of machines. In the NESTAR system a ''queen'' PET microcomputer controls access to a dual eight-inch floppy disk and to a printer. Several microcomputers can be added via a cluster bus as long as the mixture of Apples, PETs or TRS-80s does not exceed 15.

Sophisticated networks will undoubtedly expand the use of computers in education. Touch-sensitive screens, light pens, bubble memories, videodisc interfaces, and random audio devices will enhance the performance capabilities of the microcomputer. Most experts agree that hardware development is considerably ahead of software development and implementation. Though costs are expected to plummet, this price decrease will not be a significant factor unless there is enough software available to run on the hardware.

SOFTWARE

The need for micro software is becoming more critical as the number of machines in the marketplace proliferates. Both system software and applications software are needed by educators. System software consists of all the programs, languages, and documentation supplied by the manufacturer with the computer. Applications software refers to those programs employed by the user to perform some specific function; these may be in a computer managed math program, a word processing system, or a physics simulation.

Most microcomputers use the BASIC language, and manuals teaching BASIC accompany micros. Other sophisticated languages (e.g., FORTRAN, PILOT, Pascal) can also be taught on most microcomputers. Many buyers are deluded into thinking that they can easily learn to write programs of their own. Actually, it takes an experienced programmer to write most computer assisted and computer managed programs. Courseware development for computer based instruction demands a sophisticated background and sufficient development time.[12] Good software requires long and detailed instructions, which means that most users must procure, rather than develop, their programs.

More and more publishers are beginning to produce software for microcomputers. Production of high quality programs is expensive. Estimates vary, but the average cost of one instructional hour of courseware is $10,000.[13] Buyers are usually disappointed to find out that applications software at the elementary and secondary levels is a limited commodity. Over the past six months, however, there has been a steady growth in commercial programs with significant educational value. Although most educators who have purchased microcomputers have had a limited ability to find operable software, this trend should change and the consumer should see more programs becoming available.

Moreover, users often do not know what is available to run on their machines. Information about software availability has not been gathered into any single publication. Although most of the companies are now beginning to publish software catalogs, few compendiums list courseware available for all the major microcomputers.

Some computing organizations, such as the Region IV Education Service Center in Houston, Texas and the Minnesota Educational Computing Consortium in Lauderdale, Minnesota, have addressed this problem of limited software by transferring some of the programs stored on their large mainframes to microcomputers. This transfer mechanism, referred to as "off-loading," involves electronically moving computer programs and data files between their timeshare system and a microcomputer. Off-loading can be accomplished in two directions: "down-loading" transfers programs from the host computer to the microcomputer and "uploading" transfers the program from the microcomputer to the timeshare system.[14] But, unfortunately, the transfer time is too lengthy to be practical.

School users must have ready access to information about available courseware. Every school district does not need to conduct time-consuming research to find out about existing programs. The Northwest Regional Laboratory in Portland, Oregon recently received funding to set up a software clearinghouse for educational use. Several institutional members evaluate courseware according to the MicroSIFT criteria. Program reviews are exchanged by the network members. These reviews will eventually be published by the Northwest Lab.

Information sources about software are extremely limited. Many programs are not well documented. Currently, there are five major sources:

1. Hardware manufacturers—Naturally companies are interested in software that runs on their machines, but few have undertaken development of their own educational programs. Instead, companies like Apple and Texas Instruments have secured courseware by contract or through a royalty arrangement.

2. Commercial software development companies—About 300 small companies are now developing software for the microcomputer. At a recent computing conference at Harvard (November 1980), some large publishing companies (e.g., SRA, Ginn, McGraw-Hill, Houghton Mifflin) sent representatives to share their micro developments. Few were willing to make any public commitments about long-range plans.

3. Individual school districts and service agencies—Several school districts in Texas, New York, Pennsylvania, California, and Minnesota have made significant contributions in developing programs. The problem with much of this software, however, is that it is often developed around local curricula. The Minnesota Educational Computing Consortium and the Region IV Education Service Center in Houston are two service agencies which provide a wide array of microcomputer services to local school districts.

4. User's clubs and exchanges—These groups publish newsletters which contain operating hints and tips for particular machines. Documentation for software is also provided.

5. Courseware reviews—Several periodicals, such as *Infoworld, The Computing Teacher* and *Creative Computing,* publish courseware reviews on a regular basis. In addition, *Robert Pursor's Magazine* and *Dresden's Microware* provide program critiques on a quarterly basis.

Thus far, the paucity of programs has been emphasized. However, the lack of quality also remains a problem. Most of the computer curricula developed for the micro are "canned" versions of conventional instructional methods and materials. Too often, developers are creating micro programs which duplicate the ones already operating on minis and mainframes. In other words, the new micro technology which permits color, graphics, and sound has not yet been fully exploited or field-tested for use in computer assisted instruction.

FUTURE TRENDS

Despite the limitations pointed out, the use of microcomputers in the schools is coming. Experts and practitioners report that the microcomputer has already significantly contributed to students' learning. Several trends will further promote the microcomputer's acceptance and use.

Education and training are gradually shifting from a teacher-centered orientation to a student-centered one. The productivity of students, rather than the productivity of teachers, is rapidly becoming the basic focus in evaluating the success and efficiency of instruction. If instruction is to improve, then student productivity and ability must be emphasized. The use and acceptance of computers should flourish in a student-centered learning environment where the individual is emphasized.

Within a few years, microcomputers will be within the economic reach of the average American household and most school budgets.[15] The availability of computer games and toys has already sparked interest in the microcomputer. Not surprisingly, today's students are more computer literate than their parents. As a result of the advancement of this technology, these children will live in a much different world from their parents'. According to a recent estimate, 80 percent of the jobs facing our elementary students in 1990 do not even exist today. By 1985, seven out of ten adults will need to use a computer in their jobs. If these statistics are even half true, then the time to prepare students is now. Learning to write a computer program will become one of the basic literacy skills of the future.

Most educators would agree that life is going to be incalculably changed by the micro technology. Isaac Asimov, a futurist quoted in *Time's* special issue on the computer's impact on society, summed up the issue: "We are reaching the stage where the problems that we must solve are going to become insolvable without computers. I do not fear computers. I fear the lack of them."[16]

Can education survive if educators resist the advent of microcomputers? Probably not, according to Dr. Seymour Papert of MIT, who recently gave this testimony to Congress:

> During the 1980s small, but intensely powerful computers will become as much a part of everyone's life as the TV, telephone, the printed paper and the notebook. Indeed, computers will integrate and supercede the functions of these and other communicational and recreational home technologies. I emphasize: this will happen independently of any decisions by the education community; the driving force lives in industry. This computer presence has a tremendous potential for psychological impact, including improvement of the process of learning. It will affect adults, children and babies in homes, as well as in schools. . . . Every child will have access to computing power. . . .[17]

The application of new technology will probably be the unique challenge of the next generation and will make adaptation to rapid change critical. For the first time in history, students will deal with the world as they have made it, not as they have found it. Future generations will have the technological tools to create societal changes, providing that they have the information and value bases to proceed wisely. Educators will help their students by providing them with the kinds of skills they need to function successfully in a computer based society. Computers can be used to promote those aspects of learning for which they are best suited, freeing teachers to work with students in ways a computer cannot. The potential for improving the quality of life is great.

Patricia Sturdivant

NOTES

1. "School Computers Score at Last," *Business Week* (July 27, 1981): 66–67.

2. Carlo Pastore, "Technical Training Systems Using Microcomputers," (Paper presented at the Conference on Microcomputers in Education and Training, Arlington, VA, May 17–18, 1979).

3. "Computers Are Fun, but Can They Teach?" *Educational Testing Service Report* 25 (4) (Winter 1979).

4. J. A. Kulik, "Effectiveness of Computer Based College Teaching: A Meta-Analysis of Findings," *Review of Educational Research*, in press.

5. "The Micros Take to the Classroom," *Business Week* (June 4, 1979): 104 D–F.

6. "Vast Computing Power Is Seen as More Circuits Squeeze on a Tiny Part," *Wall Street Journal* (April 27, 1979): 1, 30.

7. "The Coming Impact of Microelectronics," *Business Week* (November 10, 1980): 96.

8. *Radio Shack 1979 Catalog* (Fort Worth, TX: Tandy Corporation, 1978), p. 79

9. Kevin Hausmann, "Statewide Educational Computer Systems: The Many Considerations," *Creative Computing* 5 (September 1979): 82–85.

10. Robert W. Baker, "PET-POURRI," *Microcomputing* (April 1981): 10.

11. *Technology Education Research Center (TERC) Newsletter* (January 1979): 28.

12. Kent T. Kehrberg, "Microcomputer Software Development: New Strategies for a New Technology," *Proceedings of the National Computing Conference* (Iowa City, IA, June 25–27, 1979), pp. 343–46.

13. Gerald T. Gleason, "Microcomputers in Education: State-of-the-Art," *Educational Technology* (March 1981): 12.

14. *Microcomputer Report of the Minnesota Educational Computing Consortium* (Lauderdale, MN: MECC Instructional Services Division, 1979), p. 19.

15. "Living: Pushbutton Power," *Time* (February 10, 1978): 48.

16. "The Age of Miracle Chips," *Time* (February 20, 1978): 44.

17. *Computers and the Learning Society: Report.* Subcommittee on Domestic and International Scientific Planning, Analysis, and Cooperation of the Committee on Science and Technology. U.S. House of Representatives, Ninety-fifth Congress, Second Session, June 1978, p. 258.

Contributors

Karen Billings is director of the Microcomputer Resource Center at Teachers College, Columbia University, New York. She is author, with David Moursund, of *Are You Computer Literate?* "Microcomputers in Education: Now and in the Future" is reprinted from *Kilobaud Microcomputing* (June 1980, vol. 6, pp. 100–02). Copyright 1980 by *Kilobaud Microcomputing*. Reprinted by permission.

Dennis Brisson is managing editor for *Kilobaud Microcomputing*. "Making the Grade at Keene High School" is reprinted from *Kilobaud Microcomputing* (June 1980, vol. 6, pp. 108–10). Copyright 1980 by *Kilobaud Microcomputing*. Reprinted by permission.

Geraldine Carlstrom teaches second grade at Lincoln Elementary School in Chisholm, Minnesota. "Operating a Microcomputer Convinced Me—And My Second Graders—To Use It Again . . . And Again . . . " is reprinted from *Teacher* (February 1980, vol. 97, pp. 54–55). Copyright © 1980 by Macmillan Professional Magazines. Used by permission of the Instructor Publications, Inc.

Charles H. Douglas, now deceased, was formerly an associate professor of music at the University of Georgia, Athens. "A Selected Glossary of Terms Useful in Dealing with Computers" is reprinted by permission from *Educational Technology* (October 1979, vol. 19, pp. 56–66).

John S. Edwards is coordinator, Instructional Support Services, Office of Instructional Development, University of Georgia, Athens. "A Selected Glossary of Terms Useful in Dealing with Computers" is reprinted by permission from *Educational Technology* (October 1979, vol. 19, pp. 56–66).

Susan N. Friel is division head of science, Lesley College, Cambridge, Massachusetts. "Computer Literacy Bibliography" is reprinted by permission from *Creative Computing* (September 1980, vol. 6, pp. 92, 94, 9–97). Copyright © 1980 by Creative Computing, 39 East Hanover Avenue, Morris Plains, New Jersey 07950. Sample issue $2.50; 12-issue subscription $20.

Douglas Glover is the owner-operator of The Logical Place, a retail establishment in Tullahoma, Tennessee, catering to the needs of gifted youth. He has degrees and has pursued work in business management and gifted child education at the University of South Alabama, Mobile. "Computers . . . Are All Dinosaurs Dead?" is reprinted from *G/C/T* (September/October 1978, vol. 1, pp. 16–17, 46 –50). Reproduced with permission of *G/C/T*, the world's most popular magazine for parents and teachers of gifted, creative, and talented children. PO Box 66654, Mobile, Alabama 36660.

Larry L. Hatfield is an associate professor of mathematics education at the University of Georgia. "A Case and Techniques for Computers: Using Computers in Middle School Mathematics" is reprinted from the *Arithmetic Teacher* (February 1979, vol. 26, pp. 53–55). Copyright © 1979 by the National Council of Teachers of Mathematics. Used by permission.

Kevin Hausmann is instructional coordinator, Minnesota Educational Computing Consortium, St. Paul, Minnesota. "Statewide Educational Computer Systems: The Many Considerations" is reprinted from *Creative Computing* (September 1979, vol. 5, pp. 82, 84–85). Copyright © 1979 by Creative Computing, 39 East Hanover Avenue, Morris Plains, New Jersey 07950. Sample issue $2.50; 12-issue subscription $20. "Tips on Writing Instructional Software for Microcomputers" is reprinted by permission from the *AEDS Monitor* (vol. 18, nos. 4, 5, 6). Copyright 1979 by Kevin Hausmann.

Gray Horner is principal lecturer, Stranmillis College, Belfast, Ireland. "Micro-Computers and the School

Library'' is reprinted from *The School Librarian* (December 1979, vol. 27, pp. 339–40). Reprinted by permission.

Lee M. Joiner is professor and chairperson, Department of Special Education, Southern Illinois University, Carbondale, Illinois. ''Potentials and Limits of Computers in Schools'' originally appeared in *Educational Leadership* (March 1980, vol. 37, pp. 498–501). Reprinted with permission of the Association for Supervision and Curriculum Development and L. M. Joiner, S. R. Miller and B. J. Silverstein. Copyright © 1980 by the Association for Supervision and Curriculum Development. All rights reserved.

Kent T. Kehrberg is affiliated with the Minnesota Educational Computing Consortium, St. Paul, Minnesota. ''Microcomputer Software Development: New Strategies for a New Technology'' is reprinted from *AEDS Journal* (Fall 1979, vol. 13, pp. 103–10).

Earl J. Keyser, Jr. is an instructional analyst for TIES (Teacher Information and Exchange System) in Minneapolis, Minnesota. ''The Integration of Microcomputers into the Classroom or Now that I've Got It, What Do I Do with It?'' is reprinted from the *AEDS Journal* (Fall 1979, vol. 13, pp. 113–17).

Dan Levin is associate editor of *The Executive Educator* and the *American School Board Journal*. ''Microcomputers: Out of the Toy Chest and into the Classroom'' is reprinted, with permission, from *The Executive Educator* (March 1980, vol. 2, pp. 19–21). Copyright 1980 by *The Executive Educator*. All rights reserved.

David Lubar is associate editor of *Creative Computing*. ''Educational Software'' is reprinted from *Creative Computing* (September 1980, vol. 6, pp. 64, 66, 68, 70, 72; October 1980, vol. 6, pp. 56, 58–60). Copyright © 1980 by Creative Computing, 39 East Hanover Avenue, Morris Plains, New Jersey 07950. Sample issue $2.50; 12-issue subscription $20.

Donald H. McClain is manager of instructional services, Weeg Computing Center, The University of Iowa, Iowa City. ''Selecting Microcomputers for the Classroom'' is reprinted by permission from *AEDS Journal* (Fall 1979, vol. 13, pp. 55–68).

Frederick W. Michael, Jr. is a microcomputer marketing manager in the area of education for Bell & Howell Audio-Visual Products Division. ''Funding

Sources for Microcomputers'' is reprinted fom *Instructional Innovator* (September 1980, vol. 25, pp. 26–28). Reprint permission has been granted by Bell & Howell, 7100 N. McCormick Road, Chicago, Illinois 60645.

Inabeth Miller is librarian to the faculty of education, Harvard University, Graduate School of Education, Monroe C. Gutman Library, Cambridge, Massachusetts. ''The Micros Are Coming'' is reprinted by permission of *Media & Methods* (April 1980, vol. 16, pp. 32–34, 72, 74).

Sidney R. Miller is associate professor, Southern Illinois University, Carbondale, Illinois. ''Potentials and Limits of Computers in Schools'' originally appeared in *Educational Leadership* (March 1980, vol. 37, pp. 498–501). Reprinted with permission of the Association for Supervision and Curriculum Development and L. M. Joiner, S. R. Miller and B. J. Silverstein. Copyright © 1980 by the Association for Supervision and Curriculum Development. All rights reserved.

Stuart D. Milner is an education specialist at the National Training Center, Internal Revenue Service, Arlington, Virginia. ''Teaching Teachers about Computers: A Necessity for Education'' is reprinted by permission from *Phi Delta Kappan* (April 1980, vol. 61, pp. 544–46). Copyright © 1980 by Phi Delta Kappan, Inc.

David Moursund is editor of *The Computing Teacher*, Department of Computer and Information Science, University of Oregon. ''Microcomputers Will Not Solve the Computers-In-Education Problem'' is reprinted from *AEDS Journal* (Fall 1979, vol. 13, pp. 31–39).

Ronald E. Nomeland is acting chairman and associate professor of the Department of Educational Technology, Gallaudet College, Washington, DC. ''Some Considerations in Selecting a Microcomputer for School'' is reprinted by permission from *American Annals of the Deaf* (September 1979, vol. 124, pp. 585–93). Copyright by The Conference of Educational Administrators Serving the Deaf, Inc., and the Convention of American Instructors of the Deaf, Inc., 814 Thayer Avenue, Silver Spring, Maryland 20910.

Donald T. Piele is an associate professor of mathematics, University of Wisconsin—Parkside, Kenosha, Wisconsin. ''Micros 'GOTO' School'' is reprinted from *Creative Computing* (September 1979, vol. 5, pp. 132–34). Copyright © 1979 by Creative Computing, 39 East Hanover Avenue, Morris Plains, New Jersey 07950. Sample issue $2.50; 12-issue subscription $20.

"Resources Are Macro for Micros" is reprinted from *Instructional Innovator* (September 1980, vol. 25, pp. 29–30). Reprinted by permission from the Association for Educational Communications & Technology, 1126 Sixteenth Street, NW, Washington, DC 20036.

Nancy Roberts is associate professor in the graduate school of Lesley College, Cambridge, Massachusetts. "Computer Literacy Bibliography" is reprinted by permission from *Creative Computing* (September 1980, vol. 6, pp. 92, 94, 96–97). Copyright © 1980 by Creative Computing, 39 East Hanover Avenue, Morris Plains, New Jersey 07950. Sample issue $2.50; 12-issue subscription $20.

Burton J. Silverstein is researcher, Department of Special Education, Southern Illinois University, Carbondale, Illinois. "Potentials and Limits of Computers in Schools" originally appeared in *Educational Leadership* (March 1980, vol. 37, pp. 498–501). Reprinted with permission of the Association for Supervision and Curriculum Development and L. M. Joiner, S. R. Miller and B. J. Silverstein. Copyright © 1980 by the Association for Supervision and Curriculum Development. All rights reserved.

E. Keith Smelser is director of Personnel and Information Systems, White Bear Lake Public Schools, Minnesota. "MicroComputers: Fad or Function" is reprinted with permission from *AEDS Monitor* (November 1979, vol. 18, p. 27).

Dennis K. Smeltzer is associate dean of Instruction and Learning Resources, Olney Central College, Olney, Illinois. "The Media Specialist and the Computer: An Analysis of a Profession's Attitude Towards a New Technology" is reprinted from *T.H.E. Journal: Technological Horizons in Education* (January 1981, vol. 8, no. 1, pp. 50–53).

Howard B. Spivak is an adjunct assistant professor, Department of Mathematics, Statistics, and Computing in Education, Teachers College, Columbia University, New York. "Classrooms Make Friends with Computers" is reprinted from *Instructor* (March 1980, vol. 89, pp. 84–86). Copyright © 1980 by The Instructor Publications, Inc. Used by permission.

"Student Use of Computers in Schools" was originally prepared by the National Center for Education Statistics, US Department of Education, Jeanette Goor, project director, March 20, 1981. The material is in the public domain.

Patricia Sturdivant is coordinator of computer based instruction for the Region IV Education Service Center in Houston, Texas. The introduction for this text was written by Ms. Sturdivant.

Kathy Tekawa is managing editor of *Interface Age* magazine. "Computers in the Playground: Sesame Place" is reprinted from *Interface Age* (October 1980, vol. 5, pp. 14–15, 120). Copyright © Kathy Tekawa.

F. J. Teskey died early in July 1980. He was librarian for Stranmillis College in Belfast, Ireland and vice-chairman of the School Library Association, 1979–80. "Micro-Computers and the School Library" is reprinted from *The School Librarian* (December 1979, vol. 27, pp. 339–40). Reprinted by permission.

David B. Thomas is associate research scientist, Weeg Computing Center, The University of Iowa, Iowa City. "Selecting Microcomputers for the Classroom" is reprinted by permission from *AEDS Journal* (Fall 1979, vol. 13, pp. 55–68).

Stuart A. Varden is an adjunct assistant professor, Department of Mathematics, Statistics, and Computing in Education, Teachers College, Columbia University, New York. "Classrooms Make Friends with Computers" is reprinted from *Instructor* (March 1980, vol. 89, pp. 84–86). Copyright © 1980 by The Instructor Publications, Inc. Used by permission.

Daniel H. Watt is director, Computer Resource Center, Cambridge, Massachusetts. "Computer Literacy: What Should Schools Be Doing about It?" is reprinted by permission from *Classroom Computer News* (November/December 1980, vol, no. 2, pp. 1, 26–27).

R. Kent Wood is professor and director, Utah State University Videodisc Innovations Project, Department of Instructional Technology, Logan, Utah. "So You Want to Buy a Computer?" is reprinted from *Instructor* (March 1980, vol. 89, p. 86). Copyright © 1980 by The Instructor Publications, Inc. Used by permission.

Robert D. Woolley is director of the curriculum materials center at Utah State University, an instructional development specialist with the instructional development division of the university and assistant professor in the instructional media department. "So You Want to Buy a Computer?" is reprinted from *Instructor* (March 1980, vol. 89, p. 86). Copyright © 1980 by The Instructor Publications, Inc. Used by permission.

Section I
Considerations in Selection

- Questions to be asked before investing in a microcomputer.
- Advantages of microcomputers over other systems.
- Procedures to be used in developing purchasing specifications.
- Capabilities and/or options to be expected from the microcomputer unit.
- Onsite application considerations prior to purchasing.
- Steps to take in planning for statewide support and acquisition of microcomputers.

So You Want to Buy a Computer?

by R. Kent Wood and Robert D. Woolley

Unless you've got $600 or so in your pocket, you probably won't be able to rush out and buy your own computer. But that doesn't mean your case is hopeless. There *are* other ways for you to get your hands on one that won't leave you bankrupt.

Check with your school system to see if there's already a computer available for your use. If not, contact your superintendent's office about the possibility of obtaining grant monies to purchase a system. You should become involved in the selection process, too; but bear in mind that your task won't be an easy one. With such a variety of hardware available, it's difficult to know which system is the right one for you and your school.

Before you set foot in a computer store, think about the following areas and ask yourself these questions:

1. *Audience:* Who will be using the computer? What is the level of sophistication? How many users will be served by the system? What interests and curriculum areas are likely to be represented?
2. *Applications:* Why do you want to purchase a computer? What do you want it to do for you?
3. *Software:* What commercial software is available to meet your needs? Which computers have software you can use? Will you want to create your own programs?
4. *Ease of use:* Is the computer you're considering useable with a minimum of technical skill? Does its design take into consideration human capabilities, limitations, and "kid use"? Can the computer be adapted for multiple uses?
5. *Reliability:* Does the computer have a good reputation with other users? Has it been evaluated favorably in trade literature and other sources? Have you talked to others who use the computer in ways similar to the way you will use one?

6. *Maintenance:* Is local service available? Can local dealers or service centers provide in-depth maintenance? Are service contracts available at a reasonable cost?
7. *Documentation:* Are the owners' manuals designed for those who are unfamiliar with computers? Are personnel available to teach basic use of the computer if necessary?
8. *Computer languages:* What computer languages will you want to use? Does the computer have language flexibility? Is the computer you're considering well suited to simple languages?
9. *Display capabilities:* Can the computer be used with existing school television monitors? Do you want color graphics?
10. *Expandability:* Can the system be expanded in the future with more memory, a voice synthesizer, and music? How much will it cost to expand the system? Is it possible to use the system in conjunction with other systems?
11. *Cost:* Is the computer you're considering cost effective in meeting your needs? Do desired features considerably increase the cost of the system?
12. *Environmental considerations:* Are your school rooms carpeted? (Static charges can damage computer software. Large static charges can render a microcomputer temporarily inoperative.) Is your school in a dry climate? (Ideal humidity for computer operation is 40 percent to 50 percent. If your school is in a dry climate, computers should be placed in uncarpeted areas or protected by anti-static mats.) How many electrical outlets are available for computer use? (Some microcomputers require three or more electrical outlets for operation.)

Once you establish your needs, look for a computer that will meet them. Microcomputers have a lot to offer educators. A school that views computers realistically and doesn't try to make them perform tasks they were not designed to handle will not be disappointed. Although it's difficult to predict what final effect computers will have on our schools, it is evident that they are becoming easier to use and will be performing a wider variety of functions in the near future. Microcomputers are here to stay. And remember: calculators and television sets had their beginnings, too. . . .

Some Considerations in Selecting a Microcomputer for School

by Ronald Nomeland

A review of literature, whether it be professional journals or home periodicals like *Time, Popular Mechanics,* etc., has indicated a technical revolution that is creeping upon us these days—the microcomputer, often known as a personal or home computer. Today's presentation will be focused on the microcomputer, which is a complete system and has applications in education. Let me quote Johnson (1978):

> In terms of effect on education, the advent of computers that ordinary people can afford is the most important and exciting thing that's happened . . . making an analogy with reading and writing, it's like the invention of the printing process. (p. 8)

The chip technology has already transformed our society. It has enabled the price of products such as TV games, digital watches, and calculators to go down. In 1971, a Sharp Electronics pocket calculator sold for $395; today a more sophisticated model sells for $10.95. The pocket calculator has made the slide rule obsolete. Once the world's largest producer of slide rules, Keuffel & Esser Co., stopped producing them in 1972 ("The Computer Society," 1978).

A one-fourth inch square chip, which innocently resembles a railroad switching yard under a microscope, has the computing power of what was known as a room-size computer with hundreds of vacuum tubes. To cite an example, the original IBM 1620 installed at Gallaudet College in 1962 handles 20,000 characters, or 20K bytes, but a desk-top stand-alone microcomputer is now capable of handling as much as 64K bytes of data.

The possibilities, to say the least, are mind-blowing. However,

On the other hand, educational institutions have not been leaders in the use of any kind of technology. They follow the consumer market thrust. The principal way traditional educational institutions are going to be affected by the appearance of computers is a result of the fact that kids, some kids at first, have computers at home, and start coming to school with expectations about what they will find there and what they will be able to do there. (Johnson, 1978, p. 9)

Unfortunately, as another author states it, selecting a home computer is not as easy as using it. For that reason, the goals of this presentation are to provide you with the advantages of having microcomputers in educational settings; furnish assistance in preparing specifications; and offer hints on what to look for. Affectively, the effort is to make you more knowledgeable and feel more confident when dealing with vendors on microcomputers.

In this paper, the definition of a microcomputer is as follows:

A microcomputer consists of five basic and fundamental electronic elements:

(1) a central processing unit (CPU)—a "processor";
(2) single or multiple read-only memories (ROM) for preassembled control program storage;
(3) one or more random access memories (RAM) for data and/or program storage;
(4) an expandable universal input-output (I/O) bus (that is, a connection, path, or circuit for peripheral equipment); and
(5) a computer clock (Sippl, 1977, p. 129).

Throughout the paper the terms microcomputer, micro, or microsystem will be used interchangeably.

SOME ADVANTAGES OF MICROCOMPUTERS OVER STANDARD SYSTEMS

Microcomputers possess unique features which can be considered advantageous to those of standard computer systems. School administrators might be gun shy, especially as far as new technology is concerned. They might get as far as saying that anything that is "fun" is extravagant—and some might consider microcomputers as such. Most kids are fascinated by the popular TV games, most of which have little or no educational value—maybe with the exception of developing psychomotor skills. However, microcomputers are more than TV games. Microcomputers are scaled down versions of large computers, with their own unique features, some of which are available with the large computers, and often at higher costs.

1. *Low cost*. Home computers are being sold for as low as $599 complete, but for schools, a practical micro would cost from $1,000 to $3,000 each.
2. *One-time cost*. Time-sharing and leased communication line costs are eliminated with the one-time cost of purchase of the microcomputers. In many cases the rental costs exceed the price of a microcomputer. For instance, one terminal (including all the available courseware) rents for $1,000 per month, or $12,000 per year. One year's lease can be invested in the purchase of as many as six microsystems.
3. *Portable*. The microcomputers are small and light, thus they are more portable than the leased terminals. Moreover, since the microcomputers are self-contained, they are portable and can be transferred from one classroom to another without relocating the communication lines. I have known of a school which puts its micro on a cart; thus it can be transported to any of the classrooms. In addition, micros are not so sensitive to room temperature variations as a large computer.
4. *Color and graphics*. With the microcomputers it is easy to obtain color and graphics. Of course, no color is available with a black-and-white display. The capabilities of getting certain colors on the screen is within the microcomputer itself which also has the capabilities to display bar graphs and the like. Line drawings would be best done by a graphic digitizer which will be explained later.
5. *Computer support*. When a microcomputer is obtained, you get full computer support within the package. This eliminates the so-called "crash" or unscheduled down time by the central computer which has infuriated many teachers. When the central computer is down, all terminals are down. With four microcomputers in a school, if one is down, the other three will still run, thus affecting a minimum number of users.
6. *Customizing*. The capabilities of a microcomputer can be tailored to your particular needs. Thus, instead of being dictated by a large computer or time-sharing system, the school can take advantage of the flexibility of a micro. The flexibility allows the school to allocate various capabilities to different parts of the school, depending on usage or needs of the particular program.

Some of the advantages of microcomputers are related to today's issues in education. For example, the portability facilitates the relocation of the micro from one school to another should the school population be shifted or a school close because of declining enrollment. The one-time purchase eliminates the long-term expense of leasing computer systems and communication lines. The customizing feature of the micros provides for the school to maintain its own records for accountability studies. Even with the movement of "back to basics," the microcomputers can be useful. Drill and practice materials can be obtained at a low, one-time expense; for example, a price of $7.50 for a cassette or $3 to $7 for a diskette. They can be used by a number of students; thus they are cost effective. Moreover, the courseware can be duplicated.

In response to the ramifications of P.L. 94-142, it will be possible for the schools to keep an accurate track of their special students on a microcomputer. Furthermore, the customizing of the micro, with specialized courseware and attachments, provides a tailored approach for different types of special students. One firm provides an oversized touch-sensitive keyboard, each key measuring 1 inch square, for those afflicted with cerebral palsy. In a residential school setting a student can check out a cassette or diskette and bring it to the dormitory to do his/her homework, be it drill and practice, tutorial, or simulation.

PROCEDURE IN DEVELOPING MICROCOMPUTER SPECIFICATIONS

After you have reviewed the literature and/or gone to one or two conferences on microcomputers, you might be overwhelmed with so many brands and possible options that you do not know where to start. Thus, it is advisable to sit at the drawing board to determine the basic needs and options for your microsystem. The first step will be to:

1. *Define objectives.* What will the system be used for? Who will use it? How will it be used? Why will it be used? Where will it be used? After these have been determined, the next step will be to:

2. *Perform a needs analysis.* In this process first consider (a) a summary of current systems and then (b) a description of the proposed system. While reviewing the current system, that is, if you have access to time-sharing or already own a mini or micro, consider the available computer programs (software), equipment (hardware), and personnel. For example, if you have courseware on your present system, ask yourself what are the new options teachers are looking for, if not satisfied with the present courseware.

After evaluating the current system and personnel you can then describe the proposed system. Do you wish to maintain the time-sharing capabilities? If so, determine what should remain in the central computer and what should be transferred to the micro. Make a list of your (a) immediate needs, and (b) long-term needs. After you have put these down on paper, it is time to attack the most important part of your project which is to:

3. *Develop system specs.* Instead of saying "I will buy Brand X and see what it can do for me," it is crucial that you develop specifications and see what the vendors can do for you. The specs should include the following:

(a) Statement of objectives: You already have them for your preliminary planning. They are useful to vendors; they might help tell you in what manner their system meets your objectives; they might even assist in refining your specs after they know what you are looking for.

(b) Compatibility requirements: If you wish to maintain your present time-sharing system, compatibility requirements should be stated. Compatibility requirements should be listed for interfaces such as keyboard, modems, printers, disk/tape, and other peripheral devices.

(c) Technical requirements: This part covers four areas of concern: software, hardware, communications (district access or else), and peripherals. These will be covered in a subsequent section of the paper.

(d) Cost proposal: This is not required, especially if you can estimate how much your proposed microsystem cost. On the other hand, if you know what your budget allows, it will help to state a proposed cost figure. Doing this will assist the vendors to offer you the most for your cost if your specs turn out to be either too high or low for the stated budget.

(e) Customer assistance: Be sure to include in the specs how the vendor will assist you in: (1) training, (2) documentation, and (3) maintenance. What form of training will be available with the microsystem? How long will the representative be able to assist the school personnel? One day? One week? Will he/she be available on call? Will the representative limit the training to one person or be accessible to several?

In your specs be sure to ask for two copies of documentation to be included with the bid. If a firm sends you only one, drop it from consideration. Many firms operate on a shoestring and are not able to afford to send two copies of documentation; the chances are that the firm is existing on borrowed time. Is the documentation legible? Does it tell you everything? For example, there was a major omission from a certain documentation—it lacked information on the location of the on-off switch on the particular microcomputer. There have been some instances where documentation was mailed several months after the microcomputer was shipped.

In regard to maintenance, a factory warranty policy should be stated. Furthermore, it might be helpful to consider a "maintenance contract" or "service contract," especially if many users have access to the microcomputer. This kind of contract usually costs 8 to 12% of the purchase price annually. For example, if the purchase price is $4,000, the maintenance contract will cost approximately $400 annually; it should include periodic inspection and adjustments. However, at any rate, machines do break down and the availability of emergency maintenance should come into consideration.

4. *Solicit vendor response.* Now that you have completed your specs, you are ready to send out your proposal and wait for responses. The names of many firms can be obtained from the periodicals which are listed in Appendix A.

5. *Evaluate proposed system.* By now you are able to narrow your choice to two, three, or even four. If possible, it will be advisable to discuss further with the vendors of your choice and make further deliberations before you select one.

WHAT CAPABILITIES OR OPTIONS?

This section specifically deals with the microcomputer itself. When you order a new automobile you are confronted with a number of options. Microcomputers like automobiles, start with a stripped-down version, and you can customize it according to your needs. By now, your needs have already been stated, and you can start considering the options for your microcomputer. The chart of capabilities, Appendix B, will be of some assistance as you go through the list of options.

1. *Processor*. The microprocessor is the heart of a microcomputer. Also known as CPU (central processing unit) it contains micro-instruction decode and control, registers, arithmetic unit, and control. These functions are grouped in different ways on chips by different manufacturers which present various characteristics and capabilities such as instruction set, word length, speed, and memory capacity. Some microprocessors are on a single chip; others on multiple chips which are more advantageous. You can select a word length of 4-bit, 8-bit, and 16-bit configuration that are adequate for schools in most cases.

2. *Programming language*. Most microcomputers employ ROM (read only memory) chips to store the control program in a special language. For example, if you want your computer to print out the word HELLO on the display it would take about 20 special machine instructions to do it. However, with the BASIC (Beginner's All-purpose Symbolic Instruction Code) control program you only need to type in: PRINT "HELLO." The ROM, which permanently stores high-level machine code, will spell out HELLO on the display before you can say "Jackie Robinson." BASIC uses the normal math signs, such as +, −, /, and *. The command for two times three is simply PRINT 2*3, and the computer will display a 6 on the screen.

   One source indicates that 80% of the language in microcomputers is BASIC. However, the problem is that there are several versions of BASIC; thus the language in Brand X might not be compatible with that in Brand Y. However, it is possible to edit the program from a microcomputer to be used in another brand microcomputer. Another common language in microcomputers is PILOT, and again, there are two versions of the language for microcomputers. Adherents for BASIC say that it is a simple useful language, but others insist that it uses up a lot of memory space. Gerhold and Kheriaty (1979) advocate the use of COMMON PILOT, claiming that it is truly a CAI (computer-assisted instruction) language.

3. *Memory size*. Most microcomputers come with a minimum of 4K byte RAM (random access memory) which means that they can store up to 4,000

characters that are programmable. Some of them can store up to 48K, 56K, or 64K bytes in one microcomputer. The memory size you will need depends on your applications; for example, drill and practice exercises will need only 4 to 8K bytes, but simulations will require more space, as much as 32K bytes. Please refer to Appendix C for additional information.

4. *Display*. Most microcomputers employ a display which resembles a TV set rather than hard copy (printers). Some firms provide CRT (cathode ray tube) display, others a plasma type display. A modified black-and-white TV monitor is offered as part of a microcomputer package by one firm. Unmodified color TV monitor and color graphic display are also available.

5. *Character set*. Are you satisfied with upper case letters only? Or will both upper and lower case be required for your applications? Not all micros are available in lower case letters. Another consideration concerns the availability of special characters, such as double or triple size characters, musical bars, and characters, etc.

6. *Number of characters per line*. This is another important feature in selecting a microcomputer. The number of characters per line range from 40 to 80. The recommended figure is from 60 to 80 characters per line, but if the application is used only for drill and practice or in an elementary school setting, the 40 characters per line limit might be adequate. Keep in mind that with an average of five letters per word you can insert only six or seven words per line, including spaces, in a 40-character per line format.

7. *Number of lines per display*. Available in 16 to 32 lines of display on a screen. The recommended figure is from 20 to 24 lines; additional lines will result in smaller characters on the screen. Conversely, less than 20 lines on the screen can be annoying; you will not be able to see enough on the display. For example, when you build a list of commands you will not be able to refer back far enough to check what you have finished.

8. *Storage*. Two basic storage systems are (a) cassette, and (b) floppy disk. The cassette system comes with a stripped-down version of a microcomputer. The cassette system might be adequate for drill and practice exercises and some other applications, but it is slower and not as reliable in accessing to data files as a disk storage system. For the money a disk is recommended.

   Mini floppy disks (diskettes) look like a phonograph record except that they have essentially smooth surfaces as opposed to grooves and are 5 inches in diameter. Regular floppy disks are 8 inches in diameter; such a disk can store up to 256K bytes. A single disk drive for a microcomputer will be adequate, but it is suggested that there is at least one microcomputer in each school equipped with a dual disk system for copying purposes or to make spares should the memory stored in the original disk be wiped out due to a malfunction.

9. *Graphics*. What are the capabilities for making graphics on the screen? Some microcomputers do not have any capabilities at all. If it is an important feature, it will be advisable to check on the availability of a graphic digitizer, which facilitates the production of graphics such as maps, line drawings, histogram, etc. While on the topic, it is imperative to consider a high *resolution* capability of the screen. The higher resolution provides for better graphic quality. In other words, with a low resolution you will notice a circle being composed of squares or rectangles all around, but the high resolution will show a nice round line representing a circle. Another important feature is the capability of producing graphics in colors.

10. *Microcomputer as a terminal*. The micro is considered an ''intelligent terminal'' because it is self-contained. However, it can also function as a ''dumb terminal'' if access to a time-sharing system is desired. Not all microcomputers are capable of interfacing with other computers, so if your requirement warrants it, be sure to choose a micro that has the capability.

11. *Additional features* are touch panel or a special keyboard which are not widely available. The touch panel feature could be critically important to the use of the terminal by young children who are not familiar with the keyboard. The special touch-sensitive oversized keyboard could be used by children who lack normal coordination. Another option is a PROM chip on which you can develop your own machine language and store it.

12. *Printer*. The minimum requirement is that each school have at least one printer for a variety of reasons. One such printer is the Centronics P-1 which prints 180 characters per second, prints both upper and lower case as well as in several character sizes. It adds approximately $600 to the cost of the total system. A faster printer, priced at approximately $2,000, produces 300 cps but does not have the flexible character size. Most microcomputer firms include suggested printers in their literature.

13. *Other peripherals*. For long-term planning, but vital to the selection of a compatible microcomputer, you might like to consider other peripherals, such as slide projector, music board, speech synthesizer, random access audio, videotape, and videodisk. Of course, they will add to the price.

14. *Software:* Many firms offer a number of software, also called utility, programs or courseware. The basic software should be included in the basic price. Utility programs might consist of a ''demo'' cassette or disk which demonstrates the capabilities of the system, or such ''canned'' programs as budgets, income taxes, etc. The courseware, as of now, is mostly in games, such as black jack, chess, Star Trek, and others. Instructional courseware is available, but the catchword is *quality*. A number of the so-called courseware have been developed by high school students on a commission basis and then marketed without ever being validated through field testing.

15. *Quality*. Additional qualitative consideration is the reputation of the firm with whom you are dealing. According to Holznagel (1978), there are some 500 firms producing microcomputers now; it is predicted that only 50 will survive in 5 years. Some firms are operating out of home garages.

PRECAUTIONS

First, it is difficult to choose a microcomputer from a wide range available. The attached matrixes will help to determine the best system for your school. In addition, be sure to consider the expansion capabilities of the microsystem in which you are interested. The possibilities are many; for example, you can have several microcomputers interacting with each other.

The attitude of the vendors is to ''let buyer beware.'' Many manufacturers are underfinanced. They advertise products before production; they are here today and might be gone tomorrow. Furthermore, do not pay for the micros until they are delivered.

It should be repeated here that like cars, stripped models lack many important features; so often the extra money invested will return greater dividends.

IN CLOSING

The purpose of this paper was to make you more knowledgeable and confident in selecting a microcomputer whether it be for your school or home. Of course the vendors will allow some silly questions. Assuming the objectives of this paper have been accomplished, the writer would like to say: The future is now! Go ahead and jump in the water!

It was mentioned previously that educational institutions (or rather the persons associated with those institutions) have been remarkably notorious in not being the leaders in the use of technology. Thus, I would like to close my paper by asking those professionals to set aside their biases and think aloud the following statement.

> One out of 10 teachers are literate in computers, but one out of four children are literate in computers. (Berrie, 1978)

REFERENCES

Berrie, P. *Classroom computing—mini vs. micro.* A paper presented at AEDS workshop on "Micro Mini Computers in Education," Des Moines, Iowa, October 19–20, 1978.

Bork, A. Machines for computer-assisted learning. *Educational Technology*, April 1978, pp. 17–20.

Gerhold, G., & Kheriaty, L. *Champagne quality CAI on beer budget.* A paper presented at ADCIS convention, San Diego, California, February 27–March 1, 1979.

Hawkins, W. J. New home computers can change your life style. *Popular Science*, October 1977, pp. 29–36.

Holznagel, D. *Preliminary considerations of microprocessors in the educational environment.* Paper presented at AEDS workshop on "Micro Mini Computers in Education," Des Moines, Iowa, October 19–20, 1978.

Johnson, J. Three views of the future of instructional computing: A conversation with Alfred Bork, Arthur Luehrmann, and Seymour Papert. *Conduit Pipeline*, Summer 1978, pp. 3–11.

Neuman, P. 'Personal' computers undercut the control of DP departments. *Administrative Management*, May 1978.

Sippl, D. J. *Microcomputer handbook.* New York: Petrocelli/Charter, 1977.

The computer society. *Time*, Feb. 20, 1978, pp. 44–59.

APPENDIX A*

Information Sources on Microcomputers

BYTE (Hardware) P.O. Box 590 Martinsville, New Jersey 08836 1 year $15.00 (12 issues)	*Interface Age* (Hardware) 16704 Marquardt Ave. Cerritos, California 90701 1 year $14.00 (12 issues)
Calculators/Computers Dymax (Elem/Secondary Ed) P.O. Box 310 Menlo Park, California 94025 1 year $10.00 (6 issues)	*Kilobaud* (Hardware) Peterborough, New Hampshire 03458 *Mini Micro Systems* P.O. Box 5051 Denver, Colorado 80217 1 year $25.00 (12 issues) Free to qualified individuals
Creative Computing (Software and Hardware) P.O. Box 789-M Morristown, New Jersey 07960 1 year $15.00 (12 issues) (now includes ROM)	*People's Computers* (Software and Hardware) P.O. Box E Menlo Park, California 94025 1 year $10.00 (6 issues)
Dr. Dobbs Journal of Computer Calisthenics and Orthodontia P.O. Box E Menlo Park, California 94025	*Personal Computing* (Software and Hardware) 1050 Commonwealth Avenue Boston, Massachusetts 02215 1 year $14.00 (12 issues)

*Appendix A: Courtesy of D. Thomas and D. McClain.

APPENDIX B*
Microcomputer Options and Capabilities

	PET 2001	PET 8016	APPLE	ATARI 800	TRS-80 MODEL III	TRS-80 COLOR COMPUTER	SORCERER II	TI 99/4	HEATH H 89	TERAK	OHIO SCI C2 - 8P
PROCESSOR	6502	6502	6502	6502	Z80	6809	Z80	TM 9900	Z80	LSI 11	6502
MEMORY MIN/MAX	8/32	16/32	16/64	16/48	4/48	4/16	16/48	16/16	16/64	28/56	4/32
LOWER CASE	Y	Y	OPT	Y	Y		Y	OPT	Y	Y	Y
DISPLAY	Y	Y	NI	NI	Y	NI	NI	NI	Y	Y	NI
CASSETTE OR DISK	C*/D*	C*/D*	C*/D*	C*/D*	C*/D*	C*	C*/D*	C*/D*	D	D	C/D*
GRAPHICS RESOLUTION			192 × 280 40 × 48	192 × 320	48 × 128	192 × 256	240 × 512	132 × 256		240 × 320	256 × 512
TEXT (LINES × CHAR)	25 × 40	25 × 80	24 × 40	24 × 40	16 × 64/32	16 × 32	30 × 64	24 × 32	25 × 80	24 × 80	32 × 64
COMMUNICATIONS	Y	Y	Y	Y	Y	Y	Y	Y	Y	Y	Y
DOCUMENTATION	Y	Y	Y	Y	Y	Y	Y	Y	Y	Y	Y
MULTIPLE LANGUAGES	Y	Y	Y	Y	Y	Y	Y		Y	Y	Y
COURSEWARE	Y	Y	Y	Y	Y	?	MAYBE	SOME		SOME	?
SPECIAL FEATURES	CHAR GRAPHIC	CHAR GRAPHIC	4/15 COLORS	16 COLORS SOUND	INTEGRATED SYSTEM	8 COLORS RS232 I/O PORT	MEMORY CARTRID	16 COLORS	CURSOR ADDR	16 BIT	6 & 9 DIGIT (FAST)
COST (16K SYSTEM)	995	1500	1330	1080	999	599	1295	775	(KIT) 1695	6615	799

NI - Not included   D - Disk   C - Cassette recorder   Y - Yes   OPT - Optional item not usually from manufacturer   *Extra Cost

* Appendix B: Courtesy of D. Thomas and D. McClain.

APPENDIX C*
Microcomputer Requirements per Instructional Type

	Drill Pract	Tutorial	Prob Solving	Program	Simu-lation	Testing	Others
Memory (RAM)	4-8K	16-32K	8K	8K	8-32K	16-32K	16-64K
Lower Case Characters		Y			Y	Y	Y
Cassette and/or Disk	C	D	C	C	D	D	D
Graphics					Y		
Printer		Y		Y			Y
Floating Point Arithmetic			Y	Y			Y
Other Languages				Y			Y
Files		Y			Y	Y	Y
Interface		Y			Y	Y	Y
Number of Lines on Display	12	24	16	24	24	16	24

Y - Yes   C - Cassette   D - Disk

* Appendix C: Courtesy of D. Thomas and D. McClain.

Potentials and Limits of Computers in Schools

by Lee Marvin Joiner, Sidney R. Miller, and Burton J. Silverstein

Both grandiose claims and dire warnings have accompanied the expansion of the role of computers in American education. Providing computer literacy has become an important goal in some secondary schools. Yet many educators still lack a clear understanding of the potential and limits of the computer in the school.

THE COMPUTER AS TEACHER

Computer-assisted instruction (CAI)—the computer as teacher—has been the focus to date of public schools' involvement with the computer revolution. A fundamental rationale is that this technology offers a special capability for individualizing instruction, thereby freeing the student from the rigidity and inflexibility of group instruction.

Commercial vendors have promoted this vision of the electronic classroom by stressing the presumed savings in direct instructional costs. According to some vendors, computer-assisted instruction also answers the question of how to provide instructional equality for students in rural schools where small enrollments limit course offerings. It is also touted as a painless, efficient way to teach basic skills to reluctant learners.

Few educators have the technical sophistication to challenge some of this hyperbole. Awareness of the relative costs, benefits, and limitations of computer-assisted instruction is frequently minimal. Consequently, teachers sometimes assume a defensive posture, fearing they will be replaced by machines. Direct experience reveals that these fears are greatly exaggerated. Successful employment of the computer as teacher depends on many human variables, including the adequacy of the "courseware" design, the "offline" follow-up activities conducted by teachers, the consistency of course objectives with student interest, and the way in which the CAI experience is integrated with the student's instructional and socialization program (Thelen, 1977).

There is also a definite limit to how much time students can profitably spend working with a computer terminal. Some authorities recommend a maximum of 20 to 30 minutes a day. The computer is an intense and demanding teacher. Students generally tire more quickly than they would in group instruction involving changes of pace, wider perceptual fields, and social experiences.

As for efficiency, research suggests that learning time can be compressed with CAI. In a recent review of literature, Thomas (1979) concluded ". . . it is clear from the studies reviewed at all levels, that CAI reduces the time required for a student to complete a unit." Edwards and others (1974) concluded, on the basis of the sparse research available at the time, that long-term retention appeared worse for CAI than for conventional instruction, but Thomas noted that studies reported since then "lean more toward equal retention."

Administrators should note that if the rate of learning were to be accelerated for all learners using CAI, there would certainly be no savings. The way schools now operate, students would cover, and perhaps retain, more material during their schooling, but there would be a need to extend the scope of the curriculum, resulting in increased instructional and material costs. On the other hand, if school systems were to adopt the provisions of California or Florida for early graduation through proficiency testing, they might save some money by adopting CAI.

THE COMPUTER AS MANAGER

Education, like most other sectors of our society, has been deluged by the paperwork of record keeping and documentation. As a result, long before questions about the adequacy and appropriateness of computer teaching are resolved, the computer will be institutionalized in the American school as a management tool.

In education of the handicapped, for example, the individualized educational programs demanded by law consume resources voraciously. In conducting individualized instruction, teachers must maintain detailed records of student performance and match students with instructional resources. These responsibilities force instructional resources to be shifted from direct service to costly clerical functions. Moreover, individual items of information become increasingly difficult to find and interpret as records accumulate.

This in itself has created a vast market for computer manufacturers and a prime job market for computer experts. Control Data Corporation, for example, is hard at work designing computer systems to assist the teacher in maintaining organized and immediately accessible information. The paperless classroom with computer-managed instruction (CMI) " . . . guides each student through a curriculum along a learning path which is designed by the student's instructor, maintaining records of student achievement for use in evaluating the effectiveness of the educational resources" (Control Data Corporation, 1977).

Beyond assisting teachers in the management of instruction, computers have already proven their value in school business management. Purchasing, budgeting, inventories, forms, management, personnel, "compliance" management, and the reporting of data requirements by the government are all part of the educational leadership role. Computers are able to perform management functions in each of these areas.

Until recently most educational applications of computing have involved the use of "time-sharing" systems in which large central computers are linked through a telecommunications network to terminals located in widely distributed schools. There are, however, a number of disadvantages to this system.

First, telecommunications between the school and the central "networked" computer may cost several thousand dollars a year, in addition to membership fees, also amounting to thousands of dollars. Second, what happens at "the other end of the line" is not well understood by school administrators. Often the information produced is not easily understood or useful to school personnel in conducting their daily business.

Third, the computer system down-time and the busy signals encountered during times of high system use, usually during school hours, further promote user disenchantment.

THE NEW WAVE: IN-HOUSE MICROCOMPUTERS

Partly as a result of these drawbacks, microcomputers designed to function on their own or to double as terminals for central processors are drawing increasing attention. One of the reasons for the expanded capability of microcomputer systems and steep declines in equipment costs has been the development of small integrated circuits, originally used in the space program. This advance has permitted an incredible degree of miniaturization with many attendant savings in manufacture and maintenance.

The demonstrated capabilities of microcomputers selling in the $800 to $1,800 range compare favorably with those of large time sharing interactive systems. Courseware is emerging that provides drill and practice, simulations, tutorial instruction, graphic displays, and animation.

The trend toward individualized instruction and precision teaching has also led to the increased use of microcomputers in management of diagnostic and prescriptive information. For example, at St. Thomas District High School in Braddock, Pennsylvania, a microcomputer was used to manage student progress and objectives (Duch, 1979). Kehler (1977) reported the successful use of microcomputers in the teaching of analytic grammar. In another recent application Baker (1978) concluded that the test scoring and psychometric analyses performed by microcomputer were as adequate as the results obtained from larger time-sharing systems.

An appealing feature of microcomputers is the ease of access to hardware they provide for students and the consequent heavy use rate. A statewide survey in 1978 of microcomputer users in Minnesota disclosed that the equipment was used almost constantly during school hours, with students consuming 95 percent of the computer time logged. One reason for the high rate of use is that, being present in the classroom and subject to the control of individual users, the machine comes to be viewed as the tool it is rather than as a mysterious oracle.

Microcomputers are no panacea, however. Despite the increasing availability of courseware from commercial sources such as Micronet TM, schools are likely, at least for the near future, to need to develop capabilities for custom programming of courseware. The Winnipeg school system, for example, spent $36,000 over three years on courseware development for microcomputers and still more development is needed (Sandals, 1979). While the programming language used with microcomputers, BASIC, is relatively easy to learn, it is rare for teachers or principals to possess sufficient programming expertise to allow them to develop their own CAI and CMI programs. This is a serious limitation because one of the presumed advantages of a microcomputer is the capability it offers for tailoring programs specifically to local needs. Where staff programming skills are unavailable, hiring a programmer will be necessary. The Ortonville, Minnesota, school system trained its own high school students as microcomputer programmers to work with teachers in creating courseware suited to their needs (Joiner and Silverstein, 1979).

Another approach to the microcomputer programming problem is to draw upon available courseware and software developed by or for users of the large time sharing systems. In Minnesota, for example, numerous local school districts have access by telephone to programs stored in the Minnesota Educational Computer Consortium's central library of programs. Many of these programs are being converted to microcomputer application by local users. After conversion, the programs are "uploaded": returned to the central library via telephone line for storage and further dissemination.

From a technical standpoint, microcomputers are a long way from perfect. A 1978 survey in Minnesota reported that educators using these systems had found a number of weaknesses, including the lack of computer-assisted instruction languages for microcomputer application; limited ability to perform repetitive calculations and limited ability to store and recall large data files.

Educators should beware of microcomputers sold as "blank slates" that must be programmed from scratch. Although these devices possess the potential to perform instructional and analytic tasks, many hours of technical assistance may be required to create the necessary programs. Mathews (1978) warns that most of today's microcomputers do not have sufficient courseware to make them useful for classroom instruction "off the shelf."

IMPLICATIONS FOR PROFESSIONAL DEVELOPMENT

To realize the full potential of microcomputers, schools should provide either preservice or inservice courses for teachers in computer-assisted instruction, computer-managed instruction, microcomputer programming, and computer applications. This may be easier than it sounds. Once exposed to using computers in their classrooms, teachers tend to become interested in developing skills so they can develop their own student-oriented courseware (Joiner and Silverstein, 1979).

An indirect benefit of involving teachers in the development of courseware is the increased sensitivity they often gain to the organization of information and the learning process. By observing students using microcomputers for instruction, teachers could also detect flaws in existing courseware. The cumulative improvements could benefit not only themselves, but everyone using the system.

COMPARING THE COSTS

Engineering and marketing trends suggest that microcomputer capabilities will increase while costs decrease (Bork, 1978; Sturdivant, 1977). There is a great deal of variation in hardware costs, however, depending on the configuration selected to meet user requirements. At present microcomputer prices range from $600 to $20,000+, depending on the type of microprocessor and auxiliary devices added.

Comparing the costs of microcomputer and time sharing systems is difficult and sometimes deceptive because they are often used in combination to complement each other. Although microcomputers themselves are relatively inexpensive, the prospective purchaser should ask a number of questions relating to the onsite application that will help determine overall costs.

1. Will the microcomputer serve as a terminal in a timesharing system? If so, what are the membership and telecommunication costs?
2. How many microcomputers will need to be acquired to adequately serve the projected demand level of the school?
3. What are the costs of: (a) teaching computer programming; (b) teaching computer literacy; (c) computer-assisted instruction such as educational games, drill and practice, tutorials, problem solving, and sensory motor training; (d) computer-managed instruction such as testing, recording student progress, student files, and IEP's; and (e) business management such as monthly reports to the school board, payroll, mailing labels, vouchers, accounts receivable and payable, student scheduling, optimized bus routes, and personnel records?

4. How will equipment distribution and programming be handled? Who will do it, at what cost?
5. Will staff need to be trained? Will this be done through inservice? Who will provide the training? At what cost, to whom?
6. How will existing courseware and software be acquired? What will it cost?
7. How will courseware and software development needs be identified? How will these needs be prioritized and met?
8. What is the anticipated life of the hardware? How should it be amortized?
9. What service provisions are available from the manufacturer? How remote is the service facility? What is the turn around time for repair?
10. What about Parkinson's Law? Will work expand to fill the available computer resources?
11. Will any material purchases be reduced by the computer application, such as workbooks or remedial kits?
12. How will computer-assisted instruction be integrated with existing curriculums?

Careful consideration of these questions will help school administrators appreciate the complexity of cost considerations relating to computers. Some of these factors could go overlooked if one were to consider only the promotional literature provided by computer manufacturers.

REFERENCES

Baker, F.; Ratanakesdatan, P.; and McIsaac, D. "A Microcomputer Based Test Scoring System." *Educational Technology* 18, 2 (1978): 36–39.

Bork, A. "Machines for Computer Assisted Learning." *Educational Technology* 18, 4 (1978):17–20.

Control Data Corporation. *Control Data PLATO CMI Author's Guide*. Minneapolis: CDC, 1978.

Duch, R. Learning Resource and Development Center, University of Pittsburgh, Personal Communication, January 25, 1979.

Edwards, J.; Norton, S.; Taylor, S.; Van Dusseldorp, R.; and Weiss, M. "Is CAI Effective?" *AEDS Journal* 7, 4 (Summer 1974).

Joiner, L., and Silverstein, B. "Micro In-House Computers." Unpublished interim report submitted to the Minnesota Council on Quality Education, February, 1979.

Kehler, T. "Teaching English Grammar Using a Microcomputer." *New Directions in Educational Computing*. Proceedings of the 1977 Winter Conference, Wilmington, Delaware, 1977.

Mathews, J. "Microcomputer vs. Minicomputer for Educational Computing." *Educational Technology* 18, 11 (1978): 19–23.

Sandals, L. "Computer Assisted Applications for Learning with Special Needs Children." A paper presented at the American Educational Research Association, San Francisco, 1979.

Sturdivant, P. "A Regional Delivery System for Computer Assisted Instruction Programs." *New Directions in Educational Computing*. Proceedings of the 1977 Winter Conference, Wilmington, Delaware.

Thelen, H. "Profit for the Private Sector." *Phi Delta Kappan* 58, 6 (1977): 458.

Thomas, D. B. "The Effectiveness of Computer-Assisted Instruction in Secondary Schools." *AEDS Journal* 12, 3 (1979): 3–116.

Statewide Educational Computer Systems: The Many Considerations

This article describes the Minnesota Educational Computing Consortium's (MECC) plan for statewide support and acquisition for educational microcomputers and focuses on the need, development and implementation of a plan.

Although the utilization of microcomputers in education is relatively new, within the next few years we can expect an exponential increase in the number of microcomputers sold to educational institutions. The growth is being spawned by a number of factors including the decreasing cost of microcomputers coupled with their increasing capabilities and the rapid growth of their use in a variety of fields throughout the country. Another important factor is the microcomputers' independence from a mainframe system which increases its portability and eliminates many communications-related problems, as well as the elimination of the ''limiting rules'' needed on central systems.

The potential of microcomputer applications has attracted the attention of hundreds of vendors ranging from garage hobbyists to major mainframe companies as evidenced by the attendees at personal computing fairs and National Computing Conferences. The resulting number of different systems makes it very difficult to stay abreast of current developments. Microcomputers will also follow the paths of other new technologies, meaning, many of the current microcomputer manufacturers may go out of business within a year or so, making it very important for microcomputer purchasers to be aware of manufacturer and vendor stability.

Many educators view the microcomputer as a panacea for a variety of educational ills resulting in expectations which are greater than system capabilities.

In many cases, the use of systems will be impeded by a lack of hardware or software features. In addition, applications software development and instructional support will not keep pace with the initial movement to microcomputer usage.

In order to meet the needs and address the problems defined above, MECC set up a special task force to accomplish the following:

1. To conduct a survey for assessing the current and future microcomputer uses and needs of MECC users.

2. To determine the strengths and weaknesses of microcomputer utilization in various instructional computing modes and environments.

3. To provide demonstrations of microcomputer use for instructional purposes.

4. To coordinate and disseminate information regarding pilot programs using microcomputers.

5. To prepare recommendations regarding the potential for large scale acquisition and utilization of microcomputers and the appropriate roles and responsibilities for MECC.

To begin addressing these objectives, the task force divided the tasks into three components: hardware, systems software, and applications software. Several Minnesota vendors were contacted and asked to supply systems for examination, evaluation and experimentation. Fourteen systems were evaluated by the task force.

MICROCOMPUTER SYSTEMS EVALUATED

```
ALTAIR ATTACHE
ALTAIR 88-1301
ALTAIR MULTI-USER
ASTRAL 2000
IMSAI VDF-80/1000
NCR 7200
OLIVETTI P6060
PET 2001
POLYMORPAICS 8813
PROCESSOR-TECH SOL
RADIO SHACK TRS-80
APPLE II (Integer BASIC)
TEKTRONIX 4051
TERAK RT-11
```

As a starting point, the task force defined a "minimal educational system." The minimal educational system must have:

(1) A microprocessor.
(2) I/O device(s). The system must include an ASCII keyboard and printer and/or monitor.
(3) A permanent file storage device. This can be of the form: floppy disk, hard disk, etc.
(4) A vendor supplied operating system.
(5) The BASIC programming language must be supported.
(6) At least 12K of user memory must be available. This excludes memory space required for the operating system and the language processor(s).
(7) All components, software and hardware must be documented. This must include instructions on the operating system, a language manual, and setup and maintenance instructions of the system.

Only those systems which met these specifications were considered. This definition also helped vendors identify which features are required in a system for educational purposes.

In looking at software features, the task force considered both whether or not a system had a particular feature as well as how important that feature was to users. Over fifty software features were identified and classified as to importance for two types of usage: Computer Science/programming and applications/programming.

The computer science/programming classification was defined as the use of a microcomputer system to meet the needs of secondary and post-secondary computer science instruction involving such topics as advanced programming, operating systems, compilers and assembly languages. This is a system used primarily by those who are interested in studying the computer system itself, therefore software flexibility is important.

The applications/programming classification includes using the microcomputer for running application programs as well as writing and running simple BASIC programs for problem solving in elementary and secondary schools. This mode requires the capability to run programs which generally range from 8 to 32K in core requirements. Since this system would also be used to run programs similar to the library programs on the existing timeshare system, down-loading capability is highly desirable, if not essential.

In trying to evaluate microcomputers against these classifications of use, each feature was given a rating of essential, desirable, or not necessary for the two classifications as defined above. Each microcomputer was given a yes or no score on each software feature. By combining the importance scores with the yes-no scores, it was possible to give each microcomputer a software feature score for both classifications of use.

Since BASIC is the most often used language, the task force also attempted to evaluate the microcomputer's BASIC language features and capabilities which they deemed important. Test scripts were prepared and run on each of the fourteen systems.

Ten scripts were prepared. The scripts were divided into two catagories, those that tested BASIC language features, and those which tested performance. BASIC features scripts included sequential file handling, random access file handling, chaining, time function, string functions, matrix operations, and formatted output. The BASIC performance scripts included time required to complete computation (calculate number of primes from 1 to 2000), number of mathematical functions available, and time required to generate and sort 100 numbers.

In looking at hardware, some 40 features were defined and each system was rated against these. Some of the typical features included were: K-bytes of RAM, ROM, or PROM; available user memory; chip type; add time; availability of RS-232 interface and a real-time clock.

In addition to working with vendors, the task force evaluation of systems included a user survey which was developed and administered to teachers in the state who were using microcomputers in their classes. Questions dealt with types of usage, features of the microcomputers which were particularly desirable, and problems which were encountered with their systems. The major weaknesses of microcomputer systems currently in use seem to be the availability of CAI languages, ability to perform repetitive calculations, and the storage and movement of large data files. However, the majority of instructional computing can be accomplished quite well using microcomputers.

Once done with defining needs, collecting data on microcomputer systems, and surveying current microcomputer users the task force made the following recommendations regarding microcomputers:

(1) State Contract: One specific microcomputer system should be available to all Minnesota educationally related agencies through a state contract.

(2) Support: Instructional service support for selected microcomputers should be defined and increased to the same level as is currently available for large timeshare systems.

(3) Microcomputer Technology: MECC should continue to analyze and evaluate microcomputer hardware and software technology, and disseminate information to the Minnesota educational community.

On October 15, 1978, MECC and APPLE Computer, Inc. signed a contract for APPLE's 32K, disc-based Applesoft microcomputer system. MECC anticipates about 400-500 units to be sold by APPLE through MECC to educational users in Minnesota during the current year.

Educational computing service agencies must develop plans early if they are to cope with the fast-growing microcomputer industry. There is absolutely no indication of this growth trend slowing down. The fear that service agencies will no longer be needed is totally unfounded. Users will still need the software support that they have in the past. However, service agencies will have to redefine what they call "service" or "support." There are four major areas of microcomputer support that must be considered:

1. Purchase, installation, maintenance, and documentation of the system.

2. Training in system operations, use of application packages and programming languages.

3. Acquisition, conversion, development, maintenance, documentation and dissemination of applications packages.

4. Response to questions, problems, and requests regarding microcomputers.

It is hoped that the comments related here will be of help to agencies faced with the problem of servicing microcomputers.

Section II
Hardware and Software Development

- Criteria for microcomputer hardware selection to enhance the instructional process.

- Comparison of the capabilities of specific hardware systems.

- Pros and cons for converting timesharing software for use on the microcomputer.

- Reasons for designing programs for user interaction.

- Concerns with the materials to be used in presenting material to students.

- Procedures used in developing software for instructional application.

- Current educational software packages available for the consumer and their possible applications in instruction.

Selecting Microcomputers for the Classroom

by David B. Thomas and Donald H. McClain

Microcomputers seem to be everywhere. They are found in automobiles, ovens, sewing machines, televisions, and most recently in electronic games. Microcomputers may be seen in department stores, stereo shops, and computer stores. Advertisements for inexpensive systems appear in *The Wall Street Journal*, Sunday editions of metropolitan newspapers, and inflight magazines. Microcomputers have been featured on the *ABC Evening News*. Micros are now available at the consumer level and have entered our consciousness.

Teachers have discovered microcomputers, and may see micros as an inexpensive means to develop computer literacy and provide computer assisted instruction to students at a cost lower than that of time-sharing systems. Many have rushed to buy one of the systems which are now available; some number of these recent purchasers will find, unhappily, that the system they have bought will not continue to meet their needs. Others may find that their instructional needs are not well served by the system they have purchased.

Selecting an instructional computer system from the large number and variety of microcomputers now available can be a challenging venture even for an individual knowledgeable in instructional computing. It can be a dilemma for the administrator or teacher not knowledgeable about computing, given the quantity or the quality of most information being distributed by computer vendors. A problem arises from the large discrepancy between the price of a basic system quoted by the company in its advertisement and the actual cost of a minimum system configuration capable of easily and efficiently supporting instructional computing.

The key to the successful selection of a microcomputer lies in the careful analysis of the instructional problem, the determination of instructional require-ments, and the specification of the required computing capability. Once the computing capability has been determined, the potential buyer can survey the marketplace for systems satisfying the specified needs. The final task is the selection of the microcomputer system that satisfies all the predetermined criteria.

This paper strives to guide the educator in the selection of a computer system, especially a microcomputer system, that will be used primarily to enhance the instructional process. We have attempted to outline a model which will help teachers perform the prerequisite activities necessary for the specification of a microcomputer system which will meet present and future instructional computing needs.

The importance of performing an analysis of the instructional needs and anticipated uses of the computing resources cannot be overemphasized. The assumption that a microcomputer will permit the same varieties of instructional computing as are available on existing large systems (or on mini computers) is simply incorrect. The faulty assumption is compounded when the user attempts to extend use of the micro to applications beyond those initially intended. The extensions are sometimes not feasible. Microcomputers can be valuable additions to an instructional program, but careful planning is necessary to avoid disappointment which might ensue with the selection of an inappropriate system.

THE MICROCOMPUTER SELECTION MODEL

All too often, one begins with the purchase of a computer terminal intended for instructional use, then attempts to determine what applications should be implemented with the new computer terminal. We suggest that this approach is backwards and that one ought to begin by identifying instructional problems for which various forms of computing may offer solutions. A five phase model, depicted by Figure 1, provides a systematic approach to the selection of a microcomputer which will meet both present and anticipated instructional needs. (Note that many of our analyses inevitably lead to the selection of microcomputers. Obviously, neither all instructional problems nor even most of them will lead to computer solution.)

Figure 1
Microcomputer selection model

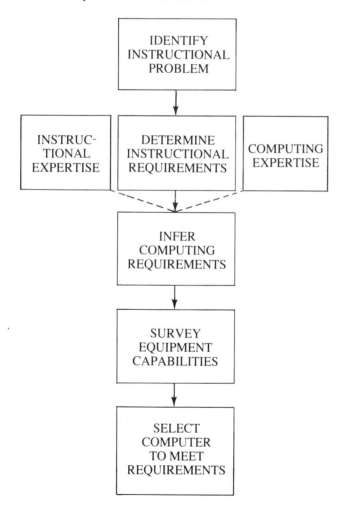

IDENTIFY INSTRUCTIONAL PROBLEM

Individualized instructional problems require that the teacher spend time with diverse student ability groups in the classroom. Some students may work on vocabulary, while others work on grammar, mathe-

matics facts, chemical symbols, or spelling. Others need the opportunity to recite, to explain, or to ask questions. We believe that the computer has much to offer the former, freeing the teacher to concentrate on the latter more frequently. It is important that the specific learning activity and a potential computer application be identifed early in the selection process. The computer is, after all, a tool which amplifies the teacher's effectiveness. But the teacher, as the responsible professional, must recognize the unique instructional problem for which a computer solution is available. The teacher who realizes that a group of students will profit from interactive drill on punctuation skills, for example, has completed the first step in the microcomputer selection process. Problems associated with the application of rules, or verbal associations, or concept learning would also serve as examples. The teacher's problem identification process likely would identify many areas where computing could provide help with the learning process. Selecting the appropriate computing tool to solve the problem will yield more satisfaction than fitting the problem to the tools already selected.

DETERMINE INSTRUCTIONAL REQUIREMENTS

Having identified an instructional problem, the teacher is best able to select a strategy for teaching the skills required of the student. We have identified 11 instructional activities or strategies for which microcomputers might be used. These strategies, although not exhaustive, represent the bulk of applications for which computers have been used in instruction (purely administrative applications have been excluded).

Drill represents a form of interactive computer-assisted instruction in which the student responds in a rather quick fashion to brief items or questions under a "flash card" format. The computer provides feedback as to the correctness of the student's answer and may adapt to the individual student by varying the number of items or the frequency of the stimuli, as a function of the student's responses.

Tutorial programs provide paragraph-like material, interspersed questions, and response-sensitive branching. These programs are usually characterized by an abundance of textual material.

Problem solving programs typically help the student in the learning of principles or rules by harnessing the power of the computer to eliminate the need for each student to complete complex calculations or engage in the manipulation of multiple logic states. These programs are usually short algorithms for which the student repeatedly supplies data to be manipulated according to the rule or principle being taught.

Programming involves the use of a computer language to provide the proper instructions which control the computer. Perhaps the major single use of computers in instruction is in the teaching of computer programming.

Simulations model phenomena of an often very complex nature in which random events are introduced to add realism to the interaction. Simulation is a valuable strategy when one needs to compress time (as in an explanation of radioactive decay) or avoid dangerous phenomena or use of expensive equipment.

Testing by computer permits the educator to exercise options not available with traditional testing methods. Items may be administered contingent upon prior responses to improve test reliability; alternate tests may be constructed easily for individualized programs; diagnostic tests may be collapsed into short testing sessions; tests may be scored instantaneously.

Computer-managed instruction (CMI) is characterized by the collection of student data and the transmission of learning prescriptions following objectives-referenced tests.

Data analysis involves the activities for which computers are most widely known. The use of standardized statistical analysis programs, list processing programs, and similar programs are a central topic in many disciplines.

Information retrieval is a much-used application in the social and physical sciences as well as in the humanities. In this application, the computer is used to select information from a large storage medium according to certain predefined rules. Typical applications are literature searches, selective mailing lists, and fact-finding.

Word processing provides an environment whereby the computer permits easy manipulation of text for reports, essays, and other paragraph material. This strategy may facilitate the student's preparation of essays by permitting easy insertion of text, correction of spelling, or reorganization of presentation without the necessity of completely rewriting the material.

Computer literacy represents the use of a computer itself as a demonstration of computer hardware and data processing capabilities. The ten strategies previously described also may be employed in this context.

Each of these 11 activities or teaching strategies has associated characteristics which in part define the instructional milieu. For example, interaction is a necessary characteristic for drill but not for date analysis; large amounts of text is a typical requirement for tutorials, but not for problem solving programs. Eleven characteristics have been identified which describe the eleven strategies defined above. These characteristics are not exhaustive, but represent the major instructionally oriented concerns associated with the activities mentioned.

The 11 characteristics of the instructional "contact" and the 11 strategies may be formed into an Instructional Requirements Matrix as shown on Table 1. The intersection of a strategy and a characteristic indicates a requirement which subsequently will be translated into a computing requirement. The problem-solving strategy may be illustrative; neither high student terminal time nor significant interaction typically take place within a problem-solving program. Graphics may be necessary for some applications, such as where the shapes of mathematical functions are being studied. It should be noted that the entries in Table 1 are intended to be illustrative rather than prescriptive.

The Instructional Requirements Matrix provides the information needed to develop a requirements list. By selecting the strategies which will be employed in the classroom, and collapsing across strategies, one obtains a list of instructional needs which the computing equipment must satisfy.

In identifying strategies it is important to take a fairly liberal view, considering the relative frequency of use of the various strategies and the strategies which will be employed in the future. This analysis, by its very nature, is quite subjective, but will provide one with weightings for the various computer system characteristics. These subjective weights are used during a subsequent phase of the selection procedure where specific computing requirements are developed.

INFER COMPUTING REQUIREMENTS

Previous phases in the selection process represent a needs assessment. The problem was identified and a solution devised which resulted in a set of instructionally oriented needs as expressed by a collapsed Instructional Requirements Matrix. These instructional needs must be transformed into computer requirements. This

Table 1
Instructional Requirements Matrix

Characteristic \ Strategy	Drill	Tutorial	Problem Solving	Programming	Simulation	Testing	CMI	Data Analysis	Info Retrieval	Word Processing	Computer Literacy
Interaction	X	X			X	X	X	X	X	X	X
Lower Case		X			X	X				X	
Graphics		X	X		X	X		X			
Large Data Source		X			X	X	X		X	X	
Specific Language			X	X							X
Multiple Languages				X							
Student Record Keeping	X	X				X	X				
High Student Terminal Time		X		X	X					X	
Large Amount of Text		X		X	X			X	X	X	
Hard Copy Printed Output			X	X	X	X	X	X	X	X	X
Packaged Statistical Programs			X					X	X		

task typically requires the combined talents of two people, one representing instructional and the other computing expertise.

Each instructional characteristic indicated in Table 1 has associated implications for the selection of hardware, whether the microcomputer or terminals, and for the selection of software.

The implications of the instructional needs may be described briefly as follows. The extent of interaction between the student and the terminal directly translates to a need for the assessment of ease of use of the computer system and its software. Requirements for lower case or graphics in the instructional setting need to be translated into hardware or software requirements. The need for a large data source or a large amount of text suggests the strong need for a disk unit, which in turn may have implications for memory size. Specific languages required for instruction have obvious software implications. If student record keeping is a requirement, then the use of a disk unit again is recommended. Should a high student terminal time be suggested by the combination of strategies, then there is need to consider the number of terminals or microcom-

puters necessary to assure that student waiting periods are not excessive. For the applications where hardcopy printed output is required, one needs to be cognizant of a microcomputer's ability to support printers or that of the terminals being surveyed. Finally, if packaged statistical programs are assumed necessary to the instructional application, both the availability of the packages and the usability of the package on various systems need to be considered.

A crucial decision at this stage is whether one ought to be investigating a microcomputer or a large system. Table 2 shows four levels of computers and recommendations for the kinds of instructional computing which are approriate for each. The mix of applications, their complexity, and their use-frequency will determine the appropriate system size. From this point forward, we assume that the instructional needs and computing capabilities which have been analyzed have resulted in the decision that a microcomputer is to be selected. The phases completed thus far provide the information needed to focus attention on the microcomputers which are appropriate for meeting identified needs.

Table 2
Computer Capabilities by Size

```
VERY
SMALL       -      (KIM, SYM, ELF, Single Board)

                 - Programming

SMALL       -      (PET, TRS-80, APPLE II)

                 - Drill
                 - Problem Solving
                 - Programming
                 - Simulation
                 - Testing
                 - Data Analysis (Small)
                 - Information Retrieval (Small)

MEDIUM      -      (PRIME, HP2000)

                 - Tutorial
                 - Data Analysis
                 - Information Retrieval
                 - Other Modes

LARGE       -      (IBM 360, 370, CYBER)

                 - All Modes
                 - Programming
                 - Data Analysis
                 - Information Retrieval
```

The following narrative describes the general capabilities or options of microcomputers that are believed to be essential in the consideration of an instructional computing system. These capabilities will be related to the various instructional activities or strategies. A survey of a range of microcomputers with different features will follow, as well as a list of points to keep in mind when making the final selection.

CAPABILITIES OF MICROCOMPUTERS

At the heart of every microcomputer is the microprocessor, the part of the system that manipulates all data and performs all calculations. Each of the different processors has sufficient power, speed, and precision for most instructional applications, making the brand name less important than some of the other features. However, one processor characteristic that some individuals believe makes a difference is whether it uses an 8- or 16-bit word length. The 16-bit processor might

have faster speed, more efficient instruction and data handling, and greater precision. High precision might be necessary for some applications such as data analysis or simulations; but in most instructional strategies, greater precision is not necessary to aid students in understanding concepts or in practicing rules.

The instructional programs and data being processed by the microcomputer are stored in the memory unit. Memory is a vital resource of a microcomputer, and the size of the memory is a very important factor in determining the types of instructional computing that can be undertaken. There are two kinds of memory in most microcomputers, read only memory (ROM) and random access memory (RAM). ROM, as the name implies, can be read but not changed, making it non-accessible as user memory. ROM contains code which may not be modified, such as system programs. In some microcomputers, the programming language software is in ROM. However, in most systems, part or all of the programming language software and even some of the system utilities are loaded into RAM along with the instructional programs. Therefore, the number which should be of concern is not the total memory, but the amount of memory available for the instructional materials. For example, on one 16K microcomputer where 1K represents approximately one thousand characters, the disk operating system and other system software take up almost 12K, leaving less than 4K of usable RAM. 16K of RAM sounds sufficient but the actual 4K is not enough for the majority of applications. Often the minimum amount of memory listed for a microcomputer is not enough, and additional memory needs to be acquired. Also, the maximum amount of memory that can be supported by the microcomputer should be considered, giving room for expansion. Memory is a very important and relatively expensive resource, but advances in the technology are lowering its cost, making larger quantities possible.

Another capability that should be considered is the character set. Many microcomputers have only upper case letters and it is desirable for most instructional applications to have both upper and lower case. Almost all of the other learning materials that a student utilizes make use of both; an educator should not settle for less when doing instructional computing. Further, the size of the characters should be noted along with the availability of special characters. The ability for the user to design an alternate character set might be a asset in certain applications and should be kept in mind.

In conjunction with the character set, the number of characters per line and the number of lines per display should be factors weighed in the selection process. The number of lines is dependent upon the display unit used by the system. A display unit of some kind (hard copy or video) is required, and if the number of display lines is too small, it can be a limiting factor on the type of instructional application. Also, the number of characters per line can limit what can be presented in an efficient and readable manner. A recommended size is 64 to 80 characters per line and 24 lines per display for video terminals.

Every instructional system must have some external storage device for keeping the curriculum materials and associated programs. Typically, this storage medium is either a cassette tape or a floppy diskette. The cassette tapes used are the typical audio tapes and their contents are input into the computer through a regular tape recorder. The floppy diskette is a thin, circular magnetic recording surface enclosed in a square envelope which has an exposed recording area. The diskettes come in two sizes, 8-inch or 5-inch. To confuse matters, the two diskette sizes can also come in double density which holds approximately twice the amount of information of the regular single-density diskette. The information on a diskette is read into the computer's memory by a disk drive. Microcomputers may have either single or multiple disk drive capability. If students are utilizing several different programs during a session, a disk capability is recommended over the tape recorder. Tape recorders are inexpensive but are very slow and sometimes unreliable, taking several attempts before successfully loading a program. It is further recommended that at least one microcomputer in a cluster be equipped with a dual-disk drive for backing-up the system and creating copies of courseware.

Many microcomputers have graphics capability integrated within the system. In some systems, this feature even includes colors, ranging from four to fifteen different hues. In selecting a microcomputer with graphics, the buyer should consider one with a resolution of 128 by 128 addressable points for a minimum. The ability to display graphical representations can be extremely useful in many types of instructional computing.

Two other features that might be necessary in some instructional applications are the existence of several programming languages and the ability to utilize the microcomputer as a terminal to another computer. Some microcomputers have available other programming languages, such as FORTRAN, PASCAL, or a CAI language, PILOT. The addition of other programming languages can be necessary in the teaching of computer science. The ability to utilize the microcom-

puter as a terminal to a larger computer system can be an asset, in that it may permit the development of programs on the larger system and then the transfer of the resulting code to the memory of the microcomputer. Also, the systems could be used in an hierarchical arrangement where the microcomputer is utilized as a stand-alone system for most computing, but when more resources are required, the larger system could be employed. In an environment where the user has access to other computer systems, it is recommended that the microcomputer be equipped with a communication interface, permitting its use as a terminal.

The last capability of microcomputers to be discussed is the ability to directly connect peripherals, expanding the system's potential. Peripherals that would be extremely beneficial in instructional computing are printers, plotters, graphic input tablets, music boards, speech synthesizers, speech recognition systems, random access audio devices, random access slide projectors, and videodisk players. A microcomputer with the flexibility to permit connection of a good selection of peripherals should be viewed favorably. When comparing peripherals, make sure software is available to support them on the particular microcomputer and that their addition will not require a major revision of existing courseware. The addition of other media to your instructional computer applications can greatly enhance its effectiveness.

Table 3 shows the capabilities of a microcomputer which are believed to be essential for each of the various instructional strategies. However, a particular application, even though classified within one of the strategies, might require capabilities other than those listed. The educator should compile a set of computing requirements, using the Instructional Requirements Matrix and employing Table 3 as an aid.

Several microcomputers having a range of capabilities are described in the survey in Table 4. During the final phase of the selection process, the potential buyer would want to create a similar survey, matching those capabilities and systems that satisfy the computing requirements generated previously.

In completing the selection process, the following questions should be asked of each of the possible microcomputers:

1. Is it flexible and easy to use?
2. Does it have good documentation?
3. What is the manufacturer's reputation?
4. Does courseware exist for it?
5. Can it be expanded?
6. What are the service options?
7. How long is the warranty?

Individuals who own microcomputers are a ready source of valuable information. Additional sources are the various personal computing magazines which periodically evaluate micros, and computer store dealers who offer more than one manufacturer's product. In the area of service, the buyer can choose from purchasing a service contract, sending the system to a factory representative, or switching boards or chips. If several microcomputers of one kind are purchased, it may be advantageous to purchase several boards or chips and do your own servicing.

The selection of a microcomputer which will be responsive to the needs you have identified and to the requirements you have generated may now follow. You should be more confident in your selection when you implement the model proposed. A system which is congruent with your present and future needs will do much to assure a successful instructional microcomputing experience.

Table 3
Micro Requirements per Instructional Type

	Drill and Practice	Tutorial	Problem Solving	Programming	Simulation	Testing	Computer Literacy	Other
Usable Memory (RAM)	4-8K	16-32K	8K	8K	8-32K	16-32K	4-8K	16-64K
Lower Case Characters		Y			Y	Y		Y
Cassette (C) and/or Disk (D)	C	D	C	C	D	D	C	D
Graphics		Y	Y		Y			
Hardcopy		Y		Y		Y	Y	Y
Decimal (Non Integer) Arithmetic			Y	Y	Y			Y
Other Programming Languages				Y				Y
Files		Y			Y	Y		Y
Communication Capability		Y		Y	Y	Y		Y
Number Lines Display	12	24	16	24	24	16	12	24

Table 4
Comparison of Microcomputer Systems

	PET 2001	PET 8016	APPLE	ATARI 800	TRS-80 MODEL III	TRS-80 COLOR COMPUTER	SORCERER II	TI 99/4	HEATH H89	TERAK	OHIO SCI C2 - 8P
PROCESSOR	6502	6502	6502	6502	Z80	6809	Z80	TM 9900	Z80	LSI 11	6502
MEMORY MIN/MAX	8/32	16/32	16/64	16/48	4/48	4/16	16/48	16/16	16/64	28/56	4/32
LOWER CASE	Y	Y	OPT	Y	Y		Y	OPT	Y	Y	Y
DISPLAY	Y	Y	NI	NI	Y	NI	NI	NI	Y	Y	NI
CASSETTE OR DISK	C*/D*	C*/D*	C*/D*	C*/D*	C*/D*	C*	C*/D*	C*/D*	D	D	C/D*
GRAPHICS RESOLUTION			192 × 280 40 × 48	192 × 320	48 × 128	192 × 256	240 × 512	132 × 256		240 × 320	256 × 512
TEXT (LINES × CHAR)	25 × 40	25 × 80	24 × 40	24 × 40	16 × 64/32	16 × 32	30 × 64	24 × 32	25 × 80	24 × 80	32 × 64
COMMUNICATIONS	Y	Y	Y	Y	Y	Y	Y	Y	Y	Y	Y
DOCUMENTATION	Y	Y	Y	Y	Y	Y	Y	Y	Y	Y	Y
MULTIPLE LANGUAGES	Y	Y	Y	Y	Y	Y	Y		Y	Y	Y
COURSEWARE	Y	Y	Y	Y	Y	?	MAYBE	SOME		SOME	?
SPECIAL FEATURES	CHAR GRAPHIC	CHAR GRAPHIC	4/15 COLORS	16 COLORS SOUND	INTEGRATED SYSTEM	8 COLORS RS232 I/O PORT	MEMORY CARTRID	16 COLORS	CURSOR ADDR	16 BIT	6 & 9 DIGIT (FAST)
COST (16K SYSTEM)	995	1500	1330	1080	999	599	1295	775	(KIT) 1695	6615	799

NI - Not included   D - Disk   C - Cassette recorder   Y - Yes   OPT - Optional item not usually from manufacturer   *Extra Cost

Microcomputer Software Development: New Strategies for a New Technology

by Kent T. Kehrberg

The Minnesota Educational Computing Consortium (MECC) has been supporting instructional computing in Minnesota through a large centralized time-sharing system. As a result of a task force study in the Spring of 1978, MECC now also will be supporting the use of microcomputers in Minnesota's educational institutions. Through a bid process, the Apple II microcomputer was selected for support and software development.

This paper will present the views of the author on the development of software for microcomputers for use in educational environments. The opinions and positions stated are based on experiences with both Apple II microcomputers and the Radio Shack TRS-80 in elementary and secondary educational schools.

CONVERTING TIME-SHARING SOFTWARE

Coming from a large scale time-sharing environment, the first temptation is to convert existing time-sharing software for use on a microcomputer. To a large extent, this is also what the pre-users of microcomputers in Minnesota are expecting. They see the microcomputer as allowing them portability for their computing, releasing their dependence upon phone lines, eliminating their frustrations from busy signals and providing them with a higher degree of system reliability. They plan to continue using the programs they are familiar with on the time-sharing system with their new microcomputer.

Experienced users of microcomputers (and today experience is measured in days and weeks rather than in years) see the potential for the use of the computer in new subject areas (music, art) and in expanded ways (tutorials). For these people there is less need for the conversion of existing programs. When necessary, they can still access the programs through their time-share system.

If one decides to convert programs from a time-share system to a microcomputer, the first decision must be whether to carry out a line-by-line (feature-by-feature) conversion or whether to enhance the program with graphic and sound output. If the program is significantly altered by the addition of graphics, then it may no longer agree with its documentation. Neither will it agree with the previous user's expectations of the program. On the other hand, it may be more interesting and motivational for the new user.

In general, it is a much better plan to convert an idea from a time-sharing system rather than a program. In direct conversion, the addition of graphics and sound may have to be forced—added for visual effect but not completely appropriate. But if they are not added, the program will have less appeal on the microcomputer. Likewise, the programming code on the time-share version may require substantial revision in order to produce a satisfactory version for the microcomputer. Most applications for microcomputers should be developed specifically and uniquely for the microcomputer—using only pre-existing ideas from another computer system.

DESIGNING SOFTWARE FOR USER INTERACTION

Software should be designed to take advantage of the unique features of microcomputers. Usually this means making ample use of graphics capabilities. Additionally, the developer can consider the use of audio capabilities. Most microcomputers can readily control a cassette tape recorder to deliver pre-recorded instructions or audio drill material. In general, the developer should consider incorporating as many sensual experiences as possible—visual, audio, and tactile. Have the student point to an object on the screen and then use his finger as a reference point while you have the computer move a graphic display around that point. For example, the student could place his finger on the big dipper and then the computer could advance the relative position of the stars by a one-hour time period. In this way, the student can partake in the discovery of the apparent circular motion of the stars about Polaris in a more interactive manner.

Other tactile experiences can involve having the user record information on a piece of paper. Unless the microcomputer is connected to a printer or disk, records of a student's work are not recorded, and there is no evidence to the teacher that the student has run the specified program. Working into the program design some written interaction not only provides a more interactive experience for the student but also can serve as a record of the experience for the teacher.

IS THE USE OF A MICROCOMPUTER APPROPRIATE?

In the initial design of educational software for a microcomputer, it is important to ask whether or not the learning activity can best be taught with a computer. A popular program for time-sharing systems is to have the computer simulate a pendulum and then allow the student to vary the mass, period and length in an attempt to discover the effect of each. A much better experience for the student, however, is to be given a string, paper clip, and some washers. Now with the microcomputer and its graphics capabilities we are again tempted to duplicate this experiment on a machine. We can draw the pendulum, make it swing, determine the period, and so forth—all in color and with a ticking sound! Still, in most circumstances, strings and washers will provide a more complete and educationally meaningful experience for the student. It is important that we don't attempt to ''computerize'' all experiences.

There are special features of microcomputers which do enhance teaching. Computers can simulate events which may otherwise require too much time. They can simulate phenomena which may be too dangerous for the classroom or too expensive. With the graphics capabilities of the microcomputer, we can display an object in real-time and then slow it down for careful study. For example, a student can step a four-cycle engine through each piston stroke and watch for the opening and closing of valves and identify the ignition phase.

With the precise timing capabilities of microcomputers, the designer can develop software which provides students with situations in which responses can be controlled. Mathematics speed drills would not have to vary with the current load on the time-sharing system. Motivational typing drills can be developed. Experiments could be conducted in the area of psychology.

One concern of the developer may revolve around the overuse of graphics in a program. Does every program have to have entertaining graphics built into it? Will students demand (by their disinterest in a particular application) that software be entertaining? My initial concern on this topic was reduced by an elementary principal. He stated that students already demand a level of entertainment, that teachers in today's classrooms are competing with Sesame Street. Motivational graphics must be included in microcomputer software programs even for users with no prior computer experience.

DEVELOPING A MICROCOMPUTER APPLICATION

In designing a microcomputer application it is important to know the capabilities and limitations of the equipment. In particular, one must keep in mind that microcomputers do not have the memory size and computational speeds of larger systems. Many times, ideas do not have to be rejected, but accommodations must be made. Perhaps recordkeeping will have to be done on paper if files are not available. Students can be instructed to insert programs manually if chaining is not available.

Pay attention to the modes for user interaction. In addition to visual display, it may be possible to add audio output. Students might touch the screen for reference. A supplementary device such as a globe might be referred to. Design programs for active users. Monkeys can push 'return' keys to change the visual stimuli; humans can interact more fully.

Make use of graphics in your program. The quality of the graphics need not be great. Curves made out of little squares still look basically like curves. If a clock has two hands and 12 numbers, students recognize it as a clock—whether or not it is perfectly round or even has an outside border.

Plan the role of support materials into the design of your program. Can complete instructions be included in the program or should they be available in a booklet or on a sheet of paper? Perhaps some type of worksheet should be used in conjunction with the program. The student may need to design a strategy prior to coming to the computer. A record sheet for student responses may be appropriate.

Handling Text Material

In the time-sharing environment, it was common to ask the question "Do you need instructions?" at the beginning of programs. This was generally necessitated by the slow output speeds of teletypes. Few people had the time to wait for the instructions on subsequent runs of the program. On the microcomputer it is not necessary to ask such a question. You can usually display the instructions more quickly than the user can answer the question. If the instructions require more than one screen of output, a few quick carriage returns by the student will pass over them.

Commonly, some textual material is associated with a computer program. Several points should be remembered when using text material. First, display only one screen of text at a time. Do not allow the text to roll off the top of the screen. The user should be in control of the display of text. Never time the display anticipating the user's reading rate. Each frame of text should have a standard method of indicating that the material has been read. This technique should be visible on each frame. For example, a simple phrase such as PRESS "RETURN" may be sufficient and still keep the text under the user's control.

Pay attention to the readability of the text material. Readability may involve more than difficult words and long sentences. It may also include the size of the displayed characters. Larger characters need to be used for elementary children and those with special learning difficulties.

If significant amounts of text must be displayed to the student, break up the interaction between frames with questions. Many times, students tend to skip over the text by entering a few quick carriage returns. It is also wise to minimize the amount of text on the screen at any period of time. Do not write text on every possible line.

What Is Being Reinforced?

Kids are smart. After a few experiences with computers, they soon learn that certain things happen when they get a question wrong and other things happen when they get it right. Many will deliberately get questions wrong just to find out what happens. This may not be a problem as they have indicated their knowledge of the answer by actually choosing the wrong response. We must, on occasion, keep in mind that the reinforcement for a positive response should not be less motivational than the program's reaction to a negative response.

In a microcomputer version of hangman (guess the letters in the word the computer is thinking of), a boat is printed on the screen. If an incorrect response is given, the boat sinks a little lower in the water. If sufficient incorrect letters are chosen, the boat sinks and a little man is seen going down through the water with bubbles rising from his mouth. Very entertaining graphics—considering the fact that you lost! On the other hand, there is very little reward for getting the letters correct and identifying the word. A more positively motivational version might be called torpedo. If you guess the letters in the word, a torpedo is shot at the boat and the boat and the little man sink to the bottom. The more stimulating reward is now for success rather than failure.

The Dynamics of Display

With the microcomputer, several special techniques should be employed in displaying information on the screen. Many of these are needed because of the high rate of speed at which microcomputers output data. At times it may be necessary to slow down this rate by building into a program a counting loop to "keep it busy" for a few moments. For example, if two similar frames are to be presented, the student, having pressed the "return" key at the end of the first frame, may glance up only after the second frame has appeared. Mistaking the second frame for the first, the student may press the "return" key again. A programmed pause for a few seconds between frames would allow the actual change to be witnessed.

Any tables which are updated as a result of student interaction should be continuously displayed on a part of the screen. Likewise, if the student has to choose from the same set of options to answer many questions, these options should be frozen on a portion of the screen.

Never anticipate a student's reading rate. Unless a complete reading of text displayed on the screen is unessential, don't build the item into a timed loop. Rather, allow the student to continue by typing a response (remember to indicate on the screen what that response is). No timed loops should be used for any type of display unless on the same screen you give directions for continuing. Nothing is more frustrating than viewing a display and having no idea about how to continue.

Instructions for continuing from one frame or display to the next should be standardized and highlighted. PRESS "RETURN" is sufficient but could be strengthened by blinking it or printing it in an inverse character mode. Options for stopping a program partway through should also be standardized. A recommended standard term is the word END. Entering this word would bring the program to a conclusion through processing, not to an abrupt halt leaving files open, concluding messages not displayed, and system parameters incorrectly set. STOP is not a satisfactory choice, as on many systems this brings an abort to the program similar to typing a "break" key. QUIT, DONE, and so forth are other possibilities and should perhaps be anticipated in the programming, but END is preferred.

Special keys on microcomputers will sometimes clear the screen of display material. Similarly a student's response, if unanticipated, may cause graphic material on the screen to shift in position. Programming should allow a student to request a redraw of the screen or it should automatically check and redraw the screen if necessary.

The user should not have to guess at the format of the expected response. If the student must enter X and Y variables separated by a comma, then an example of the desired format should be displayed. It would be even better to ask for each variable separately. This is, after all, what microcomputers can do best—ask questions and get responses quickly.

Be consistent in the nature of responses required. When moving from frame to frame, don't mix up PRESS "RETURN" with PRESS ANY KEY or with other possible responses. It is also important not to change the rules on inputting answers. Microcomputers can be programmed to respond to the entry of a single key without the traditional "return" key. Mixing "keyed" input with "returned" input confuses the student and causes unexpected results in the program. If you want to accept "keyed" input—input where only a key need be typed—then also accept the option of typing the "return" key. Simply process the return key as extra input.

Beware of overloading the screen. If you segment a display and cause changes in various parts, it can be very difficult for the user to follow. Parts of the display could be static lists of options or some graphic shape. The "action" part of a display should be centered near the upper part of the screen. Be certain to draw the user's attention to it and allow time for eye movement prior to the event.

At the conclusion of a program it is important to give the student some type of status report. Students expect to be told how well they did. This may be a score, a percent, a message or instructions to move on to the next module. Again, some type of record sheet on which the student records his or her score may be useful.

Programming Considerations

When programming a unit on the microcomputer, take full advantage of the capabilities of the specific machine. Concern about the potential transferability of a program to other microcomputers will limit the use of features on your own system. Any hopes of standardizing the BASIC language have now been postponed indefinitely. Although the elementary statements in BASIC are common among various micros, the extended statements and graphics techniques definitely are not. The only way to convert graphics from one micro to another is by completely rewriting that portion of the program—generally by looking at the output and not at the code. If you have a general interest in the wider use of your software, choose a microcomputer which has the broadest use in education. At this time the most widely used machines would be an 8K PET, 4K Level II Radio Shack, or an Apple II using Apple Integer and having about 8K.

Remember when coding a program that it will probably be run after someone else's program and before yet another program. The last program run may have reset certain system parameters which will interfere with your program. The system's memory may have been allocated or perhaps a graphics screen was left full. Clear and reset these items at the beginning of your program. Likewise clean up after yourself at the end—the next program may have been written by someone less thoughtful.

At times, a program may have to perform a complicated calculation which requires several seconds or more of computer time. Warn the user that waiting may be necessary while a calculation is being performed. Whenever possible, the programmer can structure extensive calculations for the time periods when the user is reading the screen. For example, data could be read into variables while the user is viewing the first page of instructions.

Test the Program Thoroughly

When the program is complete, the work has just begun. Run the program with the deliberate intention of "bombing" it out. Try unexpected inputs. If it runs well, give it to a malicious user, one of those people who thrive on pointing out the weaknesses in someone else's work. If your malicious user is short on imagination, a few suggestions would include: (a) type "returns" without inputting any data, (b) type in excessively long responses, (c) enter numeric data where string data is requested and vice versa, (d) enter two "returns" in quick succession, and (e) enter an option not listed. This series of inputs should be tried for each option in the program. Lastly, give your program to a naive user—someone who has never used a microcomputer or at least knows little about the topic in your program. After passing all three of these test situations, the program will still have bugs, but fewer than before.

CONCLUSION

Constructing software for microcomputers is a combination of choosing an appropriate topic, applying the dynamics of the system, and programming for a naive user. The suggestions presented in this paper should assist in the appropriate selection of software for microcomputers and build an awareness of the care necessary in presenting material to a student. This combination should lead to new and usable software for microcomputers in education.

Tips on Writing Instructional Software for Microcomputers

by Kevin Hausmann

Now that you have that new microcomputer, you are ready to start writing programs for use in your classes. Right? Chances are that you probably have not thought of all the aspects of designing an instructional application for a microcomputer. An attempt will be made in this article to identify the major ideas that must be considered when developing an instructional application on a microcomputer.

GETTING STARTED

As with any development project, analysis before implementation of an idea is necessary. Four major items come to mind in the analysis stage.

1. Is this a reasonable application for a microcomputer?
2. What limitations do I have because of my equipment?
3. What modes of interaction should be used?
4. What support materials are required, if any?

A major mistake made by many designers is that of expecting much more than their microcomputer is capable of delivering. This is in part due to being unfamiliar with microcomputer technology or sometimes just due to the expectations carried over from larger systems. Microcomputers are like garden tractors in the tractor world. By definition still a computer, but not quite as much horsepower. Microcomputers are lacking in computional speed and memory space, compared to what many are used to from larger mainframe systems.

Secondly, one must analyze what the equipment can do. If you want to do graphics, is the resolution adequate? Is the sound generation adequate for what your objectives are in a music drill? Is the system easy enough to run so that students (say elementary) can use it? These and many other questions need answers when considering equipment.

Thought must also be given to the mode of interaction. Microcomputers not only can generate written output, but audio as well as graphical output. Animation is also a possibility. Input can be via the standard keyboard, or with tough sensitive screens, light pens, or audio. The possibilities abound in mode of interaction chosen. Lastly, one should ask whether other support material should be used. Besides additional written material, this could include, films, records, lab exercises or whatever. These are especially important if they are high cost or difficult to obtain.

IMPLEMENTING THE IDEA

The implementation phase requires some thought which is new for microcomputers. For example, care must be given to how much information is presented to the user. It used to be that a printer connected to a time-share computer could print information needed to run a program. The user could then refer back to it as often as needed since the output was permanent. Most microcomputers use a video monitor. On a monitor, once a line scrolls off the screen, it is gone and cannot be seen.

Having no printed output is only one aspect of what is oftentimes called screen or text formatting. Another is coping with the high speed at which text is printed. Text can be printed many times faster than the human reading rate. Because of this it may be desirable to slow down the rate of printing on the screen using a delay loop.

If a student must choose from a fixed set of options throughout the program, then the student should not be required to remember the options. Instead a section of the screen should be blocked off and the options continuously displayed there.

Presentation of large amounts of textual information should be avoided. After all, the importance of a computer is in its interaction. If large amounts of text need to be presented, they still should be committed to paper. However, if a significant amount of text needs to be presented here are a few hints.

1. Do not overcrowd the screen. Double spacing is suggested, as this is much easier to read. If parts of a screen are frozen, keep the action near the top rather than at the bottom.
2. If several screens are needed, do not set a specific time from one frame to another. You cannot anticipate the user's reading rate. Instead at the end of each screen, display something like, "PRESS RETURN."
3. Sometimes it is desirable to ask questions as you present the material to encourage careful reading.
4. Minimize the amount of text and graphics on a screen at any one time. Too much information of different types on a screen at the same time is confusing to the user.

To emphasize #2 above even more: In general, timing loops should be avoided, unless the application absolutely requires it. Nothing is more frustrating to a user than having to wait for a timing loop to expire when ready to go on, or to have it expire before being ready to continue.

The handling of user input is a major consideration in writing any computer application. A program should never get lost, no matter what the user has entered. The following hints should be considered in programs requiring user inputs.

1. The user should not have to guess how to enter information. If confusion is possible, always give an example. If multiple inputs are needed (like pairs of numbers), ask for them separately.
2. Be consistent with the way questions are asked and the required format for responses. Use YES and NO, or Y and N, for example. Do not require one and then the other.
3. Do not code answers unless necessary such as, 1=YES, 0=NO. String processing on most systems is as easy as numeric processing.
4. Allow for null input. Many systems do not graciously accept null inputs, so a program should make appropriate allowances.
5. Take all input as strings. If a program needs the input as a number, then convert it using system routines. This again avoids the system input messages which are usually of no meaning in the context of the program.
6. If a question must be asked again, clear the old answer off the screen before restating the question.
7. Ask a question while the information needed to answer the question is still on the screen. Some applications may require this, but in general, the student is learning, not trying to guess what is wanted.
8. Avoid jumping around the screen asking questions. The user should know where to expect questions to appear. Requesting inputs or creating distractions on the screen confuse the user.

FINE TUNING

After an application is developed and written, it is very important to adequately test the program. Many times this is best done by watching someone use the program who is totally unfamiliar with it, as your users will be when you give it to them. Another technique is to have a checklist. The items mentioned in this discussion would be part of such a checklist.

These are just a few considerations for the person just beginning to develop applications for microcomputers. Many of these ideas can also be used when evaluating software written by others for microcomputers. It is hoped that these ideas will help lead to new and more usable applications for microcomputers in education.

Educational Software

by David Lubar

Almost any use of the computer can be educational, even when instruction is not the main intent of the program. This tends to turn a review of educational software into a complex task of selection (in itself an educational experience). To narrow the field, the following types of programs will be considered: (a) those labeled "Educational" by their manufacturers, and (b) those which, while not labeled "Educational," do provide the user with new concepts, new information, or new approaches to problem solving. With these criteria established, but not inflexibly fixed, we'll look at a variety of educational software for home computers.

EDU-WARE

Edu-Pak I from Edu-Ware ($39.95) is a disk for the 48K Apple II and Apple II-plus, requiring Applesoft in ROM. The disk contains five programs: "Compu-Read," "Perception," (three programs) and "Statistics." Each program allows for several options and variations, thus creating a large software library on a single disk.

"Compu-Read," designed to improve a reader's speed and retention, begins with a choice of six different programs. "Compu-Read I" places three random letters on the screen for a brief moment. The user must type these letters after they have vanished. If he succeeds, the next set of letters remains on the screen for a shorter period of time. If he is wrong, the time of display increases. At the end, the time of display is shown, as well as the number of letters per second for both the start and end of the segment. This information helps the user gauge his progress.

"Compu-Read II" uses words instead of random letters. At this stage, the skills developed in the first program are called into service. Skills related to recognition are also emphasized and strengthened in this exercise. "Compu-Read III" displays a word on the left and four words on the right. One of the four is either a synonym or antonym for the word on the left. Once again, the words do not remain on the screen for long. The user must type the correct synonym or antonym. This involves both recognition of the words and comprehension of their relationships. The system can train a person to absorb and analyze data in a rapid manner.

"Compu-Read IV" presents a sentence, then asks the reader a question concerning the sentence. The question is always about either the subject or object, thus training the user to scan quickly for information. This technique can greatly increase reading speed. The next two programs are file builders which allow the creation of new word lists for the second and third programs. The series is well developed and seems designed to build up reading skill in discrete segments. There are options to specify the number of trials and the length of time for display. Complete statistics are given after a round, breaking the performance into several factors such as percent correct, display time of first word, display time of last word and rate of letters per second.

Next on the disk is the "Perception" series. These three programs, in high-resolution graphics, test visual perception and the ability to judge spatial relations. "Perception I" concerns lengths of lines and gives a choice of 5 tests. In each, a line must be matched to a specific, illustrated length. The line is controlled with the paddles. The options include two vertical lines on the floor of a room and two crossing horizontal and vertical lines on the rear wall of a room. Anyone who is familiar with optical illusions will realize that finding a match is not always easy. The program responds to the user's guess with the percentage of error in the estimate.

"Perception II" deals with shapes. Again, there are a large variety of options. Basically, a shape with from three to eight vertices (user selects this number) is shown in sections as a window scrolls past it. The player must pick a matching shape. In "Perception III" the match must be made on the basis of size. The player selects from a choice of seeing the shape on a blank screen or against a scale which allows comparison. He also chooses from three ways of seeing the master and test shapes. The number of vertices in the shape and the time it is displayed are also controlled by the user.

These programs develop not only spatial perceptions but also concentration. And they are fun. With all the options and variations, anyone could use the "Perception" series for a long time without tiring of it.

The last selection on the disk is "Statistics." This contains six programs, including "Chi Square Distribution," "Mean, Variance, and Standard Deviation," and "T-Test."

The disk is well done. Each program is menu driven, and comes with complete instructions. A lot of thought went into *Edu-Pak I*. It would make an excellent addition to the software library of any school, and could be used by students of almost any age. The programs mentioned above are also available individually on cassette and disk. Edu-Ware has many other educational programs (as well as some simulation programs) on the market and under development, and is also working on new versions of present programs. This process of revision insures a dynamic product. They combine talented programming with skilled educational techniques; the results are good.

STEKETEE EDUCATIONAL SOFTWARE

Cassette *TO 3* for the 16K TRS-80 ($9.95 + $1.00 p&h), from Steketee's *EDU-SOFT* series, contains two programs which can be used both in the classroom and at home, "Plot," and "Guess the Rule." "Plot" allows the graphing of single or simultaneous equations. Anything within the mathematical capability of the TRS-80, from a simple $Y=X+2$ to a complex $Y=SIN(X)/X*SOR(X)$, can be used. An equation is entered by being placed in memory as line 400. A second equation can be inserted as line 500 if a graph of simultaneous equations is desired. Since these equations become part of the program, TRS-80 conventions for math symbols must be followed. Once an equation is entered, the user has a choice of either Cartesian or Trig coordinates, as well as a choice of any desired endpoints. If the selected endpoints are too small, the line won't appear on the screen. If this happens, larger boundaries are needed. After the function is graphed, it

can be replotted with different endpoints, saved to be combined with the next equation, or deleted from memory. "Plot," which gives good visual representations of many concepts in Algebra and Trig, could be of value to almost any age group.

In "Guess the Rule," the computer selects an equation, ranging in difficulty from simple linear ones of the form $Y=X+a$ to quadratics such as $Y=aX+bX+c$. The player is then shown two pairs of X, Y values. Using this information, he must determine the rule, either by guessing the equation or by supplying a correct pair of values for X and Y. Ten equations are presented in each contest.

Another cassette, *TO 4* (same price configuration as *TO 3*), contains "Computa-Doodle" and "Simulated Computer." "Computa-Doodle," as the title suggests, is a graphics utility. The left, right, up and down arrows control a cursor which draws lines. An arrow followed by a number will give a longer line. Left arrow followed by "9," for example, will move the line nine spaces to the left, plus one for the move registered with the initial press of the arrow. The "Q," "W," "A," and "S" keys allow diagonal moves, with numbers following to give the degree of slope. Once a diagonal has been started, the slope can be changed just by pressing a different number. This allows smooth curves to be drawn. There is also a command which displays the numbers that represent the graphics in memory, and a command which moves the entire drawing on the screen. "Computa-Doodle" is well designed and easy to use.

"Simulated Computer" is an excellent program. It turns the TRS-80 into a microprocessor. Twenty memory locations (little boxes) are displayed on the screen, along with boxes for input, output, accumulator, program counter and instruction register. A group of three digit commands, for such functions as "add," "subtract," and "skip," is used to program this simulation of a computer. Once a program is entered, the operation of this "central processing unit" is graphically displayed as the user sees memory contents change and as input and output appear in the boxes. There are also modes for slowing the program, and for running in single steps. The program is a great introduction to the concept of a microprocessor. Both beginners and old pros will be fascinated by this internal view of a computer in action. "Simulated Computer" is a good first step on the way to understanding a Z-80 or a 6502 microprocessor.

Steketee programs come with good documentation, including complete instructions and suggestions for using the programs. The programs are well designed for ease of operation and contain many error traps. This cassette can definitely be used in the classroom. Individual users can also enjoy this tape. Any of Steketee's tapes can be ordered on disk for an additional $5.00.

BASICS AND BEYOND, INC.

Microcosm I for the Level II 16K TRS-80 ($19.95) contains thirty programs on two cassettes. The programs range from games and simulations to utilities and educational aids. The games are nice, though some are reminiscent of previously published ones. Several of the games could be considered educational. "South Pole" allows one or two players to try to reach the pole and return. The players decide how many men and dogs to bring, and how much food and fuel to take along. Daily reports are given as the players pick their routes toward the pole. Aside from a rather long wait while data is being displayed, the game is fun. More varied and complex is "Atlantis." Here, the player must decide on a course of action to save this mythical island from impending doom. He can try to build a dome for protection against the volcano, work toward evacuation, or try one of several other approaches. Many decisions are involved, with many possible outcomes. This is a nice simulation.

Then there are the educational programs. "Country Guess" has the player choose a country. The TRS-80 asks questions until it is able to name the country. This requires the player to know (or learn) a fair amount of Geography; otherwise he won't be able to answer correctly. "Math Table Drill" allows the user to select the number he wishes to study. The computer then presents problems in basic arithmetic which involve the number. This could be a good way to practice multiplication tables. "Spelling Drill" flashes a word on the screen, then waits for the user to spell the word. Any mistake will immediately end the attempt, but another chance will be given. "Spelling Review" allows the user to enter his own list of words for review. There are three levels, each presenting the word for a different period of time.

Microcosm I also contains data-base type programs such as "Flowering Houseplants," "Calories-Food," and "Calories-Ingredients," as well as programs for balancing checkbooks and checking memory. At this price, it is a worthwhile purchase. Included with the cassettes is a 24 page booklet which gives detailed rules for the games and background on the educational programs. The tapes and booklet are attractively packaged in a sturdy plastic binder.

EDUCATIONAL ACTIVITIES, INC.

This company markets several programs for the PET and TRS-80. Apple II-plus versions are also in the works. *Missing Facts* ($29.95) can be used by a student with no help from a teacher; the instructions are clear and simple. As in "Math Table Drill" (see above), problems are presented with one missing factor—5 +?=9—and the user has to supply this missing number. After a correct answer, the whole problem is displayed again. When the guess is incorrect, three chances are given before the computer provides the answer.

Flash Spelling ($14.95) presents words one letter at a time in large script. The whole word remains on the screen for an instant, then vanishes. At this point, the user must correctly spell the word. While there might seem to be no challenge in spelling a word that has just been on the screen, the benefit of this program is that it reinforces learning. By seeing the word one letter at a time, the student is more likely to remember the correct spelling.

Scrambled Letters ($14.95) is for two players, who take turns trying to solve jumbled words. If a player is correct, his opponent gets a new word; on an incorrect guess, the other player gets a shot at the same word. If they both miss twice, the program shows them the word. Extra points are given for speed in this contest. There is only one small problem. Some words, such as "ocean," have anagrams. A player who responded to "aceno" with the answer "canoe" would be told he was wrong. Aside from this, the program is well designed.

Introduction to Mathematics on the Computer ($29.95) is a marvelous, wide-ranging program. It presents the student with math problems at a specific selected level of difficulty. If the student does well, the level increases. The value of the program becomes apparent when the student makes a mistake. After several tries, if the answer hasn't been found, the machine restates the question as a word problem. Instead of using "5+3," for example, it says, "Maybe this way would be easier for you: If I had 3 pencils and you gave me 5 more, how many pencils would I have?" The program is also extremely patient when trying to get answers to yes/no questions during the initial set-up. This is a nice touch, and shows the care that went into the package.

Most of the EA programs make extensive use of large-size letters. The documentation consists of only an insert in the cassettes, but it provides information on changing the data bases for the spelling games, and advice on what to do when problems are encountered. Besides, the programs contain everything the user would need to know. These tapes could be of value in the classroom, and could also be used by students who want to learn on their own, or who need extra help with a subject. This is definitely a quality product line.

IMAGE COMPUTER PRODUCTS

Now that the Atari home computer has been on the market for a while, other companies are beginning to produce software for it. Image has brought out a nice cassette, *Skill Builder I* ($19.95), containing two educational programs for younger persons. Running on either the 800 or 400, "Number Hunt" has the player move from the center to the edges of a three-by-three grid, trying to find the number that matches the answer to a problem shown at the bottom of the screen. At first, the problems are very simple. If the player does well, the problems become more difficult. A single player can use the program, or two players can compete, trying to be the first to find the number. In the two player version, each player has his own grid. The control is through joysticks.

The same cassette also contains "Bingo Duel." In this game, numbers must be found on a five-by-five grid. Two players can compete, each getting a different level of problems but using the same grid, or the game can be used by a single player. Both games are well explained in the booklet accompanying the cassettes. These programs could be used by children who are learning their numbers or who are learning elementary addition and subtraction. Older children might also enjoy the competitive aspects of the games.

ATARI

The *Talk and Teach* programs from Atari represent a good concept which has produced fair to excellent applications. Using the Educational System Master Cartridge, the machine comes on with simple instructions for loading the cassette. After the program is in memory, the computer controls the tape, which gives audio output through the television to supplement the information on the screen. For some applications this is a nice idea. The Sociology set, with sixteen programs on four tapes, is well done. The first program introduces the topic, explains what will be covered, and begins to give a background of basic concepts. As text is displayed on the screen, a narrator repeats the material.

Since speech can be faster than reading, the voice is able to give extra information.

Throughout the program, the tape stops and a question appears on the screen, along with two or three possible answers. If the wrong answer is selected, there is a buzz. When the right one is found, the tape continues, often making a comment about the answer.

In the same series is a set of History tapes. These begin with the Greeks and move chronologically forward. The history lessons stress a cause-and-effect approach. Obviously the tapes took the efforts of three professionals; a programmer, an educator and a trained speaker. The lessons are put together with great care for detail, accuracy and interest. The use of text and graphics is well done, and learning from these tapes is a painless endeavor.

There are times when something is used because it is available, not because it is the best thing to use. This could be the case with the *Great Classics* selection of the *Talk and Teach* series. Each story is presented in synopsis with a style reminiscent of *Classics Illustrated*. The program pauses to ask questions, insuring that the reader grasps the plot line, but that isn't enough. The value of literature comes not from the plots, which are often ancient and borrowed, but from the way words are put together. None of the works in this sixteen-story collection, from *Julius Caesar* to *A Tale of Two Cities*, can be viewed as anything but story line. Each work is a classic because of the style and art of the writer. These tapes are pale images of the classics. If they interest a student enough to get him to read the originals, fine; but that doesn't seem likely.

Also from Atari is *States and Capitols* ($14.95). A high-resolution map of the USA is displayed. One at a time, the states are outlined. The player has to guess the state. If he is wrong, the program will tell him the answer. After that, he has to guess the capitol. Again, the correct information is provided after each guess. The game is nicely designed, but would be best used in a classroom, since individuals who used it would quickly learn the states and have no more need of the program.

CREATIVE COMPUTING (SENSATIONAL SOFTWARE DIVISION)

This review would not be complete without mention of some of the newer educational programs from *Creative Computing*. First, for the TRS-80, is *Ecological Simulations-2* ($14.95). This contains four programs: "Pollute," "Rats," "Malaria," and "Diet." In "Rats," the player tries to control a population of rats, using various poisons. He can select the length of time between reports, as well as the length of each application and weight of the poison. Trying different methods, the player learns the results of combination programs using varying amounts of poisons.

"Malaria" is a varied and interesting program. The player must select from several measures designed to limit the spread of a malaria epidemic. Attention must be split between preventative and curative measures. At the end of a round, the player is given an evaluation of his work, showing how effective each of his measures was. Bit by bit, it is possible to develop a strategy which makes the most effective use of the various measures. This game quickly becomes absorbing.

"Pollute" takes the user's selection of water temperature, kind of waste, rate of dumping, and treatment method, then shows the efforts on a body of water. It contains good error traps and other aids. In entering the amount of waste, a reply that is way too large will result in the comment: New York City has a rate of only 12 parts per million per day. The display graphs oxygen against waste in the water. This program, too, is a good learning tool.

The final simulation, "Diet," allows experimentation with various weekly diets, without the risk entailed from actual experiment. A player can learn what a week of milkshakes would do to him, or a week of sprouts and other vegetables. The output tells how much weight would be gained or lost on this diet, as well as the nutritional makeup of the food.

In these programs, a reply of "-1" as input is used whenever the player needs help in answering a question. The documentation includes detailed explanations of all parameters and variables, as well as exercises to get the user started and advice for classroom activities with the program. Also included is information on the assumptions made in the simulation. The manual itself can be an educational tool.

Another tape from *Creative Computing, CAI-2* ($11.95), is for a 16K Apple II with Integer Basic. It contains three programs designed for computer-assisted instruction. "European Maps" begins with a high-resolution display of Europe. The player is given the choice of naming either countries and capitols or just countries, as well as the option of just entering the first letter of the name of the country. During the game, a dot in the center of one of the countries will begin to flash. The player must name this country. If he is wrong, he will be given the same country twice more at other times during the game. This use of graphics for visual learning is nice, and should produce good results.

"Meteor Math," for beginning and intermediate students of math, takes the pain out of arithmetic. The player is informed of a meteor which is falling toward Earth. He must destroy the meteor with his laser cannon. But he has to answer math problems correctly before he can fire the cannon. It takes a lot of shots to destroy the meteor. If the student does well, the level of difficulty of the problems increases. This is a nicely-designed package which makes good use of graphics in presenting math problems.

The tape also contains "Music Composing Aid," which allows the entry of notes, the replay of the notes or of other saved scores, and the editing of compositions. The music, coming from the Apple's own speaker, sounds like an alto recorder. When using the system for composition, each note is played as it is entered. Notes are coded using a simple method. A C below middle C is entered as C. To go an octave higher, the composer would use CC. There is a range C below middle C to C three octaves above middle C. Along with the program is a data tape containing a Bach composition. The program encourages students to learn musical notation so they can transpose their favorite scores from sheet music into computer data. This package offers a nice variety of programs, and would be worth the price for the music routines alone.

Moving away from educational software, we get to those programs that are intended as aids for teachers. Generally, such programs are concerned with organizing data, and with saving time. First, two cassettes from Educational Associates; one very good, one fairly disappointing. The good cassette, *Readability Index* ($9.95), can be useful not just to teachers but also to those who work in children's literature; especially literature for the high-interest low-readability field. Readability gives a guideline for determining what material can be comprehended by what grade level. In the EA program, the user enters three paragraphs; the first, one from the middle, and the last. The program then gives word count, sentence count, the number of letters, the average length of a word, the percentage of the words that are on the Dale readability index, and the readability level. The Dale long list contains words that are in the vocabulary of readers at certain ages. The percentage given is an estimate; an actual check against the list would take too much time. Along with the printout is a chart for finding the grade level that is appropriate to the readability. This program is useful and well set up for ease of operation.

Considering the overall quality of EA software, their *Grade Averager* ($9.95) is a disappointment. The program allows entry of grades, either letter or numeric, for each student in a class. When all the grades have been entered for a student, an average score and letter equivalent are given. At the end of the program, a summary of all names and averages is furnished. So far, no problem. But the program does have flaws. First, once a grade is entered, it is there for good. There is no way to edit mistakes. Any change would entail redoing the whole file for that student. Also, a wrong entry that is a letter other than "A," "B," "C," "D," or "F" is taken as a signal that the entries for that student are finished. It seems that this cassette could create more work than it saves.

The *Apple II Gradebook* ($24.95) from *Creative Computing* is a disk-based utility that allows teachers to set up files containing the names of students and their scores. The user first establishes a roster by entering the names of the students. More than one class can be held on a disk. Once a roster is on file, it can be accessed to add new scores, change scores, change existing information, or add information.

A lot of thought seems to have been devoted to making this program easy for the user. After a name has been entered, the computer shows the name on the screen and asks if it is correct. Getting a "yes," the name is put on file. If the name isn't correct, the computer asks for another entry. This method should virtually eliminate user errors.

With names and scores on file, it is possible to get various statistics from the system, such as scores and averages for each student, as well as his deviation from the mean. Another nice touch: the names can be entered in any order. When they are sent to disk, they will be stored alphabetically. This system is very easy to use. Anyone who can type can have the luxury of a computer grade book. The documentation covers use of the system and recovery from any problems that might be encountered (such as accidentally hitting reset).

As should be obvious by now, there is a lot of educational software out there, and the quality seems to be getting better every month. With careful shopping, any school or individual should be able to fill all software needs for a reasonable price.

MICRO POWER AND LIGHT

Circulation ($29.95) for 32K Apples with Applesoft in ROM and one disk drive contains a nice combination of text, high-resolution diagrams, and animation. The program gives instruction on six topics: blood, heart, arteries, capillaries, veins, and lungs. Each section first introduces the concept, then tests the user's understanding by asking questions. The program makes appropriate responses to both right and wrong answers. The strong point of *Circulation* is the high degree of interaction between computer and student. There is little chance that anyone's attention will drift in the middle of a lesson. When done with a segment, the user is given the choice of reviewing the material, moving on, or quitting. There is also a game on the disk; a race between two trucks. The player has to answer true/false questions. If the right answer is given, the player's truck dashes ahead; on a wrong answer, the computer's truck wins the heat. The program, designed for students from fifth grade up to junior high, and for adults who need a refresher course, is well designed and pleasant to use. The documentation, though brief, contains complete instructions for loading the disk and for recovering from accidental resets.

STONEWARE MICROCOMPUTER PRODUCTS

Aristotle Apple ($34.95) runs on any Apple with 48K, disk, and Applesoft. It could be the answer to a teacher's prayers. The program allows the creation of tests. While this revelation might not sound exciting at first, the combination of solid programming, ease of use, and several user options makes this package very valuable. The teacher, using the "Editor" program, can create tests of three types: multiple choice, column matching, and fill in. With the multiple choice version, five choices are entered. The fifth choice is always either "All of the above" or "None of the above." These two are entered with "A" or "N," thus saving a bit of typing. The other choices can be up to 40 characters long, and the question can be as long as 75 characters. Column matching places two columns on the screen. The student picks a selection from the first column and tries to match it with the correct member of the second column. The fill-in test presents a question, then waits for the answer. The teacher has the option of entering two answers. This is useful, since some questions can be answered correctly in more than one way.

The "Editor" program also allows for changes in tests and for deletion of tests. To do mass deletion, there is a program called "Hemlock." (The connection between Aristotle and hemlock was not explained in the documentation. It was Socrates who took that unkindest cup of all.) Students can also run the tests in a "Tutor" mode that presents the questions in an interactive manner.

The disk comes with enough documentation to get anyone going. Stoneware recommends making a backup copy and saving the original in a safe place. After this, the user should run "Hemlock" to delete the example test files on the copy. If this isn't done, the sample tests will always appear when a student runs the program.

MUSE

The *Elementary Math Edu-Disk* ($39.95) runs on a 48K Apple with versions available in Applesoft or Integer Basic. This program presents math problems in large characters that are formed using the low-resolution screen. Before starting the problems, the program can give a test which determines whether the student is ready for the material. An option allows the problems to be accompanied with a voice. Coming through the Apple's speaker, the voice is understandable and adds interest to the program. During the presentation of the problems, incorrect answers produce graphic tutorials on the misunderstood concept. Blocks and numbers move around the screen, demonstrating and breaking down math operations. This part is nice, but one of the demonstrations takes a long time, and some students might lose interest. On the nice side, the disk keeps track of the student's score. The number of times a section has been worked, and the number of correct answers, is preserved until the teacher (or a budding young computer crime genius) deletes the file.

TYC SOFTWARE

The *Individual Study Center* for 16K Level II TRS-80 and Apple II with Applesoft ($39.95 plus $1.50 p&h) represents a nice idea with executions that vary from excellent to poor. The package comes with a sample data tape, a maintenance program for creating data tapes, and six programs that use the data tapes. These six programs all present tests in the form of games. "Beat the Clock" allows the user to select the level of difficulty by picking a time limit from 30 minutes for twenty questions to 10 seconds per question. A clock appears on the screen along with the questions. At the end, the player is shown the correct answers.

While "Beat the Clock" is well done, "House on Fire" has some flaws that could frustrate the player. The game opens with graphics of a burning house. Each correct answer puts another rung on a ladder. Each

mistake removes the rungs. The problem is that any question which is answered incorrectly is repeated over and over until the right answer is found. If the player doesn't know the answer, he is stuck.

Once again, the concept is good, and the ability to create data is very handy. Despite the problem with some of the games, the package could be useful in a classroom.

COOK'S COMPUTER COMPANY

Cook's produces some nice programs for the Apple II. Since they are presently reorganizing their disk selections, prices can't be quoted, but some of the programs definitely deserve mention. *Take It or Leave It* builds math ability through a game. The player competes with the computer, deciding whether to take or leave the results of arithmetic problems that are shown on the screen. The goal is to build up the score, so the player has to determine whether the result is positive or negative. *Slope* gives a variety of questions that test understanding of concepts dealing with slope and graphs. Incorrect answers are well handled. The questions range from simple to fairly advanced. *Legacy* gives multiplication practice in the form of a game. The player tries to amass more dollars than the computer by getting to the right spot on a grid first. The grid has integers at the top and side, and the correct location for each number is the spot with a row and column value that, when multiplied together, produce the target number. *Alcohol*, which strongly resembles a program from *Creative Computing*, takes the user's body weight and the amount of liquor imbibed, then gives the percentage of alcohol in the blood and the effects that will probably occur. (Seeing the result of drinking 30 shots in one hour is rather sobering experience.) The program also contains some nice comments. If a ridiculous weight is entered, the reply is, "I didn't know elephants could operate a computer. Quit kidding and enter your real weight."

This should give some idea of the variety available from Cook's Computer Company. For specific prices and available disks, it would be best to contact the company.

MICRO LEARNINGWARE

Grammar Package I for Level II 16K TRS-80 ($14.95) contains six programs that test recognition of parts of speech such as adverbs, adjectives, and pronouns. A sentence appears on the screen and the user can get one word at a time to appear in a box. Pressing "enter" when the right word is in the box produced a nod from an android on the screen. A wrong answer produces a message, but then jumps right back to the same point in the program. The package also contains a test of person, place, or thing, where the user has to put nouns in the correct box.

The math programs, *Elementary Math Packages I* and *II* ($14.95 each), contain drills, some tutorials, and a few games. The drills are fairly straightforward, but again they do not handle incorrect answers very well. The games aren't too bad; most of them are exercises in metrics. The main problem is the lack of true interaction in the educational programs.

MICROPHYS

A large selection of educational programs for the PET are available from this company at $20 per tape. *Gram-Molecular Weight* presents problems in chemistry, giving a formula and asking for the molecular weight of the molecule. If the user has trouble, the problem is broken down for him, and he is asked the weights of the individual elements in the molecule. All Microphys programs come with instructions for retrieving the student's results and grade.

Linear Kinematics presents graphs, then asks questions about acceleration, speed, and related areas. The graph shows the instantaneous speed of a car, plotted against time. Five questions are presented with each graph. Each run presents different graphs.

In his September PET column, Gregory Yob had some strong criticism against Microphys. While some of his points are well taken if the tapes are intended solely for instruction, the tapes function best when used to supplement, not replace, classroom instruction. The full line from Microphys is too long to list here, but interested educators might want to write for their catalog.

PROGRAM DESIGN, INC.

This company markets a wide selection of educational software, almost all of which is available for both Apple and TRS-80, with some available in PET format. *Astro Quotes* ($14.95) is a nice twist on standard word games. The player has to guess a quotation. Underlined spaces show the number of words and letters in the quote. Above the quote are four definitions, also sup-

plied with blanks. When a correct word is found for one of the definitions, the letters in that word are placed at all points in the quote where they appear. The maximum score is obtained by getting all four words before guessing the quote. There are three skill levels and over 150 quotes in memory.

While *Astro Quotes* is useable as either a game or educational product, PDI also markets programs with specific educational intent. *Spelling Builder* ($18.95) contains eight programs and an audio tape. The programs take the user through a few basic rules, building up spelling ability as well as facility in accenting and syllabification. The programs work well, though there is one weak point. There is no branching when several incorrect answers are given. The user has to keep trying until he gets it right. An occasional hint would be nice. Aside from that, the programs are good. The audio tape overcomes one of the major problems of spelling programs. When words are presented on the screen, the user sees the correct spelling. PDI's use of audio tape allows spelling tests that actually test the user's ability. A program is used along with the audio portion, and the words are presented in groups of ten, allowing the user to stop when he wants and continue at a later time.

Suffixes ($14.95) gives a tutorial on several common endings. There are five programs. The first present "meter" and "gram." Later programs test learning. Throughout each program there are multiple choice questions. Again, there is no branching on incorrect answers.

The PDI line seems varied and well done. All of their Apple tapes are available on disk for an extra $5. Those in need of this type of software could probably fill many of their requirements here.

TANDY CORPORATION

Radio Shack has produced a rather massive educational package for the TRS-80. The *K-8 Math Program* ($199.95) contains drills and tests in mathematics for students from kindergarten to eighth grade. The students are locked into the programs, but the teacher, by hitting two certain keys in a row, can access the system to check results and make changes in the problems. In the first four levels, correct answers are rewarded with a smiling graphic face. The package contains tapes, disks, and extensive instructions, all bound in a sturdy notebook. The math lessons have several modes. They can be used for placement, as skill-building exercises, or as tests.

The programs for the lower grades are supplemented with graphics, the upper levels use text and put prompting messages on the screen if the student doesn't give an answer within fifteen seconds. The drills go through operations in a step-by-step manner, with the student filling in one number at a time, including a carry whenever it is produced. Brighter students might become a bit impatient with this approach, but it does reinforce the proper procedure for doing arithmetic.

A young student using the system for the first time should be guided through the exercises so he knows what to expect. Once started, any child should be able to continue on his own with this package.

TEXAS INSTRUMENTS

A variety of educational cartridges are available for owners of the TI-99/4. *Early Learning Fun* is ideal for young children. It contains learning games that deal with numbers, shapes, and letters. The shape exercises are especially nice. In one, a shape appears on the right side of the screen, and the player has to match it to one of the shapes on the left side. When a choice is made, the test shape moves across the screen and pauses next to the selection. The letters section gives exercises in letter recognition, accompanied with pictures for each letter.

Beginning Grammar has sections on nouns, adjectives and other parts of speech. Each section is presented with a different theme. For example, "Adjective's Restaurant" uses the inside of a menu to present the problems. Another one uses a bus and traffic signal, with red or green flashes to signal wrong or right answers. The programs are nicely designed to ignore bad input from the keyboard such as numbers or punctuation marks. Music and sounds through the monitor add interest to the program and insure that children will have fun while they learn.

Number Magic gives several types of quizzes. The user has many options, including a choice of working against time or working without a limit. The level of the problems goes from simple to fairly difficult. All of the Texas Instrument Cartridges come with extensive booklets and make full use of the excellent sound capabilities of the TI-99/4.

PERSONAL SOFTWARE

The *Vita Facts* series for Apple, PET, and TRS-80 contains cassettes on several crucial topics, including *Heart Attacks* and *Birth Control*. Each package consists of an audio tape and a program. The audio tape contains the information. After listening to it, the user runs the program, taking multiple-choice quizzes to test his retention and comprehension. This use of audio data is nice since it allows the listener to gain a great deal of information without the eyestrain associated with long sessions in front of a monitor. The topics are valuable to older students and to adults.

MICROCOMP

While designed as a utility and data base, *Nutri-Pak* for the Apple has educational value. The user first establishes a file for himself which contains his age, sex and weight. He can then select foods from the data base, or add his own foods, and determine how these foods contribute to his daily requirements of vitamins and minerals. The program is easy to use and makes it possible to investigate different diets. Many foods are included on the disk; adding others is simple to do.

UPDATES

Time for a quick mention of some things that didn't make it into last month's review. Among the products from **Steketee** that weren't covered is a nice math program, *Speed Drill*. This presents problems with a time limit and is well designed. **Edu-Ware** also has a nice math package, *Compu-Math*. **Image** produces games as well as educational programs. These will be covered in a review of Atari software which is scheduled for a later issue. Most educational software is designed for ages from elementary school to high school. **Conduit** produces programs for college students. Their programs didn't reach here in time for this review, but will be covered in the near future.

Again, this review just touches the surface. The exclusion of any particular program or manufacturer is a matter only of fate, postal peculiarities, and deadlines, bearing no reflection on quality or lack of quality. Educators and parents should have little trouble finding a program that comes close to fulfilling their requirements.

EDUCATIONAL SOFTWARE VENDORS

Atari Inc.
1265 Borregas Ave.
P.O. Box 9027
Sunnyvale, CA 94086

Basics & Beyond, Inc.
Box 10
Amwalk, NY 10501

Cook's Computer Company
1905 Bailey Drive
Marshalltown, IA 50158

Creative Computing
P.O. Box 789-M
Morristown, NJ 07960

Educational Activities, Inc.
P.O. Box 392
Freeport, NY 11520

Edu-Ware Services, Inc.
22035 Burbank Blvd. #223
Woodland Hills, CA 91367

Image Computer
   Products, Inc.

615 Academy Drive
Northbrook, IL 60062

Micro Comp
2015 N.W. Circle Blvd.
Corvallis, OR 97330

Micro Learningware
Box 2134
N. Mankato, MN 56001

Micro Power and Light
1108 Keystone
13773 N. Central
   Expressway
Dallas, TX 75243

Microphys
2048 Ford
Brooklyn, NY 11229

MUSE
330 N. Charles St.
Baltimore, MD 21201

Program Design, Inc.
11 Idar Court
Greenwich, CT 06830

Personal Software, Inc.
1330 Bordeaux Drive
Sunnyvale, CA 94086

Steketee Educational
   Software

4639 Spruce St.
Philadelphia, PA 19139

Stoneware
1930 Fourth St.
San Rafael, CA 94901

Tandy Corp.
One Tandy Center
Fort Worth, TX 76102

Texas Instruments, Inc.
P.O. Box 10508
Lubbock, TX 79408

TYC
40 Stuyvesant Manor
Genesco, NY 14454

Section III
Applications in the Curriculum

- Ways the microcomputer might assist the teacher with instructional and administrative tasks.

- Settings where the computer has been used with preschool, primary, intermediate, middle, and high school students in teaching eye-hand coordination, mathematics, problem-solving, programming, and science.

- Techniques for using this technology with gifted/creative/talented students.

- Reasons for housing the microcomputer in the library or school media center.

Classrooms Make Friends with Computers

by Howard Spivak and Stuart Varden

For 20 years, the computer has been touted as the most revolutionary educational innovation since the Gutenberg press. But only now are we on the threshold of fulfilling that great prediction. The early problems with computers have been largely solved: hardware costs have dropped dramatically; more effective programming techniques have been designed; and, because teachers have come to recognize the usefulness of computers in their everyday lives, they are more seriously considering a role for the computer in the schools.

The question that teachers want answered, though, is, "How can a computer help me become a better teacher?" The answer: In many ways! The computer can help improve the quality of your teaching by providing a wide variety of independent instruction for students. And it can cut down on the time you take for paperwork by completing many administrative tasks for you, thus allowing you to spend more time with your students. Following are specific ways computers can become a teacher's best friend.

THE COMPUTER AS INSTRUCTOR

In "computer based instruction," the student usually works at a computer terminal that has a typewriter-like keyboard for entering information, and either a video screen or printer for displaying messages from the computer. The terminal is connected to the computer by cable or phone line, or, in the case of a microcomputer, the keyboard, display, and computer are a single self-contained unit that easily fits on a desk top.

The actual instruction can take one of the following seven commonly used approaches.

Drill and practice. This is surely the least exciting but most common use of the computer in education. Nevertheless, it is quite practical for many routine learning activities. For example, teachers can use the computer for drill with math problems, spelling words, state capitals, and history facts. This approach assumes that the students have already received instruction and are using the drill and practice to reinforce learning. The computer poses a question, the student responds, and the drill and practice program "marks" the response. Then the student may proceed to the next question.

Tutorial approach. Here the instructional material provides the student with the opportunity to test his or her understanding of a concept, subject, or topic. The computer program assumes the role of teacher and presents the material in a programmed learning format. The student gradually moves from one step to the next, usually at his or her own pace. The student is actively involved, by answering questions at each step, and the program provides immediate feedback on each response. Questions are framed as either multiple-choice answers or fill-in-the-blanks.

More sophisticated programs can monitor a student's progress through the material and introduce remedial or review segments if the student is having difficulties, or skip over some of the material if it is too easy for the student.

Inquiry approach. This approach is the most ambitious attempt to have an instructional program emulate the behavior of a human teacher. Such programs have been designed to handle unstructured, natural language responses from a student. The idea is to have the computer and student hold a discussion to examine a particular concept. Usually this discussion is in the form of question and answer.

Games. Many very effective educational experiences have been developed in the context of games. Most children enjoy playing games and computer games are no exception. Instead of merely emphasizing acquisition of facts and basic skills, however, educationally oriented computer games often develop more general problem-solving methods and strategies. For example,

1. Searching: These games involve a searching or hunting activity, such as a treasure hunt. One simple game is to have the player try to discover a number between 1 and 100 that the computer has selected. After each guess, the computer says whether the guess was too low or too high. The player is allowed a fixed number of guesses in which to discover the number. Players quickly find that some approaches for discovering the numbers are far better than others. A similar game involves searching for something on a two-dimensional plane.

   Being able to perform this activity well may appear to be a rather inconsequential accomplishment. But consider what you do when you look up a word in a dictionary or search for something on a map. If you do this well, it is because you have learned to take advantage of the fact that the material you are searching through is ordered. Developing this awareness, of course, is the game's goal.

2. Resource management: In these games, the player is given an initial allotment of resources, some playing rules, and a goal to achieve. To do well in the game, the player must deploy his or her resources wisely. One game, for example, places the player in the role of a national leader with an allotment of food, military forces, land, and population of citizens. The object of the game is to expand the country without starving the population or being overrun by an enemy country. To play well, one must develop a sophisticated understanding of both national defense and food production.

Simulations. Simulations attempt to model the underlying characteristics of a real world phenomenon so that its properties can be studied. Computer simulations have the great advantage of being able to condense time and space, and to nullify the consequences of possible dangerous behavior of the phenomenon.

Take, for example, a nuclear mishap. With a computer, it would be possible to simulate on screen its long term effects in only a few minutes. The computer could then draw conclusions about the mishap—all without harm to the students.

Creative writing. There is a popular misconception that computers deal exclusively with numbers and mathematics. Actually, this is far from the truth. There are programs called *text processors* that allow students to key in a writing assignment and then edit or change its content or format at will. This makes it easy for students to edit and revise their writing. And research shows that continual practice in editing and revision leads to greatly improved writing skills.

Graphics. For generations, textbook publishers have recognized the value of graphic art. Computer programs can now provide this valuable element. A process such as the working of an internal combustion engine can easily be depicted in steps on the student's terminal.

The different modes of instructional computing just presented are by no means comprehensive. Also, many programs successfully combine different modes. Thus, there are simulations that are also games, drill and practice exercises that use graphics, and so forth.

THE COMPUTER AS TEACHER'S AID

A computer can be a teacher's friend by handling those administrative tasks that are often so time consuming. Below are a few examples.

Testing. One of the big uses for computers in the future will no doubt involve tests. Computers can construct tests, score them, analyze them, and, for that matter, test a school's curriculum. How?

1. Test construction. Need to check a student's ability to do subtraction? With certain information in a computer, you can have a test made in minutes that measures a student's skill in it. Or do you need to check a student's ability to understand the main idea of a story? Programs can supply a test to check that skill, too.

   With some sophisticated equipment, a computer can even be used to print tests. Let's say you have stored in a computer a copy of a test you gave last year. This year you would like 14 copies of that test. No problem. A computer can generate the test and print copies for you in minutes.

   Perhaps, though, you only want 10 of the questions on that test or you want them presented in a different order. Once again, no problem. A computer can generate the test, or parts of it, in any format you wish.

2. Test scoring. A computer can score standardized tests right in your own school. But more than that, it

can analyze the scores for you, tell you what the scores mean, and produce achievement profiles. The test information could also be used diagnostically. Once you get the test information into the computer, the computer can tell you what skills need to be developed.

For example, a child misses questions 4, 6, and 14 on a test. All of those items contain subtraction work. The computer will advise what practice work the student should concentrate on. Or a child misses questions pertaining to the formation of sentences. The computer would tell you to reteach that skill.

3. Testing a school's curriculum. This offers exciting possibilities, particularly for schools that design alternative programs for students and who are under accountability pressure from parents.

Let's say your school has written a curriculum with a set of objectives. There may be 30 parts to your curriculum. It would take weeks to test students on all the parts. But is is possible to give a sampling of students five test items to see how well the curriculum is meeting your schools's objectives. The computer could then take all the subparts and analyze the answers to give an overview of how well the curriculum is meeting objectives.

Record keeping. A computer can help you keep track of records. It can store inventory counts, attendance figures, and school enrollment statistics (and even make predictions). It can balance your school budget and petty cash fund. It can maintain student files, achievement profiles, and test scores—and retrieve this information for you in seconds. To protect the privacy of students, it is possible to code a computer so that only the principal or psychologist has access to certain parts of a student's file.

A computer can also help the guidance counselor by making vocational suggestions according to the material in a student's record. Many counselors in the country are already using such programs to help with their career awareness programs.

In the classroom, a computer can help you schedule an activities calendar or make new seating charts. One teacher in New Jersey spent hours rearranging student seating charts. (He was interested in breaking up cliques that formed in his class.) The computer rearranged the class once a month for him, taking all his seating problems into account.

Text processing. As noted earlier, a computer can be your own word processor. Computers can produce letters to parents and even store a range of addresses for special mailings.

Some schools are also using the computer to produce school newspapers. The process is not unlike that of city newspapers and national and local magazines throughout the country that write, store, and process their articles on video display terminals.

The Integration of Microcomputers into the Classroom or Now that I've Got It, What Do I Do with It?

by Earl L. Keyser

One of the most pressing problems for the classroom teacher whose school has purchased a microcomputer is integration. In many cases, the teacher has had little or no input regarding the selection of this machine. Often the superintendent or media director, mesmerized by a salesperson or an ad, or sheer curiosity, purchases a microprocessor. Perhaps some thought has been expended as to its final use (what can I do with it?), but more likely thought has been expended on its capabilities (what does it do?).

This article will not attempt to point up the many evils of ineffective selection, because there are many such articles in the literature. Indeed, one might wish that the authors of these many articles had pursued question number two with greater rigor. What this article will do is to describe several computer applications and mention some ways in which a microcomputer can be integrated into real world educational settings.

Computer-assisted instruction (CAI) is commonly divided into several categories: drill and practice, tutorial, simulation, problem-solving, and (although there is some argument) computer literacy and computer-managed instruction. The microcomputer can achieve a significant impact in all of these areas, and the apparent limitations seem to be much more those of the programmer and educator than of the machine itself. Even the "lowly" TRS-80 Level I microcomputer has been used with success in such widely varied areas as college chemistry and elementary school arithmetic. The applications discussed in this article all are implemented on an APPLE II microcomputer, although most could be implemented on other microcomputers.

One of the most difficult areas to teach in language arts is poetry. Having labored in the vineyards of the muse for some years, both as author and teacher, the author has found that poetic concepts are, at best, difficult to instill in the minds of the young. But one method found to be useful is the command, "Write a poem, damn it!" Although it may be terrifying for the student at first, committing his or her thoughts to paper, even in a form one would not show one's own mother, is critical. A reading of these nascent forms immediately points out problems with tone, rhyme, meter and other more subtle aspects of language. But a constant problem for the author has been one of having to rewrite or, worse, retype the poem. The sheer frustration of this mechanical process makes that one last revision that might turn a carnation into a rose seem scarcely worth the energy.

ENTER, STAGE LEFT, THE MICROCOMPUTER AND *POET*

POET is a special version of the CAI author language PILOT. It allows the student to write poems, print them out in permanent form, and play with the language. One can easily change a line, erase a stanza, substitute one word for another and even, most exciting to the author, make the poem interactive. This is all done on a television screen device, using the keyboard and mini-floppy discs. By allowing students to modify their poems easily and with little hassle, POET encourages them to experiment, and it is in experimentation that many students find new uses for language elements which they thought they already had mastered. The delight of four sixth graders with whom I recently worked was matched only by the delight of the teacher when the kids each brought an original poem to school.

Another exciting application of the microcomputer is in the area of spelling. Certainly, many readers may remember the drudgery of learning lists of 10, 15 or 20 words every week in elementary school in order that one might pass the Friday spelling test. And, the main method of study of those words was flash cards or, occasionally, a Wednesday pretest. Imagine the delight of children when they may practice their spelling words in a number of ways, guessing at them in a hangman game and being required to write them correctly in order not to be hanged, finding the words hidden in a word maze or having the computer speak each word (from a tape recorder) and requiring the student to correctly type the word.

The hangman game is the standard one found on all computer systems, modified to allow accessing words from a file. An editor has been written which allows teachers easily to list these files, add words to them, delete words from them and correct the inevitable mistakes.

The WORDMAZE program is also found on many systems. It is modified to accept words from the master spelling word files instead of words typed at the keyboard. The wordmaze is created quite quickly and the teacher may insert a ditto master into a printer to create a master which then can be used to reproduce multiple copies of the wordmaze.

LISTEN reads the words from the spelling file and, in conjunction with a computer-controlled cassette tape recorder containing a previously prepared audio tape, drills the students on the words. Although requiring more effort than the previous two methods of presentation, this mode is most like the final test and is probably most valuable. It is not as versatile as is desired, because the words can only be presented in one order unless multiple copies of the file and multiple tapes are made in advance. Future development may store words as phonemic symbols which could be manipulated randomly and sent to a speech synthesizer.

The microcomputer uses its graphic capabilities in the science classroom. Most science teachers who have used the computer have encountered the Huntington simulations. Created by Dr. Ludwig Braun and his associates, these simulations have become the classics of CAI and have performed admirably over the years.

The implementation of these simulations on the APPLE II was relatively simple. The excitement came when graphic capabilities were added, allowing a student to obtain a graph of the results of pollution in a stream, for example, while simultaneously watching the oxygen content of the water change as the amount of sewage increases. Although an earlier simulation, NEWTN2, could not actually show a tiny boat as it attempted to cross the river, now it can. The programming was not difficult, and the excitement of the students is especially rewarding.

An area in which many people are experimenting right now is that of computer-assisted music instruction. The APPLE's unique ability to create sound with considerable ease has been noted before. But, combining this with the high-resolution graphics routines to create a score allows for drills of musical items which the computer plays.

With the advent of the ALF board and other such peripherals, high-quality sound with a wider range of pitch and duration than the basic APPLE can create have been realized. However, a program known to the computer underground simply as ''Synthesizer'' points out that many inherent capabilities of the APPLE have not been explored. In this program, five simultaneous notes are synthesized, a far cry from the standard ''do-re-mi'' which one hears as the introduction to the Star Wars program.

One of the more interesting programs which the author has seen combines music with graphics and allows the student any of several options. The student may compose a melody, have the computer play the entire melody or a portion of it, change any notes, tempo or pitch, transpose the entire song to a different key, store and recover songs from a disk file, and play the song while scoring the notes on the television screen. Without too much work, it is probably also possible to play two simultaneous notes by using techniques found in the Synthesizer program. The input, by the way, is done by turning the lowest two rows of the typewriter keyboard into a musical keyboard so that the song is, in effect, played into the computer. It would not be difficult, and the author is considering this, to wire an organ keyboard to produce a digital word and make the input device even more familiar to the musician. It is the author's belief that input must be appropriate to the user, not the other way around, as is commonly assumed in much CAI and, indeed, in much computer usage generally.

A fourth exciting area in which the microcomputer can have significant impact upon students is the more general area of lesson writing. As of 1979, educators can celebrate 20 years of CAI. But, much of that CAI is incredibly stilted in input or output, makes unreasonable demands of computer sophistication on students or is so impersonal as to be threatening to both teachers and students. With the advent of the author language, a tool for teachers to write lessons became a reality. Unfortunately, many of the languages are as technical or more technical than the general-purpose languages they were designed to replace.

However, one author language, PILOT, is a prize exception to this rule. PILOT has been implemented as both an interpreter and translator on most major computer systems and on all significant microcomputer systems. PILOT consists of eight BASIC commands (oftentimes supplemented by machine specific additions) and can be taught to most groups of students or teachers within three hours. PILOT allows the teacher/ author to print information to the student, accept information from the student, match correct answers to the student's responses and provide adequate feedback while keeping count of the correct and incorrect answers. Because PILOT is dialogue-oriented and not mathematically-oriented it is nonthreatening to many teachers who might be terribly frightened by even

another author language, not to mention BASIC or other general-purpose languages. For a further description of PILOT, please refer to the author's recent article in the *AEDS Monitor*.

Like all other instructional tools, however, microcomputers must be used properly. They are multipurpose, multitalented machines which may be used at all grade levels and in all subject areas. The principal point of this paper has been to show that microcomputers, once purchased, serve no one exclusively. Like the proverbial Genie, they possess great power to help students in molding their lives, the principal limit simply being the imagination of the user.

REFERENCE

Keyser, E. Microcomputers and PILOT: A Response. *AEDS Monitor*, 1979, 17 (7, 8, 9), 22–23.

Computers in the Playground: Sesame Place

by Kathy Tekawa

An educational playground, with playmates such as Big Bird, Oscar the Grouch and the Cookie Monster, is using microcomputers to explode the myth that learning is dull, boring and painstaking for children. The spot is Sesame Place located in Langhorn, PA and it has borrowed heavily from the children's TV show, Sesame Street, to bolster the "learning and fun" concept in a completely interactive environment.

Located within Sesame Place, a creation of the Children's Television Workshop and Busch Entertainment Corp., is a 5,700-sq.-ft. Computer Gallery which houses a collection of computer games targeted for youngsters 3-13 . . . although nearly anyone would enjoy playing with these lively systems.

Those who enter this electronic playground are greeted by a colorful array of 68 terminals mounted on iron pipes reminiscent of giant Tinker Toys. Sesame Place opened last July. Since then parents have flocked in to see for the first time how effective micros can be for their youngsters. Besides having fun, their children learned about space and gravity, motion, sound and conversation, illusions, art and patterns.

Before the opening of Sesame Place, computer games were tested extensively, using children who have no problem expressing their true feelings about the project's effectiveness.

Most of the testing was conducted by Steven Gass, assistant director of research. "A lot of research was matching the game to the need of the child according to his age group. For instance, a preschooler loves exploratory games, while the teenager or adult prefers problem-solving or logic games. We had to consider each age group's needs and program them into the software," he explains. "Most of the software was designed by us, but some were modifications of existing programs."

A major concern for those in charge of the Computer Gallery was how to give the audience instant access without making them uncomfortable. "We had to ask ourselves, how are we going to overcome the standards of traditional software? How are we going to use simple instructions . . . without heavy technical terms? Computer buffs assume that if there's a blinking cursor you input then return. This isn't routine information to the general public. Every time you want someone to input a 'return' you have to tell him."

According to Joyce Hakansson, computer games coordinator, "it's exciting to see adults learn with their children. Most of us never had any interaction with computers when we grew up, so we are novices as much as our kids. It's the child who often takes that first step to show a parent how the system works.

"Adults are usually much more fearful of making a mistake, especially in family experiences. They prefer that the child try everything first. A funny thing happens," she says. "The parent prompts the child to try using the computer as he watches over the child's shoulder, then he starts making suggestions. He'll say, why don't you try this or try that first—soon what's really happening is the adult is playing the game and the poor child is just doing what the parent says."

COMPUTERS MADE TO ORDER

All the micros in the gallery are extensively modified 48K Apples. The brick red terminals with green front plates and keyboards maintain the "playful" look found throughout the park.

The custom designed keyboards differ from conventional keyboards in that they are absolutely flat . . . and 50/1,000-inch thick. Sesame Place designed its own graphic overlays to go on top.

According to Steven Gensler, president of Unicorn Engineering, the firm which designed the keyboards, they are simple to use. "The keyboard was originally designed for the handicapped, then turned out to be ideal for children because of its large keys (1-inch square) and simple design possibilities.''

The alphabet on the keyboard runs sequentially from A-Z. ''We aren't teaching typing, just allowing children to interact with a computer. Besides, most children don't know how to type. We felt they might be fearful if they could not find the letters,'' Hakansson says. Also, there is a pallet of colors on the keyboard for the user to push if the computer asks what color he wants. Rather than typing in 'red,' he simply pushes the red key. There's also a 'yes' and a 'no' key, a space, erase and the numbers.

''An advantage to this type of keyboard is that it is software defined, so it lends itself to graphics,'' Hakansson explains. ''For instance, one of our programs is a dial-a-muppet. It has a touch-tone telephone and the child picks the muppet he wants to talk to. There are different pictures of muppets on the telephone and the user chooses by pressing a picture. A voice comes on while a drawing of the muppet appears on the screen.''

The main objective to this whole computer project, according to Hakansson, was to integrate learning with fun and eliminate the confusion a child feels when he learns to operate a computer. Hakansson, who began her career with computers at the Lawrence Hall of Science at the University of California, Berkeley, has been working on the Sesame Place project for almost two years.

''I felt it was important that, before a whole new generation grew up in fear and intimidation, it needed hands-on experience with computers. The more I saw children use computers and interact with them, the more convinced I became that it was a magnificent way to teach.''

Hakansson goes on to explain that even the most patient teachers place expectations upon their students. ''A student feels a lot of stress and pressure when dealing with the adult community—he always feels the need to perform and meet up to the teacher's expectations. You take that away when you allow the child to work with a computer, which deals with him on an individual basis. The computer—being non-judgemental—lets a child take as long as he needs to answer a question.''

While many think of a computer as a cold, complicated machine, Hakansson feels that it can generate a very personal experience, especially in programs that deal with each user on an individual basis.

TYPES OF GAMES

Some games in the gallery are designed to aid a visitor in developing hand-and-eye coordination, an-

other in logical strategies, or skills in reading. Perhaps a player would like to try a music game or a creative writing exercise. For example, youngsters use the computer to write their own Sesame Place mystery. If they don't like that, they may want to try and guess the patterns forming Oscar, Big Bird, Cookie Monster and the rest of the muppets. A business-oriented game shows a young entrepreneur operating a lemonade stand; what decision-making choice he must make to stay profitable.

Other samples include a game which has a colorful array of letters march on the screen to form a jumbled word. The player has to unscramble the letters before they march into their correct position. Another game, the Face Maker, uses the computer as a creative tool. The player chooses from various facial shapes and features to create unique characters.

The majority of the machines have a menu of two to three programs. But there are also dedicated machines, running one program since some games access a lot more files.

All the computers are token-operated with the games lasting approximately 4 minutes. ''It's a friendly 4 minutes,'' Hakansson says. ''Rather than cutting you off, the timing mechanism will check and, if the player should hit a natural ending a few seconds after 4 minutes that's fine; if he hits it before, that's fine too. It allows you to complete the exercise.''

The reason for the token-operated machines Hakansson claims, is more for crowd control than anything else. ''We feel that if people pay to get in they should have an opportunity to use the environment, but if we do not have a token operation, visitors will sit in front of the terminals for hours, not giving others an opportunity.''

What are future plans for Sesame Place? Hakansson claims they would like to open more Sesame Places around the country. ''The more we expand, the more children are exposed to 'technological' learning. Computers should be another resource in the school environment and Sesame Place is one step towards making the public more aware.''

Hakansson hopes to mass market the software developed for Sesame Place next year. She wants to integrate it with Sesame Street's learning concepts. ''Then a child at home could watch Sesame Street, turn off the TV, turn on the computer and play games, drawing on the ideas he just saw on TV.

''As the micro population explodes and becomes more affordable, parents are going to start asking whether their children are using computers in schools. I believe they will make choices dependent on that answer.''

Operating a Microcomputer Convinced Me—And My Second Graders—To Use It Again . . . And Again . . .

by Geraldine Carlstrom

In the spring my teaching usually competes with baseball, anticipation of recess and general bouts of spring fever. But last year there was no contest: My second graders were busy practicing basic math facts while they destroyed alien space ships and raced down speedways. My secret? A microcomputer.

I first became interested in microcomputers when a friend showed me the TRS-80 that she had purchased for her home. The computer, the "hardware" of the system, consists of a keyboard (similar to a standard typewriter keyboard), a television screen and a cassette tape recorder. "Software," cassette tapes containing preprogrammed materials, are used along with the hardware.

I had never taken a computer class or operated a microcomputer; therefore, I considered even the mechanics of basic operation a challenge. First my friend placed a cassette tape containing a specific program in the recorder. She showed me how to start the recorder by typing commands on the keyboard. This process "loaded" the program into the computer. We loaded and ran several of the game programs my friend had purchased with the machine. By this time, whatever wariness I'd had was gone. I was totally fascinated by the microcomputer's simplicity. And, I wanted to give my students a chance to operate one. When I asked my friend to consider letting me borrow hers for the three remaining months of the school year, she agreed.

Some of the games my friend had purchased were all right for a demonstration, but I also needed educational programs that would teach concepts. After some research, I obtained a six-program package for introducing the microcomputer and a 12-program package of basic math skill games from the Software Factory in Anoka, MN. Each package came with a teacher's guide and included reproducible student work sheets. The software packages also contained student progress sheets to be filled out and filed as the students completed each program.

Since the computer was compact and required only a standard electrical outlet, I simply placed it on a small table near my desk. This arrangement allowed me to supervise the students and troubleshoot problems; however, my concern about the children's ability to use the microcomputer soon disappeared. They had little difficulty following directions displayed on the television screen, and their keyboard skills improved with each session. Many problems were eliminated because the software was designed to anticipate possible keyboard errors. For example, if a child hit a number while typing a word, the message that appeared was "That was not a letter. Please type in a letter." This was much more helpful—and personal—than if the message read "Re-enter."

The only two technicalities students had to learn in order to run the programs were to type RUN to begin them and to press the ENTER key after each response. I had students work in groups of two or three, which gave them the opportunity to remind each other of the necessary procedures. This grouping also added to the fun of the activity.

The program themes that were part of our basic skill programs ranged from space war games to mazes. In the program titled *Pit*, for example, the objective was to get a man out of the pit before a rock rolled down the hill by answering basic math problems. Each correct answer allowed the man to climb further up the rope. The child's speed in solving the problem determined the distance the man climbed. When an answer was incorrect, the man did not move and the rock continued to fall. This technique was extremely motivating and helped the students learn speed and accuracy in solving math problems. *Beat the Champ*, a game in which the first person to make a designated score became the "champ" and was then challenged by other players, taught basic math facts using numbers 1 to 20.

The children's reaction to working with the microcomputer began with curiosity and rapidly grew to unbridled enthusiasm. Everyone wanted to do math! I soon found that the children were excitedly approaching routine drills of math facts—the same drills that were once met with groans.

Each week I took time to ask the children how they felt about using the microcomputer. They enjoyed the things they could "make the computer do" when they answered the questions correctly. Timed drills had special appeal: The children loved to "beat the computer." The personalization of the machine, especially when it referred to each student by name, was important to them. Another attraction was the microcomputer's awards of titles, such as "lieutenant," "captain" and so on, on the children's completing a certain number of activities in games like "Space War." And everyone enjoyed the keyboard for recording—in lieu of writing—answers.

Not long after we started using the microcomputer I began to hear from parents, many of whom expressed surprise at the children's enthusiasm for math. One mother summed it up when she commented, "Chris said he wouldn't mind going to school all summer if he could use the computer." I was able to let parents know how their children were progressing by simply showing them the student progress sheets that accompanied the software packages.

As for me, I found the microcomputer to be an innovative new tool for teaching. Besides its motivational benefits, it allowed me more freedom to individualize. I could spend more time with students who had specific learning difficulties while others used the computer for drill and retention.

The only problem I encountered with the computer was in loading. I sometimes had to change the volume setting several times before I could successfully load a tape. I solved this by loading one program in the morning and letting the children work with it the entire day. Besides eliminating my frustration of a possible time-consuming reloading, using one program a day kept the children anticipating future computer activities.

Although there are no hard statistics to prove that my students learned more during the three months they used the microcomputer than they would have otherwise, they were enthusiastic and they did progress in basic math facts. I associate excitement and joy with learning, and both were abundant.

A major reason for the success of the microcomputer was the educational software. The programs themselves employed the kind of animated graphics that captured the children's interest and helped promote learning, and the materials supplied in the teacher's guide met my needs. From this standpoint, I think good educational software will be the key to acceptance of the microcomputer as a classroom tool.

I've already made plans to borrow my friend's computer again this spring.

Micros "GOTO" School

by Donald T. Piele

Microcomputers can be used in the classroom for instructional activities that we associate with CAI (Computer Assisted Instruction) or CMI (Computer Managed Instruction); enrichment activities that we associate with simulations and games; making numerical calculations for the purpose of solving mathematical problems; teaching students how to program—primarily in the BASIC language; and individual exploration of original problem-solving.

This article is focused on the latter activity. It is a report of a pilot project in which a microcomputer was placed in a sixth grade classroom for 8 weeks for the purpose of developing logical thinking skills. The students were given instruction on how to program the APPLE II microcomputer to draw color graphics designs. They were then given similar problems to solve using the commands they had learned.

AN APPLE FOR THE TEACHER

In the Spring of 1978, I contacted Gordon Kunaschk, a sixth grade teacher at Bose Elementary School in Kenosha, Wisconsin. He was receptive to the idea of giving up two hours a week of class time for eight weeks to let me teach his sixth graders how to program a microcomputer. If nothing else, it would be a lesson in computer literacy. Gordie had never programmed a computer before, but he was willing to learn along with the kids if I was willing to provide a computer and the necessary instruction.

The Center for the Application of Computers at UW-Parkside supported the idea and supplied an APPLE II microcomputer for the project. This was a fortunate choice for us since the APPLE II system is easy to use: it is portable; it has a good keyboard; and most important of all, it has a very simple and natural set of graphics commands that allow the programmer to create pictures on a TV screen using 16 different colors. The ideas I wanted to emphasize about computer programming would be considerably enhanced by a graphics display. The basic programming construct of a loop, for example, could be visualized, and every problem to be solved by the students could be represented by a single picture.

GETTING STARTED

My objective for bringing a microcomputer into a sixth grade classroom was to create an environment for *active problem-solving*. The BASIC programming language statements, enhanced by the graphics of the APPLE II microcomputer, form the logical building blocks. Each lesson consists of a simple program with a short explanation of the new statements, a sample run, and a series of simple program changes for the student to do. These activities allow the student to discover how the statements in the program effect its outcome. Also, problems are posed that require the student to combine statements in sequential order to solve a problem. As a result of working on these questions, the student gets a working understanding of practical problem-solving skills such as:

1. Understand the problem, its givens and goals
2. Make conjectures and probe the problem by trial and error
3. Decide on a set of possible methods of attack
4. Evaluate each possible approach for its correctness
5. Reflect on successful solutions and generalize

Each of the following exercises was designed to provide practice for these skills. They are samples taken from a larger collection and are not contiguous lessons.

Lesson #1

Key Words: GR, COLOR, PLOT

LIST	EXPLANATION
10 GR	The computer is put in the GRaphics mode.
20 COLOR=9	
20 COLOR=&	The COLOR is set to orange. There are 16 different colors to choose from. •
30 PLOT 10, 15	The position 10 over, 15 down from the upper left hand corner is plotted.
100 END	
RUN	

Your Turn (RUN the program after each change.)

1. Change line 20 to . . . . 20 COLOR=3
2. Change line 30 to . . . . 30 PLOT 5,7
3. Add line 50 . . . . 50 PLOT 5,5
4. Add line 40 . . . . 40 COLOR=6
5. Delete line 40 40
6. Add a point that connects 5,7 with 5,5 . . . .
   . . . . 60 PLOT ?,?
7. Add line 30 . . . . 30 PLOT 39,39
8. Add line 40 . . . . 40 PLOT 40,40
9. Delete line 40 40
10. Write a program that will display the first letter of your first name in graphics.

Lesson #5

Key Words: FOR-NEXT

LIST	EXPLANATION
10 GR	
20 FOR I=0 TO 15	Begin a loop with I=0 and increase I by one each time until I=15.
30 COLOR=I	The color changes with each pass through the loop.
40 PLOT I,15	The position to be plotted changes with each pass.
50 NEXT I	End of the loop. Go back to statement 20 if I is less than 15. Otherwise go to line 60.
100 END	
RUN	

Your Turn (RUN the program after each change.)

1. Change line 40 to . . . . 40 PLOT I,10
2. Change line 40 to . . . . 40 PLOT 20,I
3. Change line 20 to . . . . 20 FOR I=0 TO 39
4. Change line 40 to . . . . 40 PLOT I,I
5. Add line 45 . . . . 45 PLOT 39-I,I
6. Change the program to draw + in graphics.

Lesson #10

Key Words: RND, IF-THEN

LIST	EXPLANATION
10 GR	A random number is chosen from
20 COLOR=9	the numbers 0 to 30 and put in X.
30 X=RND (40)	
40 Y=RND (40)	Another random number is chosen and placed in Y.
50 IF Y>20 THEN COLOR=3	If Y is larger than 20 then change the color to blue (3).
60 PLOT X, Y	Go to line 20 and repeat.
70 GOTO 20	
100 END	
RUN	

Your Turn (RUN the program after each change.)

1. Change 50 to . . . . 50 IF Y>10
   THEN COLOR=3
2. Change 70 to . . . . 70 GOTO 30
3. Change 70 to . . . . 70 GOTO 20
4. Change 50 to . . . . 50 IF X>20
   THEN COLOR=3
5. Add 55 . . . . 55 IF Y>20 THEN
   COLOR=13
6. Delete 55 55
7. Change 50 . . . . 50 IF X+Y>40
   THEN COLOR=3
8. Adjust the program to plot 4 different colors in the four different corners of the screen.

TELL & RUN

In addition to the lessons, the students were given short problems to solve. They were asked to predict the output of a given program before they observed it run on the TV screen. This gave the students a chance to test their ability to reason sequentially through the statements of a program. A few examples are given below.

#1	#2
10 GR	10 GR
20 FOR I=0 TO 10	20 FOR I=10 to 20
30 COLOR=9	30 COLOR=I
40 PLOT 2,I	40 HLIN 0,39 AT I
50 NEXT I	50 NEXT I
60 END	60 END

Other activities reversed the process and presented a picture and asked the student to write a program that would produce the same result.

COMPUTER AS A CREATIVE TOOL

The APPLE II microcomputer was left in the classroom during the week to give the class time to experiment. Students signed up in pairs to work on the exercises together. The original purpose for doubling up was to provide more computer time for the class each week. But it turned out to be valuable for a completely different reason—cooperation. The students helped each other figure out the effect of each new command. The programming exercises facilitated discussions about the behavior of each new statement. New discoveries were shared with pride and enthusiasm. The computer was the focus and facilitator for cooperative problem-solving.

STUDENT REACTIONS

After eight weeks, the students were asked to respond to a questionnaire, using a scale of 1 to 5 (1-strongly disagree, 5-strongly agree), with responses from the 6th grade class of 14 boys and 10 girls recorded.

REFLECTIONS

Only a small sample of the exercises done by the students are presented in this article. An entire collection of problems was prepared for the 6th grade class to be used on the APPLE II. At the present time, good materials are not readily available. This presents a formidable obstacle to the inexperienced teacher who wants to use computers in the classroom. As more classrooms begin using microcomputers and sharing their work with others, this problem will diminish.

Students in this sixth grade class were very enthusiastic about working with a microcomputer. In contrast, students at a nearby high school who had not been exposed to computers before were generally uninterested in learning how to use them. Perhaps by this time, the older students have other activities that are more relevant. Also, in the sixth grade the survey shows that boys and girls are equally confident and interested in programming the computer. However, in entries from 10th graders in an annual computer problem-solving contest held at UW-Parkside, the boys outnumber the girls 9 to 1. A recent survey in Creative Computing Magazine had a response with a distribution of 95.4% male and 4.2% female.

Programming the microcomputer was considered by the sixth graders to be highly motivating. They would rather spend their recess on it than go outdoors. Students came early to school and would hang around as long as they could after school. A sign-up sheet became a necessity. With practice, some of the students became resident 'experts' able and thrilled to help others—including the teacher. Some of the sixth graders entered our annual computer programming contest.

RESEARCH QUESTIONS

This pilot project suggests a number of possible topics for further investigation and research:

1. If students learn how to program a computer early, will they maintain their enthusiasm in later years?
2. If students learn how to program a computer early, will the interest and confidence level of girls, in later years, continue to match that of boys?
3. What factors influence the acceptance of microcomputers in the classroom? Graphics? Games? Programming problems?
4. What is the relationship between logical thinking skills and creative programming skill?

CONCLUSION

Computers have been used in education primarily as a *delivery system* for subject matter. This role will continue to be developed even further with microcomputers. However, a new application is emerging which is fundamentally different. Instead of the computer programming the student, the student learns how to program the computer. Arthur Luehmann describes it as follows:

> Computing constitutes a new and fundamental intellectual resource. To use that resource as a mere delivery system for instruction, but not to give a student instruction in how he/she might use the resource, has been the chief failure of the CAI effort. What a loss of opportunity if the skill of computing were to be harnessed for the purpose of turning out masses of students who are unable to use computing.

The computer as an instrument for learning logical thinking and problem-solving skills is only beginning to be understood. However, with the rapid development of low cost microcomputers in the next few years, computers—and hence computer problem-solving techniques—will become a fundamental intellectual resource.

A Case and Techniques for Computers: Using Computers in Middle School Mathematics

by Larry L. Hatfield

Computers are rapidly becoming accessible to everyone. The costs of purchase have continued to decrease, with the recent miniprocessors and microprocessors representing pricing break-throughs, and inexpensive microcomputers being promoted as personal, home computers. Though much of their suggested usages to date relate to family leisure or home management, some vendors offer packages for computer-based games and drills involving mathematical ideas. Instructional programs will become increasingly available as the marketplace develops. Today's middle school students are growing up in a computerized society. Students probably feel more comfortable (often excited and curious) with the prospects of "everyman" routinely using computers than do many adults, who still view computers as complex and futuristic.

GOALS FOR MATHEMATICAL EDUCATION

We teach mathematics in a changing world. The discipline of mathematics and its applications are part of this continual evolution and our perspectives about the teaching and learning of mathematics must reflect this changing world. Our instructional goals and practices must be examined frequently to assure that we are providing for today's students an adequate mathematical education to function in the society of, at least, the near future. With this in mind, the following ideas about effective mathematics learning and teaching are summarized to suggest some viewpoints for considering possible applications of computers into middle school mathematics classrooms.

1. Mathematics learning is primarily a person-centered, constructive process; students build and modify their knowledge from experiences with task-oriented situations characteristic of mathematics. Students must experience opportunities and develop feelings of responsibility for revising, refining, and extending their ideas as the ideas are being constructed. Instruction based on the concept of constructed ideas will allow and expect errors or shortcomings in the student's responses at certain stages; the processes of identifying and correcting these are integral to the learning. *Computers can be effective instructional contexts for such constructive approaches to learning. For example, if the learning tasks involve writing or understanding a computer program, the student may be called upon to build up a procedure, test it, find the errors or inadequacies, correct or improve it, test again, and possibly refine or extend it to a more general procedure.*

2. Solving problems is the most essential of all basic skills needed in our complex, changing world, and learning to solve problems that involve mathematics is the most fundamental goal of mathematics education. Studying the processes one uses in constructing a solution to a problem may be of great assistance in knowing generalized, perhaps heuristic, approaches to problems. *Various types of computer usages can feature mathematical problem solving and its study. Student-written computer programs can involve considerable problem solving.*

3. Most school mathematics curricula put a major emphasis on algorithms. Children learn not only computational procedures for various operations but also procedures for handling almost every mathematical task they encounter: finding solution sets, evaluating expressions, simplifying fractions, factoring, finding special numbers (e.g., prime numbers, greatest common factors, square roots, and averages), completing geometric constructions or transformations, renaming (e.g., fractions to decimals), graphing, checking (e.g., computational results), estimating, and so on. In most treatments the procedures are presented ''ready-made.'' As a result, student learning of algorithms is often imitative behavior. If we believe that mathematics ought to be a sensible response to a reasonable situation, then more attention should be given to helping children to construct procedures. Helping students to identify limitations or revisions for their created algorithms can lead to significant thinking. *Computer programs are algorithms. Middle school students can learn to construct and use computer procedures for many mainline mathematical ideas. Such activity can further important goals related to algorithmic learning.*

4. Effecting quality learning is a complex combination of many factors. A reliable, knowledgeable source of help that generates, in a patient manner, interactive reteaching, practicing, and testing for each student, along with accurate records of student responses and cumulative progress, would greatly assist the harried classroom teacher. *Computers can be programmed to provide such assistance to the teacher, and teachers, as novice computer programmers, can readily learn to write and evaluate such computer programs.*

INSTRUCTIONAL COMPUTER USAGES

Most of the exploratory usages of computers in school mathematics have occurred in the past ten to fifteen years. Major attention has been given to teaching elements of computer languages, such as BASIC or FORTRAN, and to engaging mathematics students in writing and using computer programs for various mathematical topics. This use of the computer reflects the obvious interaction of the programmable, numerical, ''logical'' machine and certain qualities or aspects of mathematics. Several other types of computer applications to teaching and learning also have been identified and explored. Let's briefly examine some of these usages of the computer before considering strategies for their implementation.

Programming

Mathematics students of all ages throughout the world are writing and executing their own computer programs. Mathematics teachers cite several purposes for students' engaging in such programming tasks: (a) building ''computer literacy'' through firsthand experiences with the capabilities and limitations of programmable machines; (b) reinforcing a taught (noncomputer) procedure through students' analyzing its steps and restrictions in order to construct a computer algorithm (program); (c) illustrating the use of a computer program as a dynamic problem-solving tool—even a poor program, as an active object, can be executed, ''debugged,'' and modified; (d) providing transfer experiences through students' using their knowledge to ''teach'' the machine to generate the desired output; (e) stimulating high levels of student motivation and persistence toward more general, perhaps elegant, programs; and (f) emphasizing methods of solving, discovering, and generalizing by building programs, studying a program's output, and extending revised programs toward algorithms aimed at handling entire classes of problems.

Middle school mathematics abounds with situations that can be approached as programming tasks: (a) finding solutions to open sentences; (b) testing for properties of number systems; (c) number theory topics—finding prime numbers, multiples, complete factorizations, greatest common factors, least common multiples, and deficient, perfect, or abundant numbers; (d) solving measurement problems—perimeter, area, volume, and angle relationships; (e) manipulating fractions and decimals—renaming, simplifying, performing the four arithmetic operations, and ordering; and (f) solving applied problems—finding averages, solving proportions, calculating percents, and figuring probabilities.

Practicing

Computerized practice has been extensively applied to school mathematics instruction during the past fifteen years. Of course, the fundamental purpose of a practice session at a computer terminal is to rehearse for more automatic recall or recognition of certain aspects of the ideas previously taught. Practicing programs usually do not deal with explanations of mathematical ideas. The role of the teacher is to develop the background understandings necessary for effective practicing to occur. Although of uneven quality, many practicing programs do exist.

Tutoring

Computer-based tutorial instruction involves the use of the machine to present an introduction or review of ideas which are not adequately known by the student. The stored program attempts to simulate a good tutor as it introduces, explains, characterizes, exemplifies, asks questions, accepts and evaluates responses, diagnoses difficulties, provides feedback and reinforcements, monitors performances, and selects appropriate placement into subsequent lessons. Tutorial programs are similar in structure and function to practice programs but often contain considerably more detailed text to be used in explaining the content of the lesson. They are usually more complex and costly to prepare and to offer than practice programs. Although much attention has been given to the experimental development of tutorial programs in certain federally-funded projects, this computer usage has not become widespread. With lowered costs for computers the prospect of such private tutoring may become more feasible.

Simulating and Gaming

As a simulation device, the computer can often be used to deal with otherwise unmanageable phenomena. The advantages of computer-based simulation include the measurement and manipulation of variables that are difficult or dangerous to assess, the opportunity to experiment when it is not otherwise possible, the control of "noise" (irrelevant variables) that might otherwise obscure the item to be measured or studied, and the compression of the time dimension to allow long-term events to be studied in short periods of time. Among the contexts of possible interest to middle school mathematics teachers are situations that use probability models as well as other physical and social science applications of mathematics. The following are some examples of simulation programs: (a) probability (flipping coins, rolling dice, blinded drawings), (b) economics (playing the stock market, purchasing via loans, ruling a developing nation), and (c) sciences (effects and control of water pollution, piloting a spaceship, chemical or nuclear reactions, genetic manipulations).

Gaming programs are simulations featuring competitive settings in which one or more players can play, score, and win. Hundreds of computer-based games exist, with many appropriate to objectives of middle school mathematical education.

Testing

The computer has been programmed to serve as a test generator and administrator. Conceivably, each student could be given a tailor-made examination where the choice of objectives as well as number and difficulty of items for each objective would be specified for each student.

USING COMPUTERS IN A SCHOOL

To many mathematics teachers the prospect of incorporating the use of a computer into their curriculum appears as an educational "future shock." As a rapidly growing number of teachers in hundreds of schools are finding, however, the machines and accompanying materials are oriented toward the novice who has little or no programming and computer background. The computers are simple to operate, being quite "foolproof," and programming languages, such as BASIC, are easy to learn, yet powerful and flexible enough to satisfy the most advanced student. Numerous journals, oriented to the educational user of computers, provide further background as well as practical classroom suggestions and actual program listings. A variety of resource books for mathematics teachers provides detailed suggestions for developing student programming. Most computer companies sponsor educators' "users groups" that offer informative newsletters, meetings, and a clearinghouse service for exchanging computer programs among members. And professional associations, such as the NCTM, offer workshops at their meetings and written materials in their journals and supplementary publications to help teachers with computer-oriented activities.

A school typically begins a program of computer use with limited access to a computer, a single terminal or computer. Through workshops, teachers can learn to operate a minicomputer, run stored (ready-to-use) programs, and write and execute simple BASIC programs for several mathematical topics taught in the middle school curriculum. A sixth-grade teacher, for example, might decide to focus on two types of uses of the computer with his or her students during the first year of computer use, simple programming tasks and stored practicing programs. To develop the knowledge needed for students to write their own programs, the teacher might begin by discussing and demonstrating completed programs; later the students can be given incomplete algorithms which they analyze, complete, and execute. As students learn the BASIC language and how a program can be constructed, they will become more able to initiate their own programs for mathematical tasks.

The following is an example of student programming tasks for a particular unit to be studied:

The whole number system

(a) Find sums, differences, products, and quotients.

(b) Simplify number expressions.

(c) Make lists of pairs, given a function rule.

(d) Find factors (see figure 1).

(e) Determine primeness.

(f) Find all prime numbers in a given interval.

SUMMARY

Computers can be used in educational settings and for instructional purposes in more ways than are generally realized; they can be much more than a means to individualizing testing or drilling for competency in basic facts. Computers can be teaching aids that help to achieve the objectives for mathematics learning identified earlier in this article. When access to a computer is available, students will be able to use the computer for programming the solutions to problems; for simulating situations in order to test hypotheses; for gaming, as a study of probability and statistics; as well as for practicing, testing, and tutoring.

The purpose of this article is to help teachers become aware of the potential for this multiusage approach to computers.

Figure 1

```
1 REM  Jason, Period 2, Ms. Davis

10 REM ** FIND ALL FACTORS OF A NUMBER **

20 INPUT "FACTORS FOR WHAT NUMBER", N

30 FOR D = 1 TO n

40 IF N/D <> INT (n/D) THEN 60

50 PRINT D;

60 NEXT D

70 GO TO 20

80 END
```

```
FACTORS FOR WHAT NUMBER? 12
  1 2 3 4 6 12

FACTORS FOR WHAT NUMBER? 35
  1 5 7 35

FACTORS FOR WHAT NUMBER? 59
  1 59

FACTORS FOR WHAT NUMBER? 57
  1 3 19 57

FACTORS FOR WHAT NUMBER? 101
  1 101

FACTORS FOR WHAT NUMBER? 864
  1 2 3 4 6 8 9 12 16 18
  24 27 32 36 48 54 72 96
  108 144 216 288 432 864

FACTORS FOR WHAT NUMBER? 97
  1 97

FACTORS FOR WHAT NUMBER? 27
  1 3 9 27
```

Program notes:
This is an example of a structured, incomplete programming task.

Lines 1 and 10 are simply remarks, ignored by the computer during execution.

Lines 30 through 60 set up a "loop" where the set of possible divisors 1 through N are tested. The condition in line 40 tests for even divisibility, skipping on to the next trial divisor (line 60) or printing a divisor (line 50).

Making the Grade at Keene High School

by Dennis Brisson

Keene (NH) High School increased its enrollment last fall by 13. That's the number of TRS-80 microcomputers the school brought into the classroom for its computer-programming classes. Although the use of desktop computers for individualized instruction is in its infancy at the school, computer use and instruction is not a new idea. Indeed, Keene High was one of the first public schools in New Hampshire to make use of computers.

If KHS can be credited with breaking new ground in the computer-education field, then its principal trailblazer is Charles Tousley, math department head, who has taught programming at the school for the last 13 years. During that time, he has seen the school experiment with various computers. It was his pioneer spirit that recently prompted KHS to board the microcomputers-in-education bandwagon.

Tousley was well tutored in the fundamentals of computer programming. He notes with some pride, "I learned BASIC from the man who invented the language, Dr. John Kemeny." As part of a contingent of representatives from Vermont and New Hampshire public schools, Tousley studied the time-sharing system at Dartmouth College under the direction of Kemeny in 1967. Having learned the intricacies of programming, he operated the high school's time-sharing terminal, which hooked into the Dartmouth system. But this arrangement for teaching programming was expensive. "It cost $6000 a year just to rent the equipment," explains Tousley.

In 1972, Keene High discontinued this system and purchased programmable 8-bit calculators for its computer classes. In 1976, the students learned programming on a PDP-11 minicomputer, which the Cheshire Vocational Center, adjoining the high school building, purchased.

Advances in the computer industry produced other, less expensive, alternatives. The microcomputer had arrived, making individual use by students a practical means of teaching programming. Tousley's eyes brighten as he recalls, "Two years later, along came the TRS-80."

PROBLEM OF FUNDING

Early on, Tousley recognized the value of microcomputers in education as effective in increasing student achievement and in motivating students. However, finding people who shared his enthusiasm proved difficult at first. One such person who shares his vision of future school uses of micros is John Amstein, head of the science department at the school, and instrumental, together with Tousley, in setting up the school's microcomputing program.

Whereas Tousley learned BASIC just two years after its development, Amstein is a self-taught programmer and a relative newcomer to computers. Despite these divergent backgrounds, the two are working together toward a common goal: establishing microcomputer use at the school for all subjects. Tousley explains: "John, who hadn't done any work with computers at all until this year, at least has the enthusiasm I've got; he recognizes the importance of them." He adds, "We are always dumbfounded when we can't find the same enthusiasm in the people who control the drawstrings on the purses."

Obtaining funds for innovations in education, particularly microcomputers, is difficult at best, as Tousley, who follows closely the latest developments in computer education and the problems of other schools, is well aware. With school boards and administrators grappling with the rising costs of running a school, they are reluctant to defend the initial investment for computer equipment. They question, too, the cost-effectiveness of microcomputers as compared to the more traditional teaching aids.

Tousley sees this thread of thinking running throughout the nation. "We all run into the same problem: administrators and school-board members went to school when there weren't any computers. So trying to convince them that computers are a necessity in the curriculum is a heck of a hard job," he laments.

Tousley feels that the schools' money couldn't be more wisely spent. On this point, he is as persuasive as he is determined. Approaching the school board for the OK on this year's microcomputer expenditure, Tousley was armed with a convincing statistic he derived while thumbing through the help-wanted ads in a Boston Sunday paper: over 75 percent of the employment opportunities required some knowledge of computers or a related math background.

The previous year, the school board approved the purchase of two TRS-80s, which "proved so satisfactory in the classroom that we went to the board again the following year to ask for more money."

He got the money—not the $10,000 he requested from the school board, but $9000 the board allocated from a special school source, the Academy Fund. This year he's going after more money to purchase more computer equipment. He's seeking $4000 from the Academy Fund and a federal government Title IV three-year grant for $40,000. He modestly explains his success: "Basically, I recognized the importance of computers and their place in school, and I just kept after people until we got the money to get them [the microcomputers] into the classroom."

EDUCATORS' REACTIONS

Getting computers into the classroom is one thing; convincing others of their teaching potential is another. Tousley has been instrumental in encouraging and aiding area schools to establish microcomputer programs. But he has encountered obstacles. He has run up against educators who are reluctant to accept computers, to experiment and explore the potential of computers as a teaching tool. He cites administrators who dislike the prospect of curriculum changes involving computers because "it means changing all the methods they've developed over the years."

Even more myopic are math teachers "who are serious when they can't even think of any uses for computers. They can't imagine why computers are anything other than toys," Tousley says in disbelief.

Through the education of the people involved, the trend is changing, according to Tousley. "We're fight-

ing a constant battle with people who are entrenched in the old way of doing things. Hopefully, this will gradually change. I know it will," he adds optimistically.

Today's students, born in the computer era, will reap the benefits of an advanced technology that has resulted in computer-assisted instruction. But today's teachers in the high schools, and even in the grade schools, face a challenge: how to deal with the influx of microcomputers in the classroom.

At Keene High, Tousley sees a positive reaction among the teachers. He is quick to point out that the Keene High administration has been supportive of the microcomputing program, and inquisitive teachers have borrowed the TRS-80 manuals and units ("admirably suited for self-learning") to learn programming at home in order to better understand the educational value of these machines.

Next he plans to initiate workshops for the teachers about the computers and their potential for classroom teaching. His enthusiasm for, and belief in, computers is catching . . . particularly among his students.

USES IN THE CLASSROOM

Tousley's students need no supervision, nor anyone to tell them to begin class. Computer programs allow the students to practice and learn on their own, with immediate feedback on their progress. When not in use by the programming classes, the micros are in operation by the students during their free periods.

The purchase this year of the 13 Level II 16K TRS-80s was a joint project of the school's math and science departments. As presented by Tousley and Amstein to the administration, the microcomputing program involves three phases.

The first phase seeks student involvement—to familiarize the students with the fundamentals of programming and introduce them to all the capabilities of the microcomputers. Tousley has found that the best way to introduce students to computers is through hands-on experience. He concentrates on the graphics capabilities of the computers and relies heavily on computer games to spark student interest.

Game playing is a fundamental first step in learning the use of computers. But for most students, the game-playing stage lasts briefly before they realize the potential for more constructive uses and become eager to write their own applications. The school even boasts its own computerized radio station where the DJs can call up information on the latest Top 40 hits or recording star on the station's TRS-80.

"The first year of the project, we're trying to get as many people acquainted with the computer as possible. We want to mass-produce enthusiastic students," says Tousley.

As students use the computers more and as teachers become more involved, Tousley and Amstein predict that ideas for applications in the classroom will blossom. Outside of the programming classes, the computers see limited use in computer-aided instruction (CAI). The school uses some CAI programs to drill students on the concepts of algebra and basic math. CAI programs are also used in science: genetic cross-breeding, population growth and diet-calorie analysis programs for biology. A student who was in Tousley's computer-programming course last year and is a physics student in Amstein's class this year converted a sun-tracking program into TRS-80 BASIC.

Tousley's programming classes include about 32 sophomores and juniors. As seniors, with the knowledge of BASIC programming, they will be expected to write their own applications in the physics and science classes, an idea particularly appealing to Amstein, who ranks the computer as valuable a tool as the microscope to teach science.

Phase two of the microcomputing program involves creating applications programs and expanding the school's collection of science and math program tapes. Teachers would probably prefer plug-in software, but the KHS program calls for the students to write their own, thus expanding the learning process involving computers.

Although the amount of software on the market is growing, Tousley and Amstein cite the general lack of educational programs. They realize that computers as educational tools are only as effective as the programs written for them. So they plan to develop their own; the students will write their own applications for use in advanced math, geometry, calculus, physics, chemistry and biology. Compiling a library of good program tapes will take time.

In the third phase, Tousley and Amstein want to see the widespread use of computers throughout the school in all subjects. As Amstein explains, the school's immediate future goals include equipping a complete computer classroom, installing a computer in each of the school's 18 classrooms and making computers available to students in the library during their free time.

"By the third year of the program, we should have a large supply of program applications. We want people to realize that computers are not just tools for math and science, but for English, foreign languages and who knows what else," explains Tousley.

CHOOSING THE TRS-80

After investigating the various microcomputers on the market, KHS opted for the TRS-80 over the PET ("tiny keyboard design was a major mistake") and the Apple ("twice the price"). From the outset, Tousley was convinced that the TRS-80 was the computer for the job at KHS. "I can't see how anyone is going to compete against the TRS-80. It's the best one for the job. It isn't the best computer in the world, but for its price, and for what we want to do with it in school, there's no other competing model."

Quality and low cost were the two main features of the TRS-80 that prompted the school's selection. The availability of near-by service and the maintenance support offered by a local Radio Shack store also appealed to the school, as did the unit's portability, which allows it to be transported from classroom to classroom. The trigonometric-functions capability was also attractive.

Next year the school plans to buy several more TRS-80s, line printers and the Radio Shack Network System, which allows up to 16 microcomputers to use the same disk drive. The classroom setup at present features a large, modified TV-screen monitor from which Tousley can instruct the entire class. Each computer is comfortably situated on its separate desk-top area, with a place for keyboard, cassette recorder and monitor, as well as a CLOAD and CSAVE switch modification constructed by Tousley.

CLASS DISMISSED

Many educators, such as Tousley and Amstein, believe that computers are destined to have a profound influence on the way we educate our children. More educators are investigating the impact of computers on the education process—not just as tools for teaching, but to prepare the students for post-high-school education and for a world increasingly influenced by and dependent on the use of computers. Their place in the classrooms at Keene High has been assured by the enthusiastic reception by students and faculty.

After a brief period at the computers, the students are anxious to begin computer applications programs. Quiz and data programs, storage for foreign-language vocabulary and other data-storage uses are several applications the students are working with.

While no student has yet developed a program to replace the teacher in the classroom, the day is fast approaching when a computer in every classroom will become a reality.

Computers . . . Are All Dinosaurs Dead?

by Douglas Glover

Numerous articles have been written to describe on-going computer oriented programs and their successes, yet none has provided the "How To" information for an interested educator to initiate and manage such programs in his/her own environment. In keeping with G/C/T's intent to provide usable information to those involved with the G/C/T child, this article will be directed toward informing the reader how microcomputers can be reasonably introduced into an existing program for G/C/T children.

One might easily relate the traditional large-scale computer in the pre-college educational environment to the dinosaur: its dominance in the educational realm is on the wane. The reason for this situation is the development of the microprocessor—a computer on a single integrated circuit. This device, as the heart of a microcomputer, offers computing power equivalent to computers costing in the five to six digit range only a few years ago.

Even those schools which are using microcomputers or the larger minicomputers seldom seem to exercise these equipments effectively. In many programs one finds the computer used for a relatively few students to learn programming techniques or computer design. The computer may be infrequently used by an additional segment of the student population for simulations or games that are related to political science, history of business. In other schools one finds the computer used exclusively as a "teaching machine," most frequently for teaching younger children reading, math or perhaps a foreign language. The computer is a flexible, dynamic teaching aid which should be utilized across the entire spectrum of its capability. It is time to pause and take an arm's length look at the computer and its role in the school environment.

The University of South Alabama Saturday Program for Gifted Children (SGP) began offering computer programming for its students in the spring of 1977 using the University's IBM Model 370/145. This was at least a step in the right direction. However, the complexity of dealing with such a large system and its uncompromising protocol made it less than optimal, particularly for the younger children (8-9 year olds) in the class. Even this first foray into computing verified the high level of interest among the SGP students. Approximately seventy percent of those who had participated in the Spring programming course and later enrolled for a second year of the Saturday Program, also chose a second course in computer programming as one of their Fall Quarter courses. Still, the complexity of working with the IBM system caused some consternation.

In the Fall of 1977, The Tandy Corporation's Radio Shack Division announced the availability of its TRS-80 microcomputer. This self-contained, completely assembled microcomputer appeared to be the exact answer to our needs. Using the state-of-the-art Z-80 microprocessor, this system is composed of a computer/keyboard, video monitor and cassette recorder, at a total cost of $599.00. The Saturday Program had been looking for a microcomputer to use but several problems had precluded the acquisition of system prior to the entry of the TRS-80.

First, most reasonably priced (under $1800) microcomputer systems, that were available in the Fall of 1977, were sold in kit form. This required the buyer to assemble and test the system prior to putting it into service. Due to the electronics background and sophisticated test equipment required to accomplish this task, it was an insurmountable obstacle for most schools. Second, repair and maintenance service for the existing systems was either unavailable or prohibitively expensive. With Radio Shack's nationwide system of repair facilities, these roadblocks were overcome. Tandy has established a separate division, Tandy Computers, which will most probably eventually direct the corporation's computer related activities; however, the TRS-80 is now a standard "off the shelf" item at most Radio Shack stores.

In November, The Saturday Program ordered four TRS-80s. They were no more difficult to set up and operate than a simple component stereo system. Plugging in three A.C. line plugs and three interconnecting cables is all that is required to make the system operational. All connections are clearly marked. The manual provided with the microcomputer assumes that the user has no prior association with computers and thus takes the reader from initial equipment setup through all the programming techniques available in the computer's resident BASIC Language. The manual is written in a step-by-step, programmed instruction approach which will permit its use either as a resource book for the teacher or as a student text.

The primary use of the SGP microcomputers is to teach computer programming to students in the age range of 8 to 18 who elect this subject. During their first quarter of programming, the students are taught the computer language BASIC. The objective is to familiarize the student with the computer and how it can be made to work for him/her. Some simulations and computer games are used as motivators during the quarter. It became apparent that many of the kids would take this course repeatedly for the simulations/games alone, without ever mastering BASIC. To ensure their concentration on the task of learning to program, a post-test has been introduced on which a score of 90% must be achieved in order for the student to select a subsequent programming course. If a program intends to offer computer time to students beyond an introductory level, the participants must be guided and challenged just as with any other course for G/C/T youth. The SGP present modus operandi is to have the advanced programming students identify one or more objectives which they will work toward during the quarter. These objectives might concentrate on improving their skills in graphics techniques or in the development of programs for home use. The students work independently on their projects, using their instructor as a resource person for advice or/and assistance as required.

Using the independent study approach to advanced programming students can reap other benefits for both the program and the student. The student may elect to develop one or more programs relevant to his activities in another of his subjects. Such a student could be of valuable assistance to a teacher who wishes to include some computer related activities in his/her course.

Beyond the student directed independent study, these advanced programmers could be encouraged to do specific developmental tasks related to the administration, planning or curriculum of the program itself. There are an almost unlimited number of software items that could be developed by these programmers which might make a significant contribution to the direction in which the program grows.

The student programmers' growth and development are simply functions of the teacher's own creativity in keeping them challenged. If the teacher follows the guidelines described above, she/he can keep these more capable students deeply involved in their own research and development activities while the majority of classroom time could be devoted to beginning programmers or those who are having difficulty mastering programming concepts.

Now, what about students who are not in programming courses? Teachers should consider using the microcomputer to add spice and motivation in their courses in much the same way as other audio-visual equipment can be used. Beyond the rudimentary machine functions which any other computer user must learn (it takes approximately five minutes to teach anyone), the computer does the rest of the work. Programs should be written in a fully interactive mode (i.e., self-prompting and error correcting) so that the time wasted by instructions from the teacher will be minimized. An example of such a program accompanies this article. This program, "Dinosaurs," is written in Radio Shack Level I BASIC and was developed for use with a course for six to eight year olds entitled, "Are All Dinosaurs Dead?" This type of program is easily developed and can be expanded or reduced depending upon the capabilities of the microcomputer available. The example program requires the TRS-80 with 16K of user memory. With very little effort the program could be reduced in scope to fit the smaller TRS-80 with 4K of user memory. (The reader should not be frightened off because of a little technical jargon such as 4K or 16K of user memory. Within an hour, she/he will find the terms coming quite naturally.)

What are the hard facts an interested G/C/T teacher must have to sell his/her administration on such a project? How should the program be implemented and how much will it cost? Many G/C/T programs which offer courses in computer programming might more appropriately call these courses "Introduction to Computers" because the kids get little or no opportunity to have hands-on experience with the computer. *G/C/T kids have little interest in watching others operate equipment!* They must be actively involved. The Saturday Program has found that the most desirable ratio of students to the computer input/output (I/O) device is two to one for classes on programming. The I/O device might be a printer or video terminal in a large computer time-sharing system, while the microcomputer such as the TRS-80 has its keyboard and video display integral to the microcomputer system.

The rationale for the two to one ratio has evolved over several quarters of operation. Due to the usual time constraint of one hour per class, three or more students per I/O device will not allow each student to have sufficient hands-on opportunity to work with the programming techniques being taught. Hands-on activity is the key to continued interest and achievement in this subject area. The SGP violated its own rule in this regard one quarter with disastrous results. Because of the large number of applicants for programming, the classes were set up with a three to one ratio with the result that students who participated in these larger classes did not have sufficient applications time to learn the programming techniques. Many of them became disenchanted with the whole idea because of their competition to get a share of computer time. Those who were more persevering made the best of the unfortunate situation and they signed up for a second opportunity to learn the material during the following quarter. Needless to say the ratio of students to I/O device is back to the proven two to one.

One might logically ask, "if two to one is good, why wouldn't one to one be even better?" Ironically enough, even if there is an I/O device for each student in the Beginner's Programming Classes, during the initial learning/investigative stage, the students will gravitate toward working in pairs to solve programming tasks. Learning a computer language is much like learning any foreign language. The combination of learning the language and applying the language to problem solving situations often causes even the most dedicated "lone wolf" to seek association with his peers to accomplish a task. One might view this interactive environment as one of the major advantages to teaching computer programming in this manner.

The number of systems a G/C/T program is to acquire will be a function of the educator's creativeness in locating funds and/or his/her persuasiveness with the local school administration. If there is absolutely no computer equipment on site, an initial investment in one or two systems could get things started. An individual adept at proposal writing certainly should seek outside resources and try for a larger number of systems.

An interesting cost comparison can be shown between the relative merits of adding printers or video terminals to existing large computers available to a school system or beginning from "scratch" by purchasing an independent microcomputer. Consider the cost of two of the more common I/O, terminal equipments:

Lear Sigler, ADM-3A, video terminal $895.00
or
Digital Equipment Corp DEC Writer II, printer
terminal $1495.00
vs.
Radio Shack TRS-80, microcomputer $599.00

The terminal cost only includes the equipment (hardware) and does not include such items as installation and line lease fees for the terminals. The microcomputer has no additional costs! From a cost effectiveness standpoint, the TRS-80 wins hands-down. A program can purchase three complete microcomputer systems for the cost of two Lear Sigler, ADM-3A video terminals, or FIVE microcomputer systems for the approximate cost of only two DEC Writer IIs.

The arguments are strongly in favor of the microcomputer from virtually all points of view. The microcomputer is:

- More cost effective.
- Dedicated to exclusive student use (The G/C/T program doesn't have to be concerned with being preempted by some priority task, an experience one cannot escape as a time sharing customer on a large computer).
- A more effective system to teach programming because of its simplicity of operation.
- More easily repaired and maintained.
- A system which can be utilized and taught to children by personnel who are not computer professionals!

The computer has proven itself to be a powerful education device. With the advent of the TRS-80 microcomputer, it is well within the reach of every program for G/C/T children.

THE PROGRAM

```
10      REM **DINOSAURS**
15      REM **A SCIENCE GAME DESIGNED FOR THE TRS-80
20      REM **BY DOUGLAS GLOVER
25      REM **COPYRIGHT 1978
29      CLS
30      P.A. (64), "              **DINOSAURS**"
35      P.:P. "A SCIENCE INSTRUCTIONAL GAME FOR THE TRS-80"
40      P.:P. "FOR MY LIST OF DINOSAURS, PRESS ENTER.": IN.A$
100     P. "THE DINOSAURS IN MY MEMORY ARE:"
110     P.T. (20), "1.   DIPLODOCUS"
115     P.T. (20), "2.   PLESIOSAURUS"
120     P.T. (20), "3.   PTERANODON"
125     P.T. (20), "4.   STEGOSAURUS"
130     P.T. (20), "5.   TRACHODON"
135     P.T. (20), "6.   TYRANNOSAURUS"
140     P. "SELECT THE DINOSAUR OF YOUR CHOICE AND ENTER THE NUMBER.":IN.A
145     ON A G. 200, 400, 600, 800, 1000, 1200
146     IF (A < 0) + (A > 6) T. GOS. 3120
147     G.100
200     CLS:P.A. (192), "          DIPLODOCUS"
205     P.:P.T. (20), "(DIH-PLOD-UH-KUSS)":P.
210     P. "A.   DIPLODOCUS WAS ONE OF THE:"
211     P. "     1.   SMALLEST DINOSAURS"
212     P. "     2.   LARGEST DINOSAURS":IN.A
216     ON A G. 220, 230
217     IF (A < 0) + (A > 2)T. GOS. 3120
218     G. 200
220     P. "WEIGHING 25 TONS OR 50000 POUNDS—WOULD YOU CALL"
221     P. "THAT TINY??????"
223     GOS. 3090
224     G. 210
230     P.:P. "RIGHT! IT WAS THE LARGEST OF ALL DINOSAURS WITH A"
231     P. "RECORDED LENGTH OF 87.5 FEET."
232     P.:P. "NOW FOR QUESTION B., PRESS ENTER.":IN.A$
240     CLS: P.A. (256), "B. BECAUSE OF ITS SIZE AND SLOWNESS, IT SPENT"
241     P. "     MOST OF ITS TIME:"
242     P. "     1.   IN WOODLANDS"
243     P. "     2.   IN THE DESERT"
244     P. "     3.   IN THE WATER":IN.A.
250     ON A G. 260, 270, 280
251     IF (A < 0) + (A > 3)T. GOS. 3120
252     G. 240
260     P. "DIPLODOCUS WOULD BE HAZARDOUS TO A FOREST'S HEALTH!"
264     GOS. 3090
266     G. 240
270     P.:P. "WHERE WOULD IT FIND WATER PLANTS IN THE DESERT?"
274     GOS. 3090
276     G. 240
```

THE PROGRAM (continued)

```
280   P.:P. "RIGHT! ACTUALLY THE SCIENTISTS THINK IT SPENT MOST"
281   P. "OF ITS TIME MUNCHING SOFT GREEN WATER PLANTS TO KEEP"
282   P. "ITS HUGE BODY FED."
285   P.:P. "NOW FOR QUESTION C., PRESS ENTER.":IN.A$
290   CLS:P.A. (256), "C. A RELATIVE OF DIPLODOCUS WHICH LOOKED VERY"
291   P. "      MUCH LIKE IT WAS:"
292   P. "      1.   ALLOSAURUS (AL-UH-SOR-US)"
293   P. "      2.   ANKYLOSAURUS (AN-KIL-UH-SOR-US)"
294   P. "      3.   BRONTOSAURUS (BRON-TUH-SOR-US)":IN.A
300   ON A G. 310, 320, 330
301   IF (A < 0) + (A > 3)T. GOS. 3120
302   G. 290
310   P. "NO! NO! THAT IS TYRANNOSAURUS' RELATIVE"
314   GOS. 3090
316   G. 290
320   P. "THIS ONE IS CLOSER TO STEGOSAURUS BECAUSE IT IS BIRDHIPPED"
321   P. "AND COVERED WITH ARMOR."
324   GOS. 3090
326   G. 290
330   P. "RIGHT! IT IS JUST A SLIGHTLY SMALLER VERSION OF"
331   P. "DIPLODOCUS, REACHING ONLY ABOUT 70 FT. LONG"
332   GOS. 3000
400   CLS: P.A. (192), "           PLESIOSAURUS"
405   P.:P.T. (20), "(PLEES-EE-US-SOR-US)":P.
410   P. "A. PLESIOSAURUS IS A DINOSAUR THAT GREW UP TO 50 FT."
411   P. "     LONG AND LIVED IN:"
412   P. "     1.   MARSHY LAND"
413   P. "     2.   DESERT CLIMATES"
414   P. "     3.   THE OCEAN":IN.A
416   ON A G. 420, 425, 430
417   IF (A < 0) + (A > 3)T. GOS. 3120
418   G. 400
420   P. "I SAID PLESIOSAURUS NOT BRONTOSAURUS!!"
421   GOS .3090
422   G .400
425   P. "YOU MUST HAVE BEEN THINKING OF COELOPHYSIS (KO-E-LO-FI-SIS)."
426   P. "IT LIVED IN A SEMI-ARID CLIMATE OF OUR SOUTHWEST."
427   GOS. 3090
428   G. 400
430   P. "YOUR GUESS IS CORRECT. PLESIOSAURUS' HOME WAS IN THE"
431   P."SEAS OF THE LATE CRETACEOUS (KREE-TAY-SHUSS) PERIOD."
432   P.:P. "NOW FOR QUESTION B., PRESS ENTER.":IN.A$
440   CLS:P.A. (256), "B. PLESIOSAURUS' PRIMARY DIET WAS:"
441   P. "     1.   FISH"
442   P. "     2.   PLANTS"
443   P. "     3.   OTHER DINOSAURS":IN.A.
445   ON A G. 450, 455, 460
446   IF (A < 0) + (A > 3)T. GOS. 3120
```

THE PROGRAM (continued)

```
447   G. 440
450   P. "CORRECT AGAIN! WHAT ELSE DO YOU EXPECT IT TO EAT,"
451   P. "A MOUTH FULL OF CEPHALOPODS (SEF-A-LO-PODS)?? YUK!!!"
452   P. "NOW FOR QUESTION C. PRESS ENTER.":IN.A$
453   G. 470
455   P. "PLESIOSAURUS WAS A CARNIVORE NOT A HERBIVORE--IF"
456   P. "YOU DON'T KNOW WHAT THOSE WORDS MEAN--THEN NOW IS"
457   P. "THE TIME TO FIND OUT."
458   GOS. 3090
459   G. 440
460   P. "PLESIOSAURUS MAY HAVE TRIED A FEW SMALL ONES BUT"
461   P. "THEY WERE NOT ITS PRIMARY DIET . . . . . ."
462   GOS. 3090
463   G. 440
470   CLS:P.A. (256), "C. SOME SCIENTISTS THINK THAT A RELATIVE OF"
471   P. "PLESIOSAURUS IS STILL LIVING TODAY. IT IS:"
472   P. "      1.   GODZILLA"
473   P. "      2.   LOCH NESS MONSTER"
474   P. "      3.   BUNYIP":IN.A
476   ON A G. 480, 485, 490
477   IF (A < 0) + (A > 3)T. GOS. 3120
478   G. 470
480   P. "GODZILLA! YOU'VE BEEN WATCHING TOO MANY JAPANESE"
481   P. "SCIENCE FICTION MOVIES!!"
482   GOS. 3090
483   G. 470
485   CLS:P.A. (256), "RIGHT! MANY OF THE SIGHTINGS OF NESSIE DESCRIBE"
486   P. "AN ANIMAL VERY MUCH LIKE A PLESIOSAUR."
487   GOS. 3000
490   CLS: P.A. (256), "YOU SILLY! BUNYIP IS A MYTHICAL SEA MONSTER."
491   GOS. 3090
492   G. 470
600   CLS:P.A. (192), "            PTERANODON"
605   P.:P.T. (20), "(TER-AN-UH-DON)"
610   P.:P. "A. PTERANODON MEANS TOOTHLESS-WING. IT WAS A:"
611   P. "      1.   LAND REPTILE"
612   P. "      2.   FLYING TIGER"
613   P. "      3.   FLYING REPTILE":IN.A
615   ON A G. 620, 630, 640
616   IF (A < 0) + (A > 3)T. GOS. 3120
617   G. 600
620   P. "WITH A NAME LIKE TOOTHLESS-WING???"
623   GOS. 3090
624   G. 610
630   P.:P. "FLYING TIGERS WERE A GROUP OF U.S. FLYERS WHO"
631   P. "FOUGHT WITH CHINA AGAINST JAPAN."
633   GOS. 3090
634   G. 610
640   P.:P. "RIGHT! PTERANODON WAS AS LARGE AS A SMALL AIRPLANE"
```

THE PROGRAM (continued)

```
641   P. "WITH A WINGSPREAD OF 27 FEET."
642   P.:P. "NOW FOR QUESTION B., PRESS ENTER.":IN.A$
650   CLS:P.A. (256), "B. PTERANODON'S DIET WAS MADE UP OF:"
651   P. "      1.   TYRANNOSAURUS MEAT"
652   P. "      2.   SMALL ANIMALS AND FISH"
653   P. "      3.   TREE BARK":IN.A
656   ON A G. 660, 665, 670
656   IF (A < 0) + (A > 3)T. GOS. 3120
657   G. 650
660   P. "WITH NO TEETH--YOU'VE GOT TO BE KIDDING!"
662   GOS. 3090
663   G. 650
665   P. "RIGHT! IT USED ITS KEEN EYESIGHT TO LOCATE THEM."
666   P.:P. "NOW FOR QUESTION C., PRESS ENTER.":IN.A$
667   G. 680
670   P. "EVEN WOODY WOODPECKER WOULDN'T GO FOR THAT!"
672   GOS. 3090
673   G. 650
680   CLS:P.A. (256), "C.   PTERANODON WAS:"
681   P. "      1.   WARM BLOODED"
682   P. "      2.   COLD BLOODED":IN.A
684   ON A G. 690, 695
685   IF (A < 0) + (A > 2)T. GOS. 3120
686   G. 680
690   P.:P. "RIGHT! SCIENTISTS THINK THAT BECAUSE THE FLYING REPTILES"
691   P. "HAD TO BE MORE ACTIVE THAN LAND OR WATER CREATURES,"
692   P. "THAT THEY MUST HAVE BEEN WARM BLOODED LIKE BIRDS"
693   P. "AND MAMMALS."
694   GOS. 3000
695   P. "FOOLED YOU DIDN'T I"
697   GOS. 3090
698   G. 600
800   CLS:P.A. (192), "             STEGOSAURUS"
805   P.:P.T. (18), "(STEG-UH-SOR-US)" "
810   P.:P. "A   STEGOSAURUS WAS ONE OF THE FIRST BIRD HIPPED"
811   P. "      DINOSAURS. IT IS BEST KNOWN FOR:"
812   P. "      1.   A SPIKED TAIL AND ARMOR BODY PLATES"
813   P. "      2.   GREAT SPEED"
814   P. "      3.   A LARGE BRAIN":IN.A
816   ON A G. 820, 825, 830
817   IF (A < 0) + (A > 3)T. GOS. 3120
818   G. 800
820   P. "RIGHT! EVERYONE KNEW TO WATCH OUT FOR ITS SPIKED TAIL."
821   P. "NOW FOR QUESTION B., PRESS ENTER.":IN.A$
822   G. 840
825   P. "NOW REALLY--IT WAS A CLUMSY, SLOW MOVING CRITTER."
827   GOS. 3090
828   G. 810
830   P. "YOU CAN'T BE SERIOUS--PEA BRAIN WOULD BE MORE CORRECT."
```

THE PROGRAM (continued)

```
832   GOS. 3090
833   G. 810
840   CLS: P.A. (256), "B.    STEGOSAURUS LIVED ON A STEADY DIET OF:"
841   P. "     1.    INSECTS"
842   P. "     2.    PLANTS"
843   P. "     3.    OTHER DINOSAURS":IN.A
845   ON A. G. 850, 855, 860
846   IF (A < 0) + (A > 3)T. GOS. 3120
847   G. 840
850   P. "CAN YOU IMAGINE HOW MANY BUGS IT WOULD TAKE TO FEED"
851   P. "A TWENTY FOOT DINOSAUR????"
853   GOS. 3090
854   G. 840
855   P. "RIGHT! IT LIVED ON SOFT PLANT MATERIAL IT COULD"
856   P. "BROWSE FOR IN WOODED AREAS."
857   GOS. 3000
860   P. "ITS MOUTH WASN'T CONSTRUCTED TO EAT MEAT."
862   GOS. 3090
863   G. 840
1000  CLS:P.A. (192), "          TRACHODON"
1005  P.:P.T. (20), "(TRAK-UH-DON)":P.
1010  P. "A.    TRACHODON MEANS:"
1011  P. "     1.    HOLLOW HEAD"
1012  P. "     2.    ROUGH-TOOTHED"
1013  P. "     3.    WEB FOOT":IN.A
1015  ON A G. 1020, 1025, 1030
1016  IF (A < 0) + (A > 3)T. GOS. 3120
1017  G. 1000
1020  P. "OOPS, YOU MUST HAVE BEEN THINKING OF"
1021  P. " LAMBEOSAURUS (LAM-BEE-UH-SOR-US)"
1023  GOS. 3090
1024  G. 1010
1025  P.:P. "RIGHT AGAIN! IT HAS MORE THAN 2000 GRINDING TEETH!"
1026  P. "NOW FOR QUESTION B., PRESS ENTER.":IN.A$
1027  G. 1040
1030  P. "TRACHODON HAS WEBBED FEET BUT IT HAD NOTHING TO"
1031  P. "DO WITH ITS NAME."
1033  GOS. 3090
1034  G. 1010
1040  CLS:P.A. (256), "B.    TRACHODON LIKED TO EAT:"
1041  P. "     1.    WATER PLANTS"
1042  P. "     2.    FISH AND OYSTERS"
1043  P. "     3.    PREHISTORIC DUCKS":IN.A
1045  ON A G. 1050, 1055, 1060
1046  IF (A < 0) + (A > 3)T. GOS. 3120
1047  G. 1040
1050  P. "RIGHT AGAIN, ITS 2000 TEETH ARE USEFUL ONLY FOR"
1051  P. "GRINDING UP PLANTS."
1052  P.:P. "NOW FOR QUESTION C., PRESS ENTER.":IN.A$
```

THE PROGRAM (continued)

```
1053  G. 1070
1055  P. "OYSTERS!!! I DON'T KNOW OF ANY DINOSAUR THAT ATE OYSTERS"
1057  GOS. 3090
1058  G. 1040
1060  P. "I THINK THE DAMP WEATHER HAS OVERLOADED YOUR"
1061  P. "MEMORY CIRCUITS."
1063  GOS. 3090
1064  G. 1040
1070  CLS:P.A. (256), "C.   TRACHODON AND THE OTHER DUCKBILL DINOSAURS"
1071  P. "      WERE UNIQUE IN THAT THEY:"
1072  P. "      1.   HAVE FOURTEEN TOES ON EACH FOOT!"
1073  P. "      2.   WERE WARM BLOODED"
1074  P. "      3.   HAD AN AIR CHAMBER IN THEIR HEADS":IN.A
1076  ON A G. 1080, 1085, 1090
1077  IF (A < 0) + (A > 3)T. GOS. 3120
1078  G. 1070
1080  P. "I THINK YOU ARE HAVING ANOTHER SCIENCE FICTION FIT!!"
1082  GOS. 3090
1083  G. 1070
1085  P. "DON'T CONFUSE THESE WITH THE FLYING REPTILES."
1087  GOS. 3090
1088  G. 1070
1090  P. "RIGHT! THIS ENABLED THEM TO DIVE UNDER WATER"
1091  P. "TO HUNT FOOD."
1092  GOS. 3000
1200  CLS:P.A. (256), "            TYRANNOSAURUS REX"
1201  P.:P.T. (18), "(TY-RAN-UH-SOR-US REX)":P.
1210  P. "A.   TYRANNOSAURUS REX IS KNOWN AS THE TYRANT KING."
1211  P. "      IT HAD THE WORST TEMPER OF ALL THE DINOSAURS!"
1212  P. "      FOR DINNER IT WOULD SELECT:"
1213  P. "      1.   A NICE BUNCH OF WATER PLANTS"
1214  P. "      2.   ANY OTHER DINOSAUR IT CAN CATCH"
1215  P. "      3.   EGGS OF THE ARCHEOPTERYX (AR-KEE-OP-TER-IKS)":IN.A
1217  ON A G. 1220, 1225, 1230
1218  IF (A < 0) + (A > 3)T. GOS. 3120
1219  G. 1200
1220  P. "UGH--NOT ENOUGH ENERGY IN THAT FOR T.R."
1220  GOS. 3090
1223  G. 1200
1225  P. "RIGHT! IT WAS A CARNIVORE OR MEAT EATER--"
1226  P. "BRING ON THE BRONTOSAURUS STEAK."
1227  P.:P. "NOW FOR QUESTION B., PRESS ENTER.":IN.A$
1228  G. 1240
1230  P. "YUK! IT WOULD TAKE 1000 EGGS TO FEED T.R."
1232  GOS. 3090
1233  G. 1200
1240  CLS:P.:P.A. (256), "B.   TYRANNOSAURUS REX IS A:"
1241  P. "      1. LIZARD HIPPED DINOSAUR"
1242  P. "      2. BIRD HIPPED DINOSAUR":IN.A
```

THE PROGRAM (continued)

```
1244   ON A G. 1250, 1255
1245   IF (A < 0) + (A > 2)T. GOS. 3120
1246   G. 1240
1250   P. "RIGHT! T.R. STOOD UPRIGHT AND TOWERED 19 FT. HIGH"
1251   P. "NOW FOR QUESTION C., PRESS ENTER.":IN.A$
1252   G. 1260
1255   P. "THE BIRD HIPPED DINOSAURS GENERALLY WERE HERBIVORES"
1256   P. "AND WERE PEACE LOVING DINOSAURS."
1258   GOS. 3090
1259   G. 1240
1260   CLS:P.A. (256), "C.    TYRANNOSAURUS REX DIED OUT WHEN:"
1261   P. "       1.   THE PLANT EATERS DIED OUT AT THE END OF"
1262   P. "            THE CRETACEOUS PERIOD."
1263   P. "       2.   A LARGER, STRONGER DINOSAUR ARRIVED ON"
1264   P. "            THE SCENE.":IN.A
1266   ON A G. 1270, 1975
1267   IF (A < 0) + (A > 2)T. GOS. 3120
1270   P. "CORRECT--T.R.'S FOOD SUPPLY NO LONGER EXISTED!"
1271   GOS. 3000
1275   P. "NO OTHER DINOSAUR WAS EVER MORE FEROCIOUS THAN"
1276   P. "TYRANNOSAURUS REX."
1278   GOS. 3090
1279   G. 1260
3000   Y=1:N=0:P.
3010   IN. "DO YOU WANT TO LOOK AT SOME MORE DINOSAUR DATA? (Y/N)";Z
3020   IFZ=1T.100
3022   CLS:P.A. (192), "TO ACTUALLY SEE AN ACTUAL MARINE MONSTER"
3023   P. "IS ONE OF THE THINGS THAT DO BEFORE I DIE I WONSTER."
3024   P. "SHOULD YOU ASK ME IF I DESIRE TO MEET THE BASHFUL"
3025   P. "     INHABITANT OF LOCH NESS."
3026   P. "I COULD ONLY SAY YES . . . ."
3027   P.T. (22), "OGDEN NASH"
3028   P.:P. "PRESS ENTER":IN.A$
3030   CLS:P.A. (256), "THANK YOU FOR PLAYING MY DINOSAUR GAME."
3040   P.:P. "I HOPE TO SEE YOU AGAIN SOON."
3050   P.:P.T. (20), "TRS-80"
3060   G. 9000
3090   F.B.=1TO8000:N.B
3095   CLS
3100   P.A. (192), "THINK AGAIN. YOU CAN FIGURE OUT THE ANSWER."
3105   FORB=1TO2000:N.B
3110   RET.
3120   CLS:P.A. (128), "TRY AGAIN, YOU MUST CHOOSE ONE OF THE"
3121   P. "NUMBERS ON THE DISPLAY."
3122   FORB=1TO2000:N.B
3123   P.:P.:RET.
9000   END
```

READING THE PROGRAM

To the uninitiated, computer programs are a confusing jumble of numbers and symbols with an occasional recognizable word, which gives one the feeling that the machine is trying to speak to you in your native tongue. To help allay your confusion, you will be "walked" through parts of the "Dinosaurs" program to show how these number/symbols/words are turned into understandable dialogue with the student.

First, this program is written in the computer language BASIC (Beginners All-purpose Symbolic Instructional Code). This language, used with most microcomputers, is unique in its ability to easily use literal English words and phrases in programs. This is a particularly strong point in the development of instructional programs and games.

Now to the program. Notice that each line is numbered. This is a requirement of BASIC and serves as a reference when the computer is executing the program. You will see it more clearly as explanatory comments are made at points of interest as the program progresses. Follow the instructions which the computer would use. This will give you the actual flow of the program as the computer would print it.

Line No. Explanation

10 This is heading information for computer programmers. It does not print out. The REM or Remarks statement is for reference only.

29 Clear the screen to begin program execution.

30 Here we provide the student with the game name, and after he presses the Enter key, a listing of dinosaurs covered by the game.

145 These are computer instructions which tell it what to do based on the student's selection of a dinosaur to be studied. Line 140 asks you to select a number from 1 to 6. When the child does this and presses Enter, the program moves to line 145. Here, based on the number selected (variable A), the computer is directed to move to line 200 (if you chose the number 1 - Diplodocus), line 400 (if you chose number 2 - Plesiosaurus), etc., through line 1200 (if you choose number 6 - Tyrannosaurus). For example, let's suppose you chose the number 2 - Plesiosaurus . . go to line 400.

292 Additional dinosaur names are provided.

400 Here we begin a three question section on Plesiosaurus. After reading the first question, suppose the child entered the wrong answer - such as the number 2. The computer moves to line 416 where it is instructed to move to line 425. Here the computer first informs the child that the answer is incorrect, then in line 427, it instructs the computer to move to a sub-routine located at line 3090. Let's go there and see what happens.

450 The correct answer is given and at the same time another scientific name is introduced.

455 Terms are introduced which may require the child to research them.

480 Humorous comments which result from an incorrect answer spark the child's interest in the question.

817 If the child chooses a number other than 1, 2, or 3, the computer has another prompting routine. Go to line 3120 to see what happens.

1026 In addition to acknowledging the correct answer, amplifying information is given.

1050 Additional information with the correct answer.

1060 Remember you are conversing with an electronic device.

1092 After you complete the series of questions, another subroutine is used. Go to line 3000 to find out what happens.

1255 Comments on the anatomy of the dinosaur.

3000 Here the student is asked whether or not he would like to continue or not. If he elects to continue (Y), the computer returns to line 100 and the dinosaur list is displayed. If he decides to stop (N), the computer gives him an Ogden Nash rhyme and says goodbye.

3090 A subroutine is a group of statements which are used more than once in the program. As a labor saving device, it is written as a subroutine and the computer is directed to it as needed. In this case, the subroutine is a prompting device which in line 3100 asks the child to "Think Again," then automatically returns (line 3110) to the question which he missed and allows him another opportunity to select the correct answer.

These program comments should have aided you in seeing how a program such as "Dinosaurs" enables the computer to interact with the student in a quest for knowledge. This program was written with two objectives in mind. First, it was designed to be a motivator for the G/C/T 6 to 8 year olds who were studying dinosaurs in the University of South Alabama's Saturday Program for Gifted Children. Second, it was written in a relatively unsophisticated manner to enable a layperson or beginner at programming to follow the logical flow of the program. Using more sophicated techniques, it would take up far less memory.

Here's luck to you in getting your own microcomputers for your program. You and your G/C/T students should benefit immeasurably.

Micro-Computers and the School Library

by G. Horner and F. J. Teskey

This is little more than an early warning shot across the bows of those who might think of claiming micro-computers in education as their particular "prize." The "prize" is as yet so far off on the horizon that many teacher-librarians are not aware of its existence, and those who are may well be tempted to turn a blind eye; it is largely an unknown factor, and unknown factors can be disturbing.

The School Library Association cracked no bottle of champagne at the launching of the non-book materials boat, and we, and education in general, are still the poorer for that. Let us at least submit a tender for the carriage of micro-computers in education.

An attempted definition of a micro-computer for the uninitiated might be useful, dangerous though definitions can be. Basically a micro-computer is a desk-top computer consisting of a key-board, a visual display unit like a television screen (it could be a television screen or a VCR monitor) and a processor with integrated circuitry, popularly known as the "silicon chip." It can be used as a complete unit on its own, or it can be linked to an outside data bank, but this brief article is concerned only with the micro-computer as a single, self-contained unit.

Programs are stored on magnetic tape cassette or floppy disc; the latter looks like an advertising gramophone record, made of a plastic flexible material, hence the term "floppy disc." Both types of storage media are just other forms of non-book materials, no more difficult to store or retreive than tape cassettes or gramophone records, and equally amenable to classification and cataloguing; thus they should cause teacher-librarians no extra problems.

In British education, computer studies are almost solely the preserve of the mathematics department, but, according to an article in *Education Guardian*, November 7, 1978, this is "an out-dated concept and a serious limitation. CEEFAX and ORACLE and all sorts of word-processing devices demonstrate that computers are no longer confined to handling numbers."

That computer studies must be taught in our schools admits of no debate; whether that teaching is the role of the mathematics department is a different question, and does not fall within the scope of this article. Our concern is with the micro-computer as a teaching tool in most subjects of the curriculum. Its use in this mode will be akin to the use of the VCR (videocassette recorder), and the teacher using it in this way will require no knowledge of computing; the skill necessary to operate it is no more difficult to acquire than is the skill to operate a VCR.

As this will probably be its major use in schools, it would seem inevitable that the library is the sensible place to house such a machine (along with the projector for film slides and the cassette player for sound tapes, etc.); the programs on tapes or floppy discs being catalogued, classified and shelved with other non-book materials and fully integrated into the library stock.

The following are the types of programs suitable for discovery-learning in a number of disciplines which can be and are being devised for the micro-computer:

(1) straightforward skill programs where the computer will present number problems, spelling tests, etc. to the child, and check and comment upon his answers;

(2) branched learning programs where the computer will take the pupil through a sequence of learning steps, testing him at each stage and providing remedial loops where necessary;

(3) simulation programs, e.g. the computer could be made to simulate the growth of a particular variety of plant. The student can be allowed to vary the conditions under which the plant is growing, and thus learn in a short period the way in which the plant will react to different growing situations.

Programs could also be developed which would allow quick retrieval of information about different classes of books in the library. For example, it would be possible to devise a program that would retrieve titles of children's novels that deal with various historical events, family life, transport, war, adolescence, school, etc. We are not necessarily advocating the educational desirability of such a program, only indicating that it is feasible.

Micro-computers could also be used to keep a complete file of the issue and return of books, the individual child's reading, indeed almost any permutation and combination of library records that a teacher-librarian could wish for. However, both these types of program require computing skill, and are outside the teaching range of the micro-computer. They are only incidentally noted at present.

The fact that as yet there are but few privately or commercially-produced programs is no excuse for teacher-librarians to put off the "evil" day. Micro-computers are about to make a grand entry on the ever-widespread use in schools during the next decade, when they will become comparatively cheap.

Section IV
Trends and Issues

- Reasons microcomputer technology is likely to influence and enhance the educational process.

- Clarification of the role of microcomputers in education.

- Problems to anticipate in using computers in instruction.

- Guidelines for the development and use of microcomputers by an individual school district.

- Media specialists' attitudes, backgrounds, and uses for this new technology.

- View of the school executive in relation to the impact of computers on education in the 1980s.

- The importance of computer literacy for all people involved in precollege education.

- Training teachers to be computer literate in order to use the technology and teach about its societal impact.

- Courses for future teachers in using computers effectively in instruction.

- Steps to expedite computer education for teachers.

- Concerns for the many problems associated with the use of computers in education.

Microcomputers in Education: Now and in the Future

by Karen Billings

Although computers are indispensable to science, business and government, they have not realized their full potential in American education. In an information society, a computer-literate populace is important, and we may go through a crisis trying to develop it.

Just as the 70s became the decade of computer technology, the 80s must become the decade of computer education. For the past 15 years I've witnessed the tremendous growth of computer technology. However, until recently, I've seen relatively little interest among school personnel to provide student access to it. The marketing of personal computers, microprocessor-based games and word-processing machines has generated a recent surge of interest. Computers have become so prolific that the educators can't ignore them any longer.

Not only has the degree of interest changed but so has the kind of interest. For example, language-arts teachers are finding a new classroom tool. For some time they have used the computer in tutorial or drill and practice modes. Now the word-processing features and text-editors have made the computer a writing tool.

THE TEACHER'S VIEWPOINT

What is exciting for one teacher is threatening to another. Although we can provide some teachers with the hardware, software and training, microcomputers may still not become a part of every classroom.

I understand why teachers 10 years ago weren't too excited about using mark-sense cards and transporting them to and from an IBM 360 at a nearby campus. Later, even with the more appropriate user languages and an extensive library of instructional programs, computers captured the interest of few teachers. Part of the problem was the justification of the cost and the inconvenience of time-sharing equipment. Furthermore, it was difficult to convince other colleagues that this was an instrument to be controlled, not feared.

Some teachers are philosophically opposed to computer use because of its 1984 image. Others refuse to get involved, sure that it's another fad that will die away like so many other curriculum innovations. Still others just don't want to bother, content to let the younger members of their staff take the responsibility.

Teachers do not think they will be replaced by a computer, but expect their role with students will change as they each learn to communicate with these machines. Could the microcomputer destroy traditional schooling altogether? Some people envision the gradual disappearance of books and the absence of schools as we know them. Teaching will be done at home on the computer with lots of drill and practice exercises.

While this scope of teaching may sound futuristic and threatening, I am convinced that software to change the classroom environment and provide a unique kind of motivation for students will eventually become available.

THE STUDENTS

Teaching with a microcomputer has given me a chance to experience a potentially important resource in American education. I see the students excited by its interactivity, open-endedness and versatility in presenting text, sound and graphics. They are really being exposed to a "mind multiplier."

The students are much less afraid of the computers than are their teachers. They have more access and more time to get involved. Programming gives the student a chance to control the computer rather than being controlled. It emphasizes the process as well as the product. I can recall few other instances in school where a student describes an action, then executes it on command. Programming has enabled some of my students to share "intellectual products" with each other.

INTO THE CLASSROOM

Some educators want to see microcomputers fit into the existing school curriculum, while others want to see them change it. To be usable tools, they must be employed in a manner consistent with the philosophy of the teacher and the curriculum of the school. Most teachers will consider themselves liaisons between computer and student. They will not become hardware experts or programmers, but they will know enough to teach students how to use the equipment. Drill programs, tutorials, games and simulations can be written to fit into almost any curriculum. But teachers must determine the ratios of those different uses, the amount of "hands on" experience and the possibility of programming. To make these decisions, teachers will have to consider their individuals skills and interests, the atmosphere in the classroom and the philosophy of the school.

To use computers successfully, teachers must know what they want the machine to do in their classroom. They need information on the development of microcomputer use in schools and on available educational software to make their own decisions about equipment and software.

A recent report by *Conduit* revealed a variety of computer uses at the college level, including complex problem solving, simulations, model building and manipulation of large data bases. Drill and tutorial uses accounted for less than ten percent of computer use in instruction, although the percentage increases when interactive services are offered.

I suspect that the percentages are almost reversed for the elementary and secondary levels. Drill and practice, together with games, account for most of the computer time.

Two obvious reasons are the age or sophistication of the users and the nature of the equipment. Teachers are under pressure to emphasize skill building and to raise test scores. Drill and practice programs can create better-skilled students, and the public would love to see the trend of declining test scores reversed. The educators must use what is on the market or produce it themselves. Games are most available commercially,

and drill and practice programs are considered the easiest to write.

HARDWARE, SOFTWARE AND PERSONNEL PROBLEMS

The use of microcomputer technology is hindered currently by a relative nonexistence of appropriate instructional software. It's also hindered by lack of information about what people are doing in education. A clarification of its role at the elementary and secondary levels is needed.

People outside education think the problem lies with the staff, not with the hardware and software. They're not exactly impressed by the quality of thinking or practice in the area of education. If we educators want money for instructional computing when everyone in the schools is being asked to cut back, we will have to convince the public of its benefits. We will have to be able to show them what the computer can do better, and not just replicate in the learning process. It's going to be a tough challenge to make the computer an appealing tool so that taxpayers will buy it, and a lasting tool so the students will really gain from it.

Since I remain so optimistic about the potential of the microcomputer, I have to be realistic when it comes to solving some of the problems of using microcomputers in education. These solutions are not immediate, easy or inexpensive, but they are possible.

People are doing what they can. Teachers and parents are buying their own microcomputers; they are buying or producing their own software. They are taking courses, subscribing to computer journals and attending conferences to learn. Administrators are helping by budgeting for microcomputers and by searching for ways to train teachers in microcomputer use.

Some school districts are supporting teams of teachers and students to produce the needed software. Typically, a teacher who is knowledgeable about programming, available software and computer equipment organizes a team of programmers (usually high school programming students) and teachers with specific needs. The teachers discuss their objectives and the programmers write accordingly. The teachers critique and the programmers revise during the process, each time coming closer to the type of programs that teachers can use directly in their classrooms.

The software curently on the market is largely the result of hundreds of different people, all writing independently of each other, for different microcomputers. The level of their programming skill varies as do their standards for their programs. Given the technical problems with using cassette tapes, we risk buying a program that's of questionable quality or one that won't load on our machine.

Some major, organized efforts to produce educational materials for use with microcomputers exist. Publishers who do this are taking risks when they enter this unpredictable market. (Can you imagine trying to do cost projections, or finding the right person to head the effort?)

QUESTIONS FOR EDUCATORS

Should a school buy one complete system (with printer, disk and memory expansion) that provides more capabilities and applications or several microcomputers that provide more hands on experiences for students?

Selection of this hardware poses philosophical questions for educators. Should we select one all-purpose machine that does limited drill and practice and that has limited programming potential? Should we, instead, select a dedicated computer that has excellent drill and practice programs, and a different machine on which students can learn to program? Should the computer be in control of the student or should the student be in full control of the computer? Is there a machine that serves both student and teacher needs in the classroom? What computer can carry out both administrative and instructional functions and is it better than buying two separate pieces of hardware?

TENTATIVE SOLUTIONS

Only when we can tell equipment manufacturers what we want the computer to do and when we can afford to pay for it, will we have the appropriate hardware. If and when we can show software houses and publishers that we will support their educational programs, we'll get the desired instructional software. As long as small businesses are purchasing more microcomputers than schools, the hardware manufacturers and software developers will direct their efforts in that direction.

It is exciting to look at the potential of the microcomputer in the classroom. It is frustrating to list all the things that must be done, but also rewarding to see the progress. The problems involved with putting microcomputers to their full use in the classrooms have complex and costly solutions, but I am confident that education will solve these problems as soon as it's humanly and technologically possible.

The Micros Are Coming

by Inabeth Miller

In the back corner of Lexington High School, far from the rush of activity, George and Steve have stumbled onto a secret. They and a small group of "mostly male" friends are joined in spirit by Bob in Hartford and Jeff in Palo Alto and an increasing cadre of students throughout public and private high schools of this nation, known to their fellow classmates as "computer freaks." They have discovered in the basements and back rooms of American schools the power, the excitement, and the diversionary possibilities of the technological monsters that most teachers and students have assiduously avoided. They have spent hours learning to program, learning to manipulate, and playing games.

But now the monster computers have spawned babies that are breaking out of traditional hiding places and appearing in elementary and secondary schools, in libraries, in resource rooms, and even in the holiest of holies—the individual classroom. These new computers (called microcomputers) are the size of typewriters, and show signs of proliferating like pocket calculators did during the mid-seventies. They are entering the classroom through a circuitous and interesting route— not by administrators ballyhooing the latest panacea, certainly not by teachers heralding technological change (although math and science teachers have lent strong support to computer-assisted instruction at all levels), but by *parents*. It is parents who are buying microcomputers for their schools. It is parents who are demanding that their children be made aware of the new "basic skill," computer literacy. It is parents who are doing the programming and teaching the teachers. The result is a bandwagon, a new crusade led by parents and abetted by a "video game-wise" generation of students to whom pushing buttons means both power and pleasure.

Before the march becomes a stampede (and it may be too late already), some sober reflection is in order.

What are microcomputers, what can they do, what are the problems involved, and how can educators maintain control over their introduction and use in schools?

WHAT IS A MICROCOMPUTER?

In the simplest terms, a *computer* is a filing cabinet, into which useful bits of information are stored and located for the user in a remarkably efficient manner. A *micro*computer is a small-size system that includes all four of the elements of its behemoth cousin, the computer: INPUT—the accumulated data that the programmer puts into the computer; MEMORY—(obvious, and the more the better); CENTRAL PROCESSING UNIT—it "thinks" logically and arithmetically, and faster than a speeding bullet; and OUTPUT—(all you ever wanted to know about . . .).

All of the information, other than that needed for operating the microcomputer, can be stored in two different ways: on cassette, or on floppy disk ("diskette"). A cassette looks exactly like an audio cassette. It plays through an ordinary audio tape recorder attached to the micro, and in the sequence that it was recorded. A diskette, which comes encased in a cardboard sleeve, resembles a wilted 45 rpm record (hence the term, *floppy* disk). Here information can be retrieved rapidly in any sequence desired. Most microcomputers have diskette capabilities which the companies sell as an "optional" feature. The information contained on the cassette or diskette is called up with the use of a typewriter-type keyboard, and displayed on a screen. Some micros have a build-in screen or "display unit"; others require attachment to a TV monitor/receiver. If a regular home-type TV set is used, an adapter is necessary.

For the micro, many attachments are possible: a *printer*, which will spew out information in printed form rather than merely on a screen; a *communications coupler* or *interface*, which will allow the computer to "talk" to other computers, mainly via telephone lines; *graphic devices*, which will allow a programmer to enter graphs, tables, pictures, photographs, maps, and even play "etch a sketch"; *audio extras*, which will enable a micro to "speak" in a reasonably natural voice.

Instructions or commands to the computer are given in one of several computer languages. These are not as complex as modern foreign languages, since they closely resemble everyday English. They function to translate instructions into binary terms understood by the computer. Different applications and degrees of difficulty demand different computer languages. The one most commonly used in microcomputers and most widely taught in secondary schools is BASIC, an acronym meaning Beginners' All-purpose Symbolic Instruction Code. A set of words and symbols, it includes such elements as RUN, PRINT, END, +, −, **. PASCAL, another language that allows a clearer programming structure, will be available as an option on some of the more popular microcomputers.

WHAT IS GOING ON WITH MICROS IN SCHOOLS?

For the individual school or classroom management, a micro could be that longed-for but never affordable secretary and bookkeeper for the teacher. Programs are already available that allow teachers to keep track of attendance, individual progress, lesson plans, lunch money, inventories, assignments, grades— *everything*. The time-saving potential, the elimination of tedious paperwork, are aspects that few teachers thus far are really utilizing. Individual school administrators are excited about the reporting capabilities. Special Education teachers and directors have found that the micro can keep track of individual prescriptions for "mainstreamed" students, as well as all the required state and federal data. With a printer attachment, reports become a machine function rather than a teacher's albatross.

"Computer literacy" is fast becoming a new buzz word. Researchers and scholars have spoken articulately for several years about the challenge that it presents. Some strong voices in government, as well as education, are looking at the problems of an educational system that is not moving fast enough to teach the skills

necessary in this technological environment. Yet, it is the parents and kids who have discovered the pervasiveness of computers in their everyday lives.

Grocery stores now use computers to produce itemized register tapes, the garage analyzes automotive problems via computer, the department store, the office, and the kitchen are part of a computerized society whose tentacles are all-encompassing. In few places other than schools is it even possible to secure an entry-level position without minimal computer skills. High schools are giving computer courses as part of a math curriculum, or as a "life skills" requirement for graduation. Junior high and elementary schools are giving increasing computer exposure to all students. A child— having received electronic math and reading games for Christmas at age four, and a calculator (instead of a pencil box) upon starting school—is neither intimidated nor uncomfortable manipulating a microcomputer.

The simplest and most common use of micros is for drill and testing. From foreign language vocabulary to reading comprehension, factual, direct response programs are available on even the least expensive of the small personal computers. A teacher does not have to be a computer expert to create such a program. Drill-type worksheets in every discipline, combined with classroom management programs, will allow teachers to assign students drill, practice, and assessment of progress in highly individualized programs. This is one area in which the commercial vendors have great interest. Their expertise in producing workbooks, transparencies, and tests is useful in a new market. However, the quality of the programs are only as good as the information entered.

Those teachers who have been using games and simulations for problem solving will find the computer a valuable ally. Initially, adaptations of scientific simulations were the only programs available. Now, through both the commercial marketplace and "user groups," a variety of historical simulations, career investigations, driver education, life problem situations, and, most recently, business decision programs have emerged. Simulations, offering a band of options with logical sequences composed of circumstance, decision, result, new circumstance, can be carried out on the computer with far greater variety than normally available in classrooms. An individual student can operate at a level entirely disassociated from the rest of the class.

Closely allied to the simulations are games made for the computer. From the simplest video ping-pong to "Othello," checkers, or chess, microcomputers will find increasing use in homes for their play value. Children's Television Workshop has ambitious plans for a Sesame Place in Pennsylvania that will contain a Game Center designed to combine learning and play. For this Center and others that CTW hopes will follow, a vast quantity of game material will be required. The game market has been quickly discovered by students. Current computer magazines regularly print new games that can be copied for microcomputer use. The use of such games as motivational devices has been advocated by educators, encouraged by salespersons, and pounced upon by students who now have found, within the confines of the school building, an alternative diversion that is not only legal but encouraged. However, use of computer games as part of an educational program that is tied to the curriculum exists in few school systems.

Music and art are linked together by a small but dedicated group of computer aficionados. With possible rare exceptions, neither computer-generated music nor computer graphics are incorporated into the traditional curriculum as complete, self-contained courses. Students, particularly in private secondary schools, have done independent studies, creating their own music or art on microcomputers. A few weeks may be devoted within art and music courses to developments in these fields or notable examples of artistic efforts. Primarily because access has been so limited, little actual class instruction on the computer has taken place. As micros enter these classrooms, much more student creative experience will emerge.

The area that shows the most promise for educators is individualized pacing of curriculum. Most textbook companies, aware of current market potential, have divisions or positions devoted to "electronic publishing." Researchers have been working on reading programs for prisons, for the armed forces, and a variety of training programs for industry. Major computer companies themselves are designing training programs for their employees utilizing small micros as the most efficient, least costly method of accomplishing individualized and small group instruction. A new software program has been recently introduced that allows the teacher to translate curriculum onto the computer without any knowledge of computer language. Schools are beginning to hire computer coordinators who will work with teachers, discussing what areas of the curriculum could best be handled by the computer, and assisting in the entire transition from design to program, from operation to revision, from teacher training to classroom assistance. In this way the computer program emerges from the curriculum, rather than being an after-thought or addendum. Curriculum workshops devoted to computer-assisted instruction and training are necessary corollaries to utilizing the exciting potential of individual tutorial and skill development that lies with classroom computers.

PROBLEMS INVOLVED

Once again educators are faced with a situation where technology has raced ahead of available materials, and continues to advance and change before any sufficient quantitative or qualitative development of software. Education has gathered battle scars galore in the never-ending conflict of machines and materials. Gullibility has been tested and appears unending as unstandardized audio and video devices play havoc with budgets, are ignored by teachers, raged at by parents, and underutilized across this nation. No cogent body of easily accessible research exists in the area of non-print materials, their selection and evaluation.

Computer software is obtainable through five sources—in-house programming, commercial vendors, computer magazines, user groups, and research efforts. In-house programming, begun by parents and teachers (particularly in science-based communities), is as effective as internally produced video, slide-tapes, or transparencies. It has an immediacy and relevance to the particular school system, and an obvious qualitative range. Some school systems are using students in a variety of programming efforts. What appears missing in many such internal programs is any overall quality control. The acceptance level is based on "humanistic" concerns rather than educational.

Commercial vendors are an increasing source of program material. Again, having no standards, it is possible to buy a language drill with inappropriate vocabulary, an inaccurate and misleading history simulation, a biased and sexist reading comprehension program. It is also possible, when the uninformed are selling to the uninitiated, to purchase materials in the wrong "language." With the lack of standardization and the incompatibility of software, it is possible to purchase the unusable.

Computer magazines are a regular source of new materials. They are primarily directed to the user, not to the educator or administrator. They provide a plethora of games, progamming techniques, and advertising for commercial materials. Most of the microcomputer companies also distribute magazines that include new products and programs.

In response to the educational need for software, user groups have developed both formally and informally throughout the country. Much valuable information, support, and programming is shared through such efforts. Once again, there is little consistency. Quality requires a process that takes considerable time and attention. Complex, ''branched'' programs that lead each student to highly individual connections must be examined in rigorous detail.

Research is presently taking place at Harvard, M.I.T., Stony Brook, and the University of Utah in both artificial intelligence and the interface of computers with other devices such as videodiscs; this will result in programs tested at a variety of school sites. MECC, the Minnesota Educational Computing Consortium, has researched and produced high-quality instructional programs. All this is vital, because without adequate software no effective computer applications can occur—another machine will simply join the arsenal of educational gadgetry.

Changing technology coupled with technological innocence presents one more mammoth stumbling block. State and federal grants have been awarded to school systems which then purchase personal computers that have no capacity to perform the required tasks. Adaptability to greater memory capacity or to other computer languages is essential if greater demands will continue to be placed upon present machines. Consider reliability and flexibility. Know what is available, what is possible, and what is affordable. Intelligent decisions require expertise and advice.

WHAT NEXT?

Education sits on the edge of an interesting precipice. There are those who proclaim that, if schools do not jump headfirst into the immediate application of computer technology, the commercial market will, through personal home computers, take over all basic skills instruction and much of the effort for both the handicapped and the gifted. Others blithely disdain the computer, as they have ignored the entire video explosion and its effects upon student learning. In each generation, opportunities for educators have been overlooked or misused, often as a negative reaction to invention.

At this time, in this field, there is an opportunity for teachers to become part of the effort to direct, control, and decide what computers will do for the curriculum and the classroom. It is a time to learn, to move with careful consideration, and to be an active participant in the development and analysis of materials. It is not a time for hesitancy, inaction, or delay. The pressure to use the low-cost microcomputer will come from many sources—parents, students, administrators, salespersons. Its potential for humanizing education, for opening teaching and learning opportunities, lies within the grasp of the classroom teacher.

MicroComputers: Fad or Function?

by E. Keith Smelser

Do you remember how excited educators got with each new innovative teaching tool? Each in its own way assisted in the "improvement" of instruction. Some worked and some didn't, but the fact of the matter was that the individual classroom teacher was the final measure of success for the teaching device. It would be interesting to see how many overhead projectors or self-paced learning machines or any of a host of other devices are still in active use in the classroom today.

Now we're learning about another "teaching tool" . . . something called a *microcomputing system*. The computer industry says these systems have great capabilities and are the answer to the many problems of public education. But just how potent and how acceptable these devices will be is a question many educators are or should be asking themselves. In other words, are the micros just a fad that will pass in a few years or will they become an integral part of our educational delivery system. In my opinion, microcomputing systems are not another educational tool that will go by the boards in a few years. In fact, their impact on education in the next few years will be significant.

Before we consider these questions any further, let me digress a moment and list some characteristics of an outstanding teacher. We would hope that this is a person who individualizes and personalizes instruction. He/she also keeps detailed records of student progress, prescribes instruction to each student according to his/her (the student's) own needs, plus provides immediate reinforcement to each student. Our super teacher also provides visual and audio stimulation in addition to treating each student fairly and as a unique person. Such a teacher is ready to work early in the day, rarely takes a break if students need help and always stays after school as long as there are tasks to do. If necessary, this teacher is available during evenings and on weekends, too.

One might ask, how do these characteristics relate to micros? In response let me suggest that the technology is nearly in place which would allow educators to relate some of the characteristics of an outstanding teacher to the potential capabilities of microcomputing systems. The missing components of a "complete delivery system" are the development of a comprehensive curriculum, the software to run the various curricular applications plus the teacher training and involvement in order to control the teaching process at the classroom level. Many teachers will resist this change to increased involvement of computers in the classroom as long as possible. There are, however, some powerful variables now in motion which will force us to consider them: namely, politics, economics, technology and the private sector. Recognizing now that microcomputing systems will be with us it is important to determine how best to use them. I'd like to suggest some guidelines:

1. *The development of an instructional delivery system which utilizes microcomputing systems should not pose a threat to the teachers.*
   Microcomputers should expand the teachers' capabilities in all areas.

2. *Insist that comprehensive curriculum work for use on micros be developed in an orderly manner.*
   Sporadic, partial development of computer related curriculum by one staff member or by a very small segment of teachers without district coordination has been the rule instead of the exception. I recommend district wide coordination of this development.

3. *Use accepted research techniques to test this method of instructional delivery.*
   If the research is inconclusive, then know enough to temper your involvement. There are already some

districts which have purchased units and are developing instructional applications without any apparent long range coordinated research/evaluation project to parallel their development.

4. *Be sure the school board and the district administration make the financial and personnel commitments necessary to support micro systems.*

    Many districts have no "new" money to allocate to this relatively new dimension, so priorities will have to be reexamined over the next few years to allow for these commitments.

5. *Inform the community.*

    Be sure the public knows what you are doing (or planning to do) with micros. Chances are they will be insisting that we increase our use of micros since many inexpensive, highly effective, off-the-shelf devices will soon be available which will teach their kids spelling, math or any of wide variety of subjects. The public will also be influenced by advertising from the private sector.

6. *Inservice, Inservice, Inservice!*

    Over the next few years districts will make commitments to develop instructional applications on micro systems. Be sure to use your district coordinator, the instructional staff, and other knowledgeable teachers and administrators in your district to provide inservice to the professional staff. If local districts want to have a local impact on their instructional delivery system in the next decade, teachers and administrators must raise their awareness in the field of micro computing systems.

7. *Walk before you run.*

    a. Design orderly curriculum projects which include micro computers in the delivery system.

    b. Utilize your district staff with assistance from the TIES (Teacher Information and Exchange System) staff.

    c. Pilot test your projects.

    d. Evaluate.

    e. Implement.

    f. Evaluate again!

Use of micro computing systems is just beginning in public education. Districts will surely experience more and more pressure to purchase them from all quarters. Be aware that there are many vendors getting into the production of micros and that the hardware we choose today might be replaced by an upgraded version or even a different brand which has more capabilities in just a few years. It is important therefore that the user insist on some compatability between pieces of equipment in order that the software and application programs won't have to go through a major conversion in order to operate on the new equipment. We as educators must *act* now to harness these systems so we won't have to *react* five to 10 years from now.

The Media Specialist and the Computer: An Analysis of a Profession's Attitude Towards a New Technology

by Dennis K. Smeltzer

To any casual observer, the role that computers are playing in education has vastly increased in recent years and the trend appears to lead towards additional involvement. Administrators, in the past, have seen the value of computer technology in such areas as scheduling, attendance, and budgeting. With the advent of the microcomputer, the classroom teacher is beginning to open the vistas of computer-assisted instruction to students. Because of the shrinking cost and the increasing availability of this technology, the computer is beginning to rival other instructional technologies as the progenitor of new educational programs.

As with any other technology, the effectiveness of the classroom computer will be dependent upon the availability of trained personnel to maintain, operate, and develop this new instructional component. The path that administrators have taken, in their utilization of the computer, has been to rely on the expertise of the computer specialist. Since the nature of administrative computer needs involve numerical manipulations and projections, the computer specialist appears to have the inherent training to provide the necessary assistance to educational administrators.

The classroom teacher, on the other hand, has a unique use for the computer. No matter whether the computer is serving as the main instructional component or as a secondary information source, the content of the computer is of primary importance to the classroom teacher and to the student. The design and the organization of that content can spell success or defeat in the effectiveness of computer-based instruction. Teachers will soon realize that the technology of the computer is only as good as the programs being run.

Initially, computer-based lessons will be purchased pre-packaged from the manufacturer of the microcomputer. There may be some question as to whether or not these corporations, which are basically hardware oriented, will be able to provide the necessary variety and quality in instructional programs that will be demanded by the educational community. As teachers begin to use the computer, they will realize that these computer programs, like any other commercially produced medium, are not necessarily designed to meet the unique instructional needs of their classroom. Increasingly, teachers will demand individually designed computer programs.

Many schools, undoubtedly, will turn to the computer specialist to design these new programs. Without reservation, these specialists have the ability to write good computer programs. The question is whether or not these programs will be educationally sound. The simple fact is that the training of a computer specialist usually does not include the psychological and pedagogical principles of education that will be needed to design effective, instructional computer programs.

On the other hand, the media specialist has the necessary training in systems design to produce instructional programs that will meet specific educational goals. The media specialist is also trained to manage and to distribute educational systems. Since the media specialist is already a component of the instructional system, (s)he will likely be called upon to provide the necessary expertise to design and to develop computerized, instructional systems.

Whether media specialists want this new responsibility may not be the question. The use of computers in the classroom appears to be an acceptable pedagogical technique and the teacher's willingness to use that technique is increasing! The classroom teacher is going to need support services in the use of the computer and the computer specialist does not have the educational background or the experience to provide that support. The media specialist, by default, will assume the responsibility of this new classroom technology.

Assuming that this premise is correct, one can begin to question whether media specialists have the necessary training and background to provide design services in computer systems. The attitude of media specialists towards computers and their uses in society, generally, and in education, specifically, will also greatly influence the media specialists' commitment to and the future success of computer-based educational systems. To answer some of these basic questions, a group of practicing media specialists were questioned to determine their background in computer science and their attitudes about the use of computers in society and in education.

METHOD

The survey instrument used in this study was adapted from a previous study conducted by Ahl (1976). Ahl's survey was designed to determine the public's attitude towards computers and the computer's role in society. The survey instrument consisted of seventeen questions divided into four major categories:

(1) Computer Threat to Society
(2) Understanding the Computer Itself
(3) Understanding the Role of Computers
(4) Computer Impact on the Quality of Life

The respondents to the Ahl survey indicated their level of agreement or disagreement to the statements on a five-point scale.

A later study, conducted by Lichtman (1979), adapted Ahl's basic questionnaire to survey the attitudes of educational administrators and classroom teachers. Lichtman used the same seventeen questions of the original instrument, but also included six additional questions dealing with specific issues between the computer and education.

The present study also used the Ahl survey as the basis of the survey instrument. In addition to two statements used from the Lichtman study, seven additional statements were developed by the investigator to analyze the subjects' attitudes concerning computer applications directly related to the responsibilities of the

media specialist. The survey also determined the computer background of the media specialists, including the most common programming languages used by this group.

The survey instrument, with the statements in random order, was mailed during the second week of January, 1980, to a select group of active members in the Texas Association for Educational Technology (TAET). The participants of the survey were randomly selected from a list of 365 active TAET members. The study included an initial group of 50 subjects of which 58% (N=29) returned usable instruments.

RESULTS AND DISCUSSION

Computer Background

The level of training that media specialists have in computer technology and its application to educational problems will greatly determine their ability to assist classroom teachers in the development of computer-based educational systems. One of the results of this study has been to show that media specialists, at least with the group surveyed, have had little training in computer technology. Only 31% of the media specialists have taken coursework in the computer sciences. Of this group, 56% had as little as three semester hours with only one person having as many as eighteen semester hours. In the past, the curricula of most media programs appear to have been devoid of any formal coursework in computer technology.

Although coursework in computers is important, the ability of media specialists to write computer programs is essential for the success of computer-based educational systems. Although a third of the group had completed college-level training in computers, only 20% indicated the ability to write computer programs with the majority (66%) indicating the ability to write in more than one language. The most common language used by this group was BASIC with 66% indicating the ability to use this language. The other computer languages used by this group of media specialists were Fortran (50%), Coursewriter (33%), COBAL (16%), APL (16%), PASCAL (16%), and machine language (16%).

Computer Threat to Society

The media specialists that were surveyed, generally, have mixed feelings about the role the computer plays in our society. The group was in total agreement that it was impossible to escape the influence of the computer. There seem to be, however, some varying attitudes as to whether or not this influence is good. The typical response found by Ahl (1976) and Lichtman (1979) to the social role that computers play is that they prevent normal social interactions and isolate people. In the responses obtained, slightly over one-third of the group felt this was true. At the same time, nearly one-quarter of the media specialists felt that the computer dehumanizes society by treating everyone as a number. An even greater percentage of the group felt that computer projections and polls influence the outcome of elections. These results seem to indicate that media specialists, as a group, recognize and accept the influence the computer exerts in their lives. At the same time, however, there is a significant minority that views this influence in a negative fashion.

Understanding Computers

Acceptance of the computer in the classroom will accrue through the understanding of this new technology. Media specialists, again, appear to be divided in their concept as to how a computer works (see Table 1). First, media specialists do not view the computer as something that is so complicated that it is beyond the understanding of a typical person. Quite on the contrary, most of the members of this group had an accurate interpretation of how a computer operates. Basically, the group felt that the machine aspect of the computer was error-free. When errors do occur in computer programs, this group of media specialists felt that the fault was due to errors by human programmers and operators. A substantial minority of media specialists also felt that these problems arose at least 10% of the time when working with the computer. In spite of the fact that computers and their programs are not error-free, most of this group did feel it possible to design data-based systems that would protect the privacy of the individual. It appears that media specialists realize that computers are not perfect, but they have an inherent trust in them.

Understanding the Role of Computers

Media specialists view the role of the computer as more of a tool to assist in problems solving than any other function. This group appears to be split as to the very role the computer should assume. Nearly half of the group felt that the computer was best suited for repetitive, monotonous tasks. At the same time, the majority did not see the computer hindering simple business operations. As far as the impact of the computer on the job market was concerned, this group felt that the computer would replace low-skilled jobs, but the computer would also create a new job market for those people. As with the other sections discussed so far, the media specialists are split in their opinions about computers, but the tendency is towards a positive attitude on the role of computers.

Computer Impact on the Quality of Life

Media specialists are more positive in their attitudes when they judge the impact the computer has on the quality of their lives (see Table 2). As a group, they see the usefulness of using a computer in credit rating data banks, but they see greater uses of the computer. This group felt that computer technology would improve such aspects of our lives as health care and law enforcement. On a more professional level, this group of media specialists strongly felt that the computer

Table 1
Response Percentage of Media Specialists' Attitudes Concerning Understanding Computers (N=29)

Statement	Strongly Agree	Agree	No Opinion	Disagree	Strongly Disagree
Computers are beyond the understanding of the typical person	3.4	3.4	6.9	62.1	24.1
Computers make mistakes at least 10% of the time	3.4	20.7	31.0	31.0	13.8
Programmers and operators make mistakes, but computers are, for the most part, error free	24.1	48.3	6.9	20.7	0.0
It is possible to design computer systems which protect the privacy of data	13.8	44.8	34.5	3.4	3.4

Table 2
Response Percentage of Media Specialists' Attitudes Concerning Computer Impact on the Quality of Life (N=29)

Statement	Strongly Agree	Agree	No Opinion	Disagree	Strongly Disagree
Credit rating data banks are a worthwhile use of computers	6.9	44.8	34.5	6.9	6.9
Computers will improve health care	27.6	51.7	13.8	6.9	0.0
Computers will improve law enforcement	27.6	55.2	17.2	0.0	0.0
Computers will improve education	41.4	41.4	10.3	6.9	0.0
[a]Computers can teach mathematics	13.8	62.1	6.9	13.8	3.4
[a]Computers can teach language arts	3.4	62.1	10.3	17.2	6.9

[a]Adopted from Lichtman (1979)

would improve education. Although they felt that the computer could be used in an area like language arts, the strength of their opinion was not as great as when the computer was being used in the teaching of mathematics. Generally, this group of media specialists were of the opinion that the computer has improved their personal lives and would continue to do so in the coming years.

The Media Center and the Computer

The role that the computer will have in the media center apears to be significant. Most of the media specialists surveyed indicated practical uses for the computer in the media center (see Table 3). Primarily, this group felt that the computer would be useful in the daily management of the center. Such uses as equipment and material inventories and periodical searches

Table 3
Response Percentage of Media Specialists' Attitudes Concerning the Media Center and the Computer (N=29)

Statement	Strongly Agree	Agree	No Opinion	Disagree	Strongly Disagree
Computers can select appropriate learning materials for teachers	20.7	55.2	6.9	6.9	10.3
If there were a computer terminal in my media center, it would help me administer the center better	41.4	34.5	17.2	6.9	0.0
Computers can maintain equipment and material inventories for a media center	44.8	51.7	3.4	0.0	0.0
Media specialists should have academic training in computer programming	24.1	62.1	6.9	6.9	0.0
Computers can design instructional programs	6.9	51.7	6.9	20.7	13.8
Computers can effectively search a library's periodical collection	37.9	62.1	0.0	0.0	0.0
Media specialists, someday, will have to develop computer programs for classroom teachers	13.8	65.5	10.3	3.4	6.9

were accepted as probable applications of the computer in the media center. The computer, according to this group, could also be used in non-administrative roles in the media center, although these attitudes were not as strong as with administrative uses. Specifically, these media specialists felt that the computer could be used to assist teachers in material selection and in the design of instructional programs. On a more practical point, this group strongly felt that the future role of the media specialist would be to develop computer programs for the classroom teacher. With this in mind, this group was in near total agreement that members of the media profession needed academic training in computer programming.

CONCLUSIONS

Media specialists are aware of the impact the computer has on our lives. As a group, they seem to have accepted the computer and the role it will play in their future. They also see the computer as a tool to solve their problems, but a tool that is prone to human error. In a rough comparison to the results of both the Ahl (1976) and the Lichtman (1979) studies, the attitudes of this group of media specialists are attuned, if not more positive, to the attitudes of the general public and other educators.

In its relationship to education, the computer is seen playing an important role. The media specialist sees the computer as a useful medium to teach a variety of subjects. Within the media center, the computer is seen assisting the media specialist in much of the daily operation of the center. The media specialist strongly recognizes the computer's usefulness in maintaining equipment and material inventories and in conducting data-based searches. Likewise, the media specialist sees adapting the computer to more non-managerial tasks such as material selection and instructional development.

Without question, the role of the computer in education will continue to grow. As the computer moves into the classroom, the media specialist will play an increasingly important part in this new educational system. The educational background of the media specialist, however, appears to be inadequate for him/her to assume the role of instructional leader in computer-based, instructional systems. Too few members of this profession have the necessary training or experience to design effective computer programs for the classroom teacher. As a group, these media specialists realize that deficiency and they see the need for a change in the training of future members of the profession.

To meet the demands that the educational community will place on us and to meet the opportunities that the computer presents to us, this profession must reevaluate its relationship to computer technology. As a profession, we must be prepared academically to fully utilize this new instructional medium. As a profession, we must not lose the opportunity to provide leadership in managing, designing, and utilizing this powerful instructional tool.

REFERENCES

Ahl, D. H. Survey of public attitudes toward computers in society. In D. H. Ahl (ed.), *The Best of Creative Computing* (Vol. 1). Morristown, NJ: Creative Computing Press, 1976.

Lichtman, D. Survey of educator's attitudes toward computers. *Creative Computing*, 1979, 5, 48–50.

Microcomputers:
Out of the Toy Chest and into the Classroom

by Dan Levin

Too big, too complex, and too expensive. For years, those were the persuasive arguments against using computers in the classroom. Now, thanks to the microprocessor, all this is changing, and classroom computers could revolutionize teaching techniques across North America.

Parents are buying their kids toy chests full of electronic games—which actually are microcomputers. Everyone in your community will notice all the new places computers are popping up—grocery stores, small businesses, living rooms. Result: Public pressure will increase on school officials to invest in computer hardware, even though academics will publish conflicting dissertations about the value of teaching with microcomputers. Some school executives who want to believe the success stories will short-circuit old curriculums and plug in regiments of micros. Those who remain skeptical will have to endure the advocates' pressure. Many will relent when they see slow learners beef up their test scores as a result of the micros' drill and practice exercises. Some will give in when they see how many graduates land high paying jobs in the computer field as a result of the programming courses they took in high school. Others will wait till they think the technology has been perfected. *Everyone* in education will feel the impact of microcomputers in the 1980s.

Every school executive we talked with who was using microcomputers for instruction responded with an unqualified endorsement. And the primary pedagogical advantage, according to curriculum specialists and teachers, is that microcomputers enable students to concentrate more on problem-solving methods than on the drudgery of calculations. "It used to be that you could give kids only one or two problems of an advanced nature because the pencil-and-paper work would wipe them out," explains Tony Jongejan, who has taught high school mathematics and computer science in Everett, Wash., for ten years. "It is easy for them to make a trivial mistake. Sometimes they can get so involved in the detailed work that they lose sight of the concept. If the computer does the tedious work, I can give many more examples, and the kids will understand the concepts better."

If you've every used a microcomputer, you know it has a great potential for educating children. But, understandably, many school people worry that the computer they buy today will be obsolescent five years from now. Costs are a worry, too. The price of electronic calculators has plummeted while the devices have become smaller and more adept at solving problems. Is that going to happen with microcomputers as well?

No one really knows. But the major advances in microcomputers probably will be made not so much in the machine itself—the hardware—but in the programming that makes the machine tick—the software. In other words, barring a major breakthrough, the micros on the market today will be as practical for teaching kids as will the 1985 models. What will change is the software: Educationally, software will be better, but you'll still be able to present a 1985 lesson on long division with a 1980 machine.

Peripherals—the devices that can be attached to the computer to increase its memory capacity or to print on paper what appears on the video screen—also will change somewhat in the coming years; these, too, will be improved. So, you have a choice: You can invest in microcomputers now or you can let the students in your schools fall behind while you wait for the unlikely day when scientists throw up their hands and say, "That's it. The microcomputer is as good as we're ever going to get it."

To sacrifice a whole generation of kids would be a big mistake, says Marilyn Spencer, coordinator of instructional computing for the Ridgewood (New Jersey) schools: "We must start now. We can't allow our students to become a lost generation on computers." David Moursund is more blunt: "It's perfectly reasonable to think about throwing away equipment. Think of cars: Some old cars did the job back then, but they look kind of funny to us now." Moursund is a professor in the computer and information science department at the University of Oregon at Eugene. He's also chairman of the elementary and secondary school subcommittee of the Association of Computing Machinery's curriculum committee and the editor of *The Computing Teacher*, a journal for people interested in the instructional use of computers at the precollege level.

Moursund's group has identified 29 problem areas in instructional computing, and the group plans to publish a series of reports for school administrators. One of the most serious problems, according to Moursund, is the lack of teacher training: "You can't just go out and buy the hardware and the software and hope good things will happen." School systems must be willing to put time and money into teaching teachers. The amount of training, he explains, depends on the goals school officials set when they buy the machines. For example, if the schools hope to teach computer programming to high school students, a college-trained person probably is necessary. To teach a short course in computer literacy, where the computer itself is the object of study, an instructor might need only a summer of inservice training. "It doesn't take a lot of new skills to teach computer literacy to kids," says Tony Jongejan, the mathematics and computer sience teacher. "Most kids are in class just to learn something about computing, so the teacher ought to be able to get by."

If the schools plan to use microcomputers for Computer Assisted Instruction (C.A.I.), a one or two-day workshop should suffice, according to Moursund. C.A.I. comprises a series of methods in which the student responds to information the computer provides and vice versa. Moursund and others believe C.A.I. is most effective with slow learners, learning disabled, and handicapped children. Some experts say that in 20 years, younger students will learn half of all the lower-level skills—such as basic arithmetic and spelling—by C.A.I. and that teachers will concentrate primarily on teaching higher-level skills, such as mathematical formulas and syntax.

One school system that realized the importance of staff training is the Scarsdale (New York) public schools. After deciding that the schools had an *obliga-*

tion to teach computer skills to students, the system established a computer committee to plan a budget for buying microcomputers, to deal with curricular matters, and to plan inservice activities. Today, more than 150 Scarsdale teachers have taken an introductory programming course or a computer literacy course at Columbia University Teachers College in New York. They learn how to operate the computer smoothly as well as about the general role of computers in society. And it's not just mathematics teachers, says Assistant Superintendent for Curriculum Richard Sprague; English, art, and science teachers have taken the courses as well. The Scarsdale schools teach computer literacy to fifth and sixth graders and programming to high schoolers. There are two micros in each of five elementary schools, eight in the junior high school, and 17 in the high school. The schools, located in one of New York's wealthiest suburbs, have spent $16,000 in local funds for computer training for two years running, although Sprague says Title IV federal money is available to purchase both hardware and software. Next year, the schools plan to sink more money into better software.

The problem of poor software, educators we talked to unanimously agree, is the most troublesome aspect of microcomputers. "Most of the stuff on the market is still *Star Wars* and junk like that," says Tory Esbensen, coordinator of elementary curriculum and instruction in Edina, Minn. "The computer hobbyists are not educators. There are ten games for every educational program." Scarsdale's Sprague agrees: "We don't want kids to associate the computer just with games."

For the three best selling machines (the Radio Shack TRS-80, the Commodore PET, and the Apple II), some good software is available, says Karen Billings, director of the Microcomputer Resource Center at Columbia University Teachers College. But several problems remain: Much of it doesn't fit teachers' needs; software developed for one machine cannot be used on a competitors' model; and most important, good software is expensive.

A common mistake among school systems is to blow the budget on hardware at the expense of software. "Educators must create the market for software," says Billings. Today, the dissemination of software generally is poor; it's in the hands of the microcomputer manufacturers and a sort of underground network of hobbyists and academics that operates through newsletters and advertisements. Once you buy a program from a "hacker," as members of this network are called, you might be stuck if the program doesn't work. Thus, many school systems still rely heavily on the manufacturers.

Poor quality software and the incompatibility of one company's software on another's machine led the Minnesota Educational Computing Consortium (MECC) not only to set up a software dissemination network, but also to endorse a single manufacturer's microcomputer equipment for use in the state's schools. Today, Minnesota school systems (and schools elsewhere) can purchase software from MECC and receive it via telephone hookup in a matter of minutes. MECC also runs workshops for teachers. Other school systems around North America rarely are as lucky as those in Minnesota, where the state legislature earmarks in the neighborhood of $4 million annually for MECC to help schools make the best use of computers. In most school systems, an enthusiastic young mathematics teacher will lobby for a microcomputer, use it in a classroom or two, and possibly run an after-school computer club. With no clear school system commitment to the microcomputer, the instructor has to fend for himself for high quality software.

In spite of the software problem, however, school systems are experimenting with micros. Many schools place one or more in their libraries; teachers can send slow learners there for remedial work. Or, a few micros might be brought into a room for a class on computer literacy.

Alexandria (Virginia) Superintendent John Bristol thinks he has a better idea: Every fifth grader in his suburban Washington, D.C., school system must take a two-week computer literacy course. But instead of hav-ing some kids look over others' shoulders or take turns on the machine, Bristol has developed a road show of 30 microcomputers that visits the district's elementary schools. In the computer literacy class, each child has his own machine. "I don't want watchers; I want doers," declares Bristol, who laughs off suggestions about the difficulty of moving the micros from school to school. In fact, Bristol hopes to see the day when the micros used in schools can be sent home under the students' arms and plugged into the kids' television sets. That way, says Bristol, the family gets involved in the instructional process; commercial television viewing is curtailed; and the youngster is established as someone special in the home. Kids will be showing their dads how to use computers, Bristol predicts, and this will get education into the home in a nonthreatening way. The Alexandria superintendent advocates using micros in classrooms rather than having terminals attached to a mini or a large main frame computer because, "When a main frame goes down [stops working], I've got 30 kids staring at blank terminals. When one micro goes down, I still have 29 kids working." Minnesota's Tory Esbensen agrees: "I don't like being tied by Ma Bell's umbilical cord."

What school officials must remember is that the microcomputer is a *tool* for teaching; it does not *replace* the teacher. But it's an *easy* tool to use: Unlike the bulky computers that many students have used in the recent past, microcomputers do not require great expertise on the part of the instructor or the user.

Computer Literacy: What Should Schools Be Doing about It?

by Daniel H. Watt

The term computer literacy is coming into widespread use without a clear, generally agreed upon definition. I think that the concept remains poorly defined for several reasons. First, the everyday concept of literacy is not clearly defined, having different meanings in different contexts. Second, computer technology is proliferating so rapidly in all phases of our lives that any particular notion of the *specific* knowledge necessary to be computer literate tends to be surpassed as quickly as it is formulated. Third, now that there is widespread agreement that computer literacy is of fundamental national importance, many people with diverse goals are trying to attach that label to their own particular ideas. Yet we need to formulate a concept of computer literacy that we can use to develop the new educational programs we will require during the next few years.

DEFINING LITERACY

My definition of computer literacy is based on an interpretation of the common meaning of literacy. Dictionary definitions of literacy usually include phrases such as ''the ability to read and write'' and ''the state of being well informed, educated.'' These definitions include no specific standards. The concept of what it means to be literate can vary from culture to culture, and from group to group within a given culture. Literacy has to be viewed as a continuum, from a minimal ability to read news headlines at one extreme to the literacy skills of a professional writer or skilled academic at the other. In between are a set of skills, understandings, knowledge and values that play a large part in determining how well a person can function in society.

When I consider a person literate, I usually mean that she can read and write well and can use reading and writing fluently in many contexts and for many purposes. She regularly uses her literacy skills to satisfy personal needs, to conduct family affairs, to meet requirements of daily life and to meet the needs of her school, job, business or profession. Further, a literate person in our society will have had a range of experiences with the literature of our common cultural heritage. She will be able to read, understand, interpret and make judgments about a news article or a literary work, and will be able to compare the works of different writers.

On the other hand, I do not expect a literate person to be a professional writer, to be able to read fluently in a special field or even to spell perfectly all the time. I expect a literate person to have general command of language and literature, with all that that entails, but not necessarily to have achieved mastery of all language and literary skills.

A more complex aspect of literacy is its effect on a person's intellectual functioning. The ability to read and write can affect one's access to and storage of information, one's organization of ideas and even one's logical reasoning. All of these can affect daily functioning in profound ways. Simply put, a literate person can make use of a wider range of intellectual strategies than those available to someone who is non-literate.

How does someone grow up to be literate? I can suggest some major elements of the process. Literacy pervades our culture. Children almost absorb it by growing up in a society of literate adults. Older playmates, parents and teachers are all carriers of the culture of literacy. In school, all teachers—not just teachers of English—are presumed to be literate and to infuse literacy and the appreciation of literacy into all teacher/student interactions. From the earliest years of schooling, students both *use* literacy skills in a wide variety of everyday tasks of importance to them, and build new skills through teacher-directed activities.

COMPUTER LITERACY

With this understanding of what literacy means, I can describe computer literacy as that collection of skills, knowledge, understandings, values and relationships that allows a person to function comfortably as a productive citizen of a computer-oriented society. I have divided the concept of computer literacy into four distinct, but interrelated, areas:

1. The ability to control and program a computer to achieve a variety of personal, academic and professional goals. This includes the abilities to read, understand and modify existing computer programs, and to determine whether or not the program and/or the data it is using are correct and reliable.

2. The ability to use a variety of preprogrammed computer applications in personal, academic and professional contexts. This includes the abilities to make informed judgments as to the suitability of a particular software tool for a particular purpose, and to understand the assumptions, values and limitations inherent in a particular piece of software.

3. The ability to understand the growing economic, social and psychological impact of computers on individuals, on groups within our society and on society as a whole. This includes the recognition that computer applications embody particular social values and can have different impacts on different individuals and different segments of society. It includes the understanding necessary to play a serious role in the political process by which large and small scale decisions about computer use are made, and to transcend the dependent roles of consumer or victim.

4. The ability to make use of ideas from the world of computer programming and computer applications as part of an individual's collection of strategies for information retrieval, communication and problem solving. This aspect of computer literacy corresponds to the effect of learning to read and write on intellectual functioning and is probably the most difficult to incorporate specifically into educational programs, since the effects themselves are still not entirely clear.

CRITICAL IDEAS

As more and more schools begin to incorporate computer literacy into their programs and seek to use computers to enhance learning in other curriculum areas, I would like to raise certain considerations as critical for any computer-related programs.

Our understanding of what is meant by computer literacy will continue to expand rapidly. Observing the proliferation of computers and computer applications in our society, we are forced to recognize that the knowledge a competent citizen needs will expand with the increasing significance of computers. By introducing a particular set of computer literacy objectives into existing curricula, schools will not have *solved* the problem of computer literacy education. The infusion of computer literacy objectives into existing curricula is only a first step: school systems should be prepared for a process of continual expansion and redefinition of all computer-related programs during the next few years.

Who is in control of the computer may be one of the critical issues of the next few years. I believe that citizens of the 1980s and 1990s must understand the ways in which they can control computers and the ways in which computer systems and programs can be and are being used to control and manipulate *them*.

A student's first encounter with a computer should put the student in charge. Many educators hold that computer programming is an "advanced" subject that we should save for high school or, in some cases, junior high school, while we expose younger students to a variety of preprogrammed instructional materials. I believe that precisely the opposite is true. Using child-appropriate computer languages such as LOGO, children should learn to control the computer, just as they learn to read and write in the earliest grades.

When students do interact with pre-programmed material, teachers should inform them of the justifications for such interaction and encourage them to evaluate both the software being used and the underlying rationale for using it. In this way, they will be developing a sense of personal understanding and control of computing on both the personal and societal levels. If students are to grow into intelligent users of computers, consumers of computer technologies and citizens capable of making decisions about computer use, all of these experiences must be built into their educational programs. We must design computer literacy activities that avoid unthinking acceptance or criticism of computer applications.

PROBLEMS OF EQUITY

Closely related to the issue of control is the problem of equity. Many educators have expressed the hope that the widespread use of computers in schools will enhance the education of those who have been excluded from the full benefits of our society. Unfortunately, certain trends now apparent may lead to exactly the reverse: a widening gap between a well-educated elite and a less-educated majority. In a society in which more and more jobs depend on computer-related skills, those who possess such skills will hold the most important positions. Those with a low level of computer literacy may find themselves increasingly relegated to menial or economically marginal positions.

Students from well-to-do families, or those who attend suburban or private schools, are already beginning to gain significant advantages in terms of learning to program computers and to use a variety of computer applications. Many families in suburban districts already have home computers, and the number of such families will continue to expand rapidly.

Schools may offer the only opportunity for many students to learn computer skills. It would be tragic if inner-city schools and schools in working class communities decide that they can't afford to purchase computers for their students or that the development of computer literacy is not the highest priority for use of the computers they do have. Ironically, many urban school districts have introduced computer-assisted instruction in an attempt to upgrade the basic skills of their students. This mode of computer use, in which the computer tells the student what to do, seems ideally suited to producing "second-class citizens" in a computer-based society.

A related concern is the domination by male students and teachers of many educational computing situations. Many high schools report that equal numbers of males and females take introductory computing courses, but that advanced courses and computer clubs are predominantly male. With computers and computer skills assuming increasing social importance, the danger that computing activities may reinforce male/female role stereotypes must be explicitly recognized and positively dealt with in curriculum materials, teacher training and program implementation.

COMPUTER LITERACY FOR TEACHERS

It is hard to imagine students becoming computer literate without computer literate teachers. When we understand how children growing up in a literate culture acquire the knowledge, skills, understanding and values that the conventional concept of literacy encompasses, we recognize that developing a computer literate school staff is a major aspect of education for computer lit-

eracy. The inclusion of computer literacy units or courses in the existing curriculum tends to bypass the long-range issue of staff development. We should see such a program as merely a first step—ultimately inadequate if not part of a long-term growth and development effort.

Educators face yet another question of priorities. Universal computer literacy is a basic skill of the 1980s and deserves a major role in the school curriculum. To educate students for computer literacy, schools must develop leadership, curricula and computer-literate teaching staffs, while acquiring the necessary hardware and software. While many aspects of this development will be intangible, two tangible aspects will undoubtedly be money and time.

Computer literacy will cost money. Equipment, software, curriculum, leadership development and teacher training will all require substantial investment. The money is not likely to come from a major increase in local budgets, or from state or federal largess. Rather, it must come from a reallocation of a diminishing pool of funds at the local level.

Computer literacy will take time. It takes a minimum of about one year to train a resource teacher who can begin to provide real leadership. It will require a substantial commitment of in-service training time for those teachers who have major responsibilities in this area, and some in-service training time for all teachers. Like the money needed to support computer education, time will have to be reallocated from other areas.

REDEFINING LOCAL PRIORITIES

The responsibility for computer literacy education is spread throughout many levels of our educational system. Federal programs, which are likely to increase somewhat during the next few years, have provided some support for research and development. Some states have formed consortia to centralize planning, curriculum development, teacher training and equipment acquisition. A few schools of education have begun embryonic graduate programs in computer education. Some computer manufacturers have offered substantial discounts to schools in their local areas, thereby supporting the acquisition of equipment.

In concentrated high-tech areas, industry councils are lobbying for and supporting a variety of technical education programs. Textbook publishers, in alliance with microcomputer manufacturers, are beginning to develop computer-related programs, although these are mostly oriented toward computer-assisted instruction rather than computer literacy. Finally, we have seen national and regional educators' groups emerge to facilitate the exchange of information and ideas.

Support from outside the schools will remain a minor factor without a major redefinition of local priorities. I believe that whether or not schools will be a serious factor in educating a computer literate public by 1990 is an open question. The failure of schools to make a major committment in this area now can have disastrous consequences for both the education of the public and the future of public education.

Teaching Teachers about Computers: A Necessity for Education

by Stuart D. Milner

Computers are here to stay. Computer usage is no longer a skill needed only in certain professions and occupations. Classroom use of computers offers opportunities for enhancing elementary and secondary teaching in many subject areas—opportunities that are being missed because many teachers at all levels do not know how to use computers in the classroom and are not prepared to teach about their impact on our society.[1]

Why does this situation exist? Why are today's students being short-changed?

The answer lies in a whole set of problems. Training and experience requirements for certification for teaching computer-related courses are generally lacking. Many educators know very little about the potential for computer applications in the classroom. Teacher training programs and courses are few and far between. Computers seem to have a low priority in relation to other areas. This, coupled with the lack of incentives for teachers to learn about computers, points to the need for greater administrative commitment and recognition.

These problems cannot be dealt with independently. Each meshes with the others. We need a multi-level approach to dealing with them as a whole. But let's look at them one by one.

Currently, only four states in the U.S. certify teachers of computer science. To illustrate the critical nature of this need, consider the situation in a large school system that requires mathematics teachers to take 24 hours of mathematics content, but requires no computer courses at all to teach computer science. Nor are teachers required to study computer education in order to teach courses that involve computing in an adjunctive manner, e.g., computer applications in social sciences. Consequently, there is much legitimate criticism of computer misuse and of ill-prepared or unqualified teachers of computing.

Computer systems and instructional materials are proliferating at an amazing rate.[2] Yet many teachers and administrators are unaware of what the systems can do and what instructional materials exist. It follows that few can use computer-related materials effectively.

Granted, a few programs in computers and computer education are offered to teachers and future teachers, notably at Teachers College, Columbia, and the University of Illinois. However, university-based programs are generally lacking in relation to other disciplines. Furthermore, available courses are often optional and are not well integrated into degree programs. In fairness, however, we should note that universities are not providing such training because they do not feel the demand.

Many educators do not seem to see the relevance of computing in the curriculum and therefore give it a low priority. High school teachers, in particular, tend to complain that there is no "room" for computing in existing curricula. However, computer-related materials are being incorporated into textbooks and other classroom materials, signaling a philosophical advocacy for computing by curriculum developers. Marvin Minsky of the Massachusetts Institute of Technology has said: "Eventually, programming itself will become more important even than mathematics in early education."[3] If he is correct, we may have serious problems ahead unless we include teacher training in computer usage as a standard element of the curriculum.

Because computer science is a new discipline to many teachers, there is a seeming reluctance to study it. It involves both new ways of thinking and new approaches to pedagogy. But, paradoxically, teachers seem to recognize the need for training in computers. In a recent survey conducted by the Minnesota Educational Computing Consortium, 85% of 1,300 teachers surveyed agreed or strongly agreed that the secondary school student should have minimal understanding of computers.[4] However, only 39% of the entire group agreed or strongly agreed that their own training was adequate for using computers in instruction.

Administrative commitment and recognition are necessary for effective and widespread use of computers in education. Many administrators, however, are unaware of the different applications that exist and the extent of their potential benefits. Yet some administrators appear to recognize the need for more trained teachers. J. Richard Dennis surveyed 686 secondary school principals in Illinois and found that: 1) 71% saw a need for computer science teachers, 2) 55% saw a need for state certification in computer science, and 3) 82% felt that some computer science is valuable in the background of any teacher.[5]

Justine Baker conducted a survey of 78 superintendents in 50 states regarding their preferences concerning the roles of computer science and teacher training in secondary schools.[6] Respondents stated their preferences with respect to: 1) a computer science department in each secondary school, 2) every teacher required to take three computer science courses, 3) a computer science department and every teacher trained in basic uses of the computer, and 4) none preferred. Respondents were divided into users and nonusers of computing. A majority of the users preferred option 3, and a majority of the nonusers preferred either option 1 or 3.

Generally, administrators seem to have mixed feelings about computer education for teachers. Perhaps a comprehensive national survey would provide data on administrators' attitudes for the purpose of planning and decision making.

In spite of problems and inhibiting factors, prototypes for educating teachers are available. I have edited a volume summarizing existing and previous approaches for educating teachers in the instructional uses of computers.[7] University-based programs, though few, include regular B.S. degree and summer M.S. degree programs. In addition, nonprofit organizations and consortia such as the Minnesota Educational Computing Consortium, the Oregon Council for Computer Education, and Project LOCAL have been very effective in disseminating ideas and materials to schools. Finally, federally funded programs such as the National Science Foundation's Programs in Pre-College Teacher Development and Information Dissemination in Science Education, as well as Title IV-C programs of the U.S. Office of Education, offer still other ways to educate teachers.

How much should a teacher know about computer use in education? This is a complex question for which there is no simple answer. However, we can deal with it on the basis of what is taught, what certification and experimental requirements exist, and what is believed necessary by experts. The matter of certification must be dealt with by school decision makers. The other matters can be dealt with through the framework presented in Figure 1. The figure deals with the kinds of courses and experiences that are necessary for various types of computer-related teaching. It is based on my experiences in providing computer education courses to a variety of teachers, as well as recommendations for courses by the Association for Computing Machinery (ACM).

Here are descriptions of the suggested courses:

Instructional Design: An Introduction—This course is designed to provide a basis for understanding and applying principles of instructional technology in education. It includes: 1) an overview of instructional technology; 2) aspects of instructional planning, development, implementation, and evaluation (e.g., task analysis, behavioral objectives, presentation strategies);

Figure 1
A Framework for Training Needs

TYPES OF TEACHING \ COURSES/EXPERIENCE	Instructional Design	Designing CBLM	Programming	Hardware & Software Organization	Computer Uses in Education	Computers & Society
Computer-Assisted Instruction	X	X	X		X	
Computer Science, Data Processing			X	X		X
Computers and Society			X	X		X

and 3) selected means for individualizing learning (e.g., CAI).

Designing Computer-Based Learning Materials (CBLM)—Depending on background and interests, the student learns how to design, implement, and evaluate instructional materials using computers. The primary projects are computer-based instructional or management modules. The student demonstrates mastery of selected computer programming techniques germane to project development. The content includes: 1) computer programming for instruction, 2) review of prototype computer-based materials, 3) development of instructional or management modules, 4) implementation, and 5) evaluation.

Programming—The Curriculum Committee on Computer Science of ACM recently recommended two courses in programming. In the first course, recommended content includes the development of algorithms and the design, coding, debugging, and documentation of programs written in widely used high-level programming languages. Computer organization is also introduced. In the second course, students are introduced to structured programming concepts, string processing, searching and sorting, data structures, and recursion. Analysis of algorithms is discussed.

These two courses or some equivalent are relevant to teachers who either major or minor in computer science or who engage in the other types of teaching described in Figure 1.

Hardware and Software Organization—The ACM has recommended and described other courses in computer science that would follow the two programming courses. These courses involve organizational and design aspects of computer hardware and software. At the freshman and sophomore levels, the courses recommended for a major in computer science are: assembly language programming, introduction to file processing, and introduction to computer organization. More advanced undergraduate courses in operating systems and computer architecture, data structures, and programming languages are also suggested. When specific planning for teachers occurs, some subset of these may need to be selected, especially for teachers who minor in computer science. Terry Frederick has provided an example.[8]

Computer Uses in Education—The purpose of this course is to provide a basis for developing, implementing, and evaluating computer uses in education. The following topics should be dealt with: 1) computer systems fundamentals, 2) instructional usage modes, 3) considerations in developing and evaluating computer-based instruction, 4) representative projects, and 5)

issues and problems. In such a course students get "hands on" experience in various applications and demonstrate competence through some form of instructional evaluation or development effort.

Computers and Society—A course in computers and society for teachers should include components dealing with systems fundamentals, programming, applications in a wide variety of areas, and implications of the applications. Many excellent textbooks are available, including, for example, Stanley Rothman and Charles Mosmann, and Donald Sanders.[9]

In order to expedite computer education for teachers, school decision makers must 1) identify needs, 2) establish goals, 3) develop certification requirements, and 4) implement teacher education and support options.

The framework discussed here can help in identifying training needs, establishing goals, and developing requirements for teaching computer-related courses. Although comprehensive national, state, and local action is required, certain actions could be taken immediately. For example, all preservice teachers could be required to take a course in computer programming.

Various types of teacher training and support activities are possible. Some of these have been practiced by schools identified as exemplary in a recent study by the Human Resources Research Organization.[10] The activities are included in the following list:

1. Consulting by professional staff or outside experts
2. Department meetings and demonstrations
3. Workshops offered for inservice teachers who may not wish to commit themselves to entire courses
4. Summer curriculum development teams for teachers with previous development experience
5. Paid released time
6. Staff development within school systems
7. Memberships paid in professional organizations
8. Travel paid to professional meetings
9. University classes

What about microcomputers? The revolution in the computer industry brought on by microcomputers such as the Radio Shack TRS-80 and the APPLE II has begun to make an impact on education. Many schools are likely to own at least one microcomputer within the next few years.

As my colleague, Carol Hargan, and I have stated previously,

> While the rewards for using microcomputers can be great, a certain amount of commitment on the part of administrators and teachers for planning, implementing, and evaluating

computer use is vitally important. The complexity of the technology and relative inexperience of most educators in using microcomputers make this imperative. Moreover, teachers and administrators must recognize how essential inservice training is for effective use of computers in instruction. While the amount of training may vary, some sophistication is necessary. Given the proliferation of microcomputers, unless serious attention is given to upgrading teachers' competencies, students may well become more computer literate than their teachers.

Educators should not ignore the implications of the microcomputer revolution. Andrew Molnar of the National Science Foundation sees computer literacy as the next crisis in American education. Only a few years ago most educators felt that the role of computers in education would be defined some time in the future. Microcomputers have changed all that—the future is now.[11]

Finally, improvement of teacher education in computer use requires the resolution of all the problems identified. I have offered a framework for thinking about and planning for teacher education here and have suggested the changes needed. Widespread and effective use of computers in education requires such action.

NOTES

1. Stuart D. Milner, ed., *Topics in Instructional Computing, Vol. 1: Teacher Education* (New York: Association for Computing Machinery, 1975).

2. Robert J. Seidel, "It's 1980: Do You Know Where Your Computer Is?," *Phi Delta Kappa,* March 1980, pp. 481–85.

3. Marvin Minsky, "Form and Content in Computer Science," *Journal of the Association for Computing Machinery*, March 1970.

4. Minnesota Educational Computing Consortium, *Computer Literacy Study—an Update* (St. Paul, Minn.: The Consortium, 2 June 1978).

5. J. Richard Dennis et al., *Computer Activities in Illinois Secondary Schools* (Urbana, Ill.: Department of Secondary Education, University of Illinois, June 1977).

6. Justine Baker, *Computers in the Curriculum.* Fastback No. 82 (Bloomington, Ind.: Phi Delta Kappa Educational Foundation, 1976).

7. Milner, op. cit.

8. Terry Frederick, "Computer Science Education for Students Training to Be Teachers," in Milner, op. cit.

9. Stanley Rothman and Charles Mosmann., *Computers and Society*, 2nd ed. (Chicago: Science Research Associates, 1976) and Donald Sanders, *Computers in Society*, 2nd ed. (New York: McGraw-Hill, 1977).

10. Carol Hargan and Beverly Hunter, *Instructional Computing: Ten Case Studies* (Alexandria, VA: Human Resources Research Organization, 1978).

11. Stuart Milner and Carol Hargan, "Microcomputers: The Future Is Now," *Practitioner*, October 1979.

Microcomputers Will Not Solve the Computers-in-Education Problem

by David Moursund

Some people mistakenly believe that microcomputers will solve the computers-in-education problem. Unfortunately, there are many problems associated with the use of computers in education. Microcomputers are helping to solve some of these problems, but are also helping to create others. This paper is concerned with instructional use of computers at the precollege level. It identifies a number of problems and discusses the role microcomputers play in these problems. Then it introduces the Association for Computing Machinery's Elementary and Secondary Schools Subcommittee; this subcommittee has been making a substantial effort to identify problems involving the instructional use of computers and to lay a foundation for their solution.

This paper begins with a brief historical perspective. ENIAC, the first general purpose electronic digital computer, was build on a university campus. Indeed, many of the early (1946–1951) computers were built on campuses and were used by students and faculty as research and learning aids. Thus the history of instructional use of computers begins with the beginning of computers.

As computers became commercially available in the early 1950's, their use spread quickly to educational administration throughout higher education, and eventually into precollege education. A few high schools began to make instructional use of computers in the late 1950's.

Second-generation computers, third-generation computers, time-shared computer systems, and mini-computers created booms to computers in education. By the early 1970's computer usage in higher education was commonplace in administration, instruction, and research. By the mid-1970's more than half of all pre-college school systems in the United States were mak-ing administrative use of computers (Bukoski & Krotkin, 1975).

Finally came microcomputers—the answer to many computer educators' dreams. Now that every school could afford the hardware, surely we could expect all schools to begin making extensive instructional use of computers! But of course this has not been the case. The process of educational change is slow and there are many problems in computer education besides hardware. So far computers have had a very modest impact upon instruction at the precollege level. The typical high school graduate, having had little or no interaction with computers, is not computer literate.

GOALS

Many individuals and some organizations have stated goals for the instructional use of computers. A summary of a typical set of these goals is: (a) all students should have a level of computer literacy commensurate with their overall level and areas of education, (b) computer-assisted learning (that is, teaching/learning using computers) should be used when it is educationally and economically sound, (c) all students who have a need for knowledge in computer science above the computer literacy level should be provided appropriate opportunities to obtain this knowledge (East & Moursund, 1979).

These goals need more careful definition before they can be adopted or implemented (Course Goals in Computer Education, 1979). But even in this crude form it is evident that they are hardware independent. Microcomputers are making it more feasible for schools and school systems to give serious attention to adopting such a set of goals. But microcomputers by themselves do not achieve any of these goals.

The first goal, computer literacy, is aimed at all students and all disciplines. The student taking auto mechanics courses should develop a working knowledge of applications of computers in this field. The student taking advanced mathematics courses should have a working knowledge of the capabilities and limitations of computers as an aid to solving mathematics problems encountered in these courses. Notice the emphasis upon the ''working'' level of knowledge. It is difficult to give a definition of computer literacy that is universally acceptable or which lends itself to easy measurement. But a computer is a tool—an aid to problem solving. Students need to understand this idea, and to learn to use the tool in whatever disciplines interest them. (For a more detailed discussion of computer literacy see Neill, 1977).

The second goal speaks to computer-assisted learning. At the current time CAI is having almost no impact on most students. But there is considerable potential for change. There is substantial experimental evidence to support the contention that in a wide variety of instructional situations CAI is at least as effective as conventional modes of instruction. When we couple this with the increasing costs of teachers and the decreasing costs of ''computer power,'' we see why the CAI advocates are so enthusiastic.

The third goal speaks to more advanced instruction for a more limited number of students. Most of our high schools offer courses in biology, chemistry, physics, second year algebra, etc. Many high school students are capable of learning the content of a typical first year college-level computer science course.

THE PROBLEMS

There are so many barriers to accomplishing the goals stated in the previous section; some of these barriers are the lack of: (a) sufficient and adequate computer hardware, (b) appropriate software, (c) appropriate courseware (books, course outlines, etc.), (d) adequately trained teachers, (e) adequately trained school administrators, (f) adequate support from school boards, parents, and taxpayers. Now, think about these problems in the light of microcomputers. Keep in mind that microcomputers are not ''inexpensive'' relative to the amount of discretionary funds available to a typical teacher or school. Most elementary school teachers do not yet have available a classroom set of calculators, but a classroom set of calculators costs considerably less than one microcomputer.

Of course, it is evident that microcomputers can have a major impact on the hardware barrier. Schools and individual teachers can afford much more computer power than previously. Those that have been putting money into time-shared systems now have an alternative that may provide much more capability for the same amount of money. Many schools that do not have access to a computer are now acquiring several microcomputers.

But even then, microcomputers do not completely solve the hardware problem. Many exciting applications of computers involve very large data base and/or very large programs. For example, a computerized career information system may require a large data base of several million characters which is updated periodically. Or, consider the PLATO sytem and the capabilities it provides. While microcomputers can do part of this, they cannot do it all.

Barriers (b)-(e) are not overcome by microcomputers. Indeed, microcomputers actually contribute to these barriers. Consider software, for example. Over the years educators have made considerable progress in developing software and figuring out how to distribute it. Much of the progress is based upon time-shared computing, standardized high-level languages, and computer-user groups. These existing mechanisms are not set up to cope with the rapid proliferation of a wide variety of microcomputers, new vendors, and novice users.

Or, consider teacher and administrator knowledge. By and large whatever knowledge they have was acquired on time-shared and/or large batch processing computers. Thus microcomputers have helped to make this knowledge outdated. The knowledge gap appears to be growing rather than shrinking.

Finally, consider the sixth barrier. Microcomputers have received widespread publicity and are beginning to become a household item. Thus parental and taxpayer support for their use in schools is growing. Also, since their cost is relatively small, some microcomputer capability can come into the schools using funds currently in the budget. Thus microcomputers are helping to remove the sixth barrier.

ACM ELEMENTARY AND SECONDARY SCHOOLS SUBCOMMITTEE

The Association for Computing Machinery (ACM) was founded in 1947 and has a long history of involvement in the computer education field. In June of

1978, an Elementary and Secondary Schools Subcommittee (ES³) was formed from the merger of the Secondary Schools Committee and The Teacher Certification Subcommittee. The new subcommittee is concerned with all aspects of instructional use of computers at the precollege level and with related problems. For example, it is concerned with teacher preparation at the preservice as well as at the inservice levels.

ES³ began by announcing its existence and goals in a news release to many national periodicals. Perhaps two dozen publications carried the news that ES³ was seeking input and that one could participate in its activities via correspondence. Interested people were asked to state and briefly discuss what they saw as some of the major problems of instructional use of computers at the precollege level. They were asked to suggest possible solutions.

Hundreds of people responded. All of the responses were read, and the problem areas were divided into categories. While the responses were still coming in, a two day working session of ES³ was held in Washington, D.C. This was December 2 and 3, 1978, during the fall ACM National Conference. Participants in this working session were asked to provide detailed input in defining several of the major problem areas and making suggestions for solutions.

As a result of the hundreds of responses and the two-day working session it was decided to establish a number of task groups. Each task group was to delineate clearly its problem area, describe what it intended to do, and tell how it would know when the task was done. Several of the task groups began work during the Washington meeting.

Shortly after that meeting a list of 29 task groups, along with brief descriptions of their problem areas, was prepared and mailed out to the 400 people then on the ES³ mailing list. A check-list of these task groups was included, and people were asked to volunteer their services to one or more task groups. Again it was pointed out that people could participate via correspondence, and widespread participation was encouraged.

Response has been very good. Task group leaders or coleaders have been identified for each task group. Over 200 people have returned the task group check list and have been put into contact with leaders of the groups they checked.

A second working session of ES³ was held on February 21, 1979, in Dayton, Ohio. Various task group leaders reported on progress they were making, and work continued in defining the goals of some of the groups. Plans for disseminating the subcommittee's

work were made. The intent is to do two things during the coming year. As task groups make progress on their preliminary reports, the results will be distributed to all people on the ES³ mailing list. The intent is to provide for some immediate dissemination and to get as much feedback as possible. Next, the intent is to prepare and publish a substantial report, of perhaps 200-300 pages in length, in June or July of 1980. This will include the task group reports that have been reviewed by people in the task groups, people on the ES³ mailing list, people who attended the working session and appropriate higher levels of ACM committees. It is expected that this report will be of considerable value to people and school systems interested in instructional use of computers.

As a result of the February meeting an attempt was made to decrease the number of task groups. Via mergers, four of the groups were eliminated. If you would like to be on the ES³ mailing list or to participate actively in the work of some task group(s), write to the author of this paper, chair of ES³. A list of the ACM Elementary and Secondary School Subcommittee task groups is given below:

1. Acquisitions
2. Administrators and School Boards
3. Arguments Supporting Computers in Education
4. Art, Music, and the Humanities
5. Articulation
6. Business Curriculum and Vocational Education
7. Computer-Assisted Learning
8. Computer Literacy
9. Computer Science
10. Elementary School Curriculum
11. Ethical and Social Concerns
12. Handicapped, and Special Education
13. Humanities Curriculum (Merged with Task Group 4)
14. Teacher Education
15. Large Data Base Systems
16. Liaison and Dissemination
17. Mathematics Curriculum
18. Mentally Gifted
19. Microcomputer Group (Merged with Task Group 24)
20. Minorities and Women
21. Periodical Literature
22. Preservice Teacher Education (Merged with Task Group 14)
23. Programming Contests
24. Local, Regional, or National Computer-Oriented Groups
25. Science Curriculum
26. Social Studies Curriculum

27. Scouting and Other Organizations
28. Software and Courseware Exchange
29. Teacher Certification Requirements (Merged with Task Group 14).

A third working session of ES[3] was held June 4 and 5 in New York City during the 1979 National Computer Conference. There a number of the task groups made formal presentations of their progress. Writing sessions were held by several of the groups, and considerable progress was made. Working sessions will continue to be held in conjunction with the national computer meetings that are sponsored or cosponsored by the ACM. Thus the subcommittee will hold a working sesison in Detroit sometime during October 29-31, 1979, and it will hold a working session in Kansas City during the winter 1980 Computer Science Conference. People interested in the work of ES[3] who can attend these meetings are welcome to attend and participate.

SOME ES[3] TASK GROUPS

We can understand better what ES[3] is trying to do by examining some of the specific problems it is addressing. The first, alphabetically, is acquisitions. Most people have some idea about how to buy a car. They have seen cars all their lives, ridden in cars, driven cars, read about cars, etc. Still, buying a car is rather a traumatic experience for most people. Now, consider acquiring a computer. The corresponding lifetime of experience and gathering of knowledge is lacking. Indeed, the potential purchaser may be a complete novice in the field. How does one identify needs, and insure that a particular computer system will fill these needs? What are the "red tape" procedures that one must go through to satisfy school, district, state or federal purchasing requirements? How does one deal with a vendor to avoid being "taken?"

These are difficult questions, and are made more difficult by the proliferation of microcomputers and their vendors. The ES[3] acquisitions task group will provide some guidelines and checklists of procedures to follow. It will provide samples of appropriate paperwork and contracts. It cannot remove the need for knowledge on the part of the purchaser, but it can reduce the knowledge and time needed to make an adequate acquisition decision.

The second task group is titled Administrators and School Boards. Administrators and school board members who read this AEDS publication are probably quite knowledgeable about computers, and can appreciate the special problems faced by teachers trying to learn to make instructional use of computers. But such people are still in the minority. Most school administrators have a low level of computer-education literacy. The ES[3] task group is working both to increase this level by preparing appropriate materials and to see that these and existing materials get into the hands of administrators.

Most educators associate the word "computers" with mathematics, science, and perhaps business. Thus it may come as a surprise to see an ES[3] task group working on art education, music education, and the humanities. But at the college level, computer usage in all of these fields is becoming quite common. Consider music education, for example. Computers can be used as an aid to composing and performing music. Many colleges use computers as an aid to teaching music; there is even a periodical magazine devoted to computers in music, the *Computer Music Journal*. For an example from the humanities, consider linguistics. Computational linguistics is now a well-established field, and ideas on transformational grammars are fairly commonly discussed in certain English courses. Stylistic analysis, or merely programs to determine readability, are common applications.

Perhaps 80% of all jobs in the computer field are closely related to business. But in most secondary schools computers have had little impact upon the business curriculum. Ideas of the use of computers in accounting or of computerized word processing have been slow to enter the curriculum. The typical high school business-oriented graduate has little insight into the electronic revolution that is hitting the modern business office. The Business Curriculum and Vocational Education task group is working on these and other problems.

Computer-assisted learning (CAL) includes all aspects of use of a computer as an aid to teaching/learning. CAL is well entrenched in many medical schools, some college courses, and in a few precollege situations. Alfred Bork, one of the leading proponents of CAL, continues to suggest that by the year 2000 perhaps 50% of all instruction in the United States will be by CAL. This would certainly be a major change in our school system. Right now relatively few people even are thinking about the types of changes that CAL can and will make or whether we want these changes to occur. The CAL task group is more of a thinking and planning group rather than a materials development or implementation group. It will help to build a firm foundation for others who are interested in this apsect of educational planning and change.

The Computer Literacy task group is focusing mainly at the secondary school level. The goal is clear-cut—all students should become computer literate. But a precise definition, involving measurable behavioral objectives, has not yet been completed. How computer literate are current students? How does the use of computers in schools or the teaching of a computer programming course affect computer literacy? What is a workable plan of attack for a school that would like all of its graduates to be computer literate?

The task group that has generated the most interest is the one concerned with the Elementary School Curriculum. One can gain some insight into the problem just by considering calculators. What would it do to the mathematics curriculum if every student had a calculator and was allowed to use it except in a few special instances when use was specifically prohibited? Eventually we will have to deal with this problem and the similar one for computers. And as computers become available, what do we want kids to learn about them? Do we want kids to learn to program, or do we want to restrict them to using library programs? If they are to learn to program, what languages(s) should be used? If they are to be restricted to using library programs, what programs should be in the library?

The list of task groups is long, and no attempt will be made to discuss each one. Rather, this paper will end with consideration of the single most important one—Teacher Education. We can produce more, better, cheaper hardware, software and courseware. All of these things can be mass produced, or produced at one place and "mass distributed." But without knowledgeable and supportive teachers the results will be disappointing and often a failure.

Progress in solving the teacher education problem has been very slow. Hardly any colleges of education require computer work for their teacher education candidates. Use of computers as an educational medium is barely mentioned in most educational media courses. Most college of education faculty are not computer literate in any reasonable sense of the term.

When we couple this with the magnitude of the inservice teacher training problem, we can appreciate why the progress of computers in education has been slow and will continue to be slow. We now know enough about inservice teacher training to realize that a short workshop or even a one-term evening course is inadequate for most teachers. The educational use of computers is not simple. It takes substantial training and experience for most teachers to reach a point where they can effectively integrate teaching using computers and teaching about computers into their classrooms. Very few precollege teachers have reached this point.

CONCLUSION

The barriers to progress in making increased instructional use of computers can be divided into two categories. Into one category we put things like hardware, software, and courseware. Each lends itself to group effort, mass production, or more money as a solution. Into the other category we put those barriers that depend upon knowledge of the individual teacher or school administrator. And it is here that we find the major and continuing bottleneck. Without knowledgeable teachers and supportive administrators, progress will be painfully slow. With them, progress is rapid, even in light of inadequate hardware, software and courseware.

REFERENCES

Bukoski, W. J., & Krotkin, A. L. *Computing Activities in Secondary Education*. Washington, DC: American Institutes for Research, 1975.

East, D. & Moursund, D.: *KNOW-PAC on Calculators and Computers in the Classroom*, Oregon Department of Education, 942 Lancaster Drive NE, Salem, Oregon 97310, 1979.

Course Goals in Computer Education, Tri-County Goal Development Project, Commercial-Educational Distributing Services, PO Box 8723, Portland, Oregon 97208, 1979.

Neill, M. *An Empirical Method of Identifying Instructional Objectives for a High School Computer Literacy Curriculum*, University of Oregon, unpublished Doctoral Dissertation, 1977.

Appendices

Appendix I
A Selected Glossary of Terms Useful in Dealing with Computers

by Charles H. Douglas and John S. Edwards

This glossary attempts to explain terms with which one needs to be familiar in order to function successfully in the microcomputer environment. The terms have been selected from advertisements, catalogs, microcomputer manuals, dictionaries, textbooks, and conversations with persons who work with microcomputers. We have tried to interpret the definitions in non-technical language. In those cases where this was not possible, technical terms used in definitions were included as entries in the glossary. These terms are italicized in the text of the definitions. We have also included a cross-reference category to refer the reader to terms which are closely related to the entry term. Hopefully this glossary will provide a launch pad from which you may pursue knowledge and use of microcomputers to the extent of your needs.

GLOSSARY

ACCESS TIME
　　The interval of time between the calling for information from a *storage address* and the delivery of that information. In general, *tape* has a longer access time than *disc* (or *disk*, as it is sometimes spelled).

ACOUSTIC COUPLER
　　A device attached to a *computer* terminal to transmit and receive audio tones via telephone lines. A type of *modem*.

ADDRESS
　　A label (name or number) that designates a location where information is stored in a *memory* device.

A/D INTERFACE
　　A/D (Analog/Digital) A circuit which changes an input voltage fluctuation (continuous), such as results from a musical tone, into digital information (discrete) for processing by the computer. It also converts digital information to analog.

ALGORITHM
　　An orderly step-by-step procedure, like a recipe, that consists of a list of *instructions* for accomplishing a desired result, or for solving a problem. Usually expressed in mathematical terms. In computer programming, an algorithm is expressed as a *flowchart*.

ALPHANUMERIC
　　A set of symbols. Can be letters (A-Z) and/or numerals (0-9), and/or special punctuation, mathematical, or *graphic* symbols.

ARCHITECTURE
　　The internal, preset arrangement or organization of a computer which determines how the computer operates. The interconnections of registers, logic units, control logic, etc. That which makes one *microprocessor* different from another.

ASCII
　　Pronounced "Ask-ee." *A*merican *S*tandard *C*ode for *I*nformation *I*nterchange. *Binary number codes* for letters, numbers, symbols, and special characters that have been accepted as standard by the computer industry. This standard specifies which number will stand for each character. All *personal computers* use this standard. SEE: BAUDOT CODE, BCD CODE.

ASSEMBLER

A program which converts English commands or expressions, usually in mnemonics, into machine language in *binary form* for processing by the computer. Assembler language and *assembly language* are synonymous.

ASSEMBLY LANGUAGE

A *computer language* that uses mnemonic names to stand for one or more *machine language* instructions. Assembly language is similar to "shorthand," used to avoid the tedious use of long strings of zeros and ones found in machine language. The advantage of using assembly language instead of a *high-level language*, such as *BASIC*, is speed of execution, but a high-level language is usually easier for a human being to understand.

AUXILIARY MEMORY (STORAGE)

Storage available in a computer, in addition to its own memory banks; it can be either *disc* or *tape*. SEE: MASS STORAGE.

BASIC

An acronym for *Beginners All Purpose Symbolic Instruction Code*. A *high-level* conservational, interpretive, programming language in wide use. Always written in capital letters, BASIC was invented by Kemeny and Kurtz at Dartmouth College in 1963. It permits the use of simple English words and common mathematical symbols to perform the necessary arithmetic and logical operations to solve problems.

BASIC-IN-ROM

This term indicates that the programming language *BASIC* has been stored in *ROM Memory*.

BATCH PROCESSING

A method of processing information in logical groups.

BAUD

A rate of information flow. Given in *bits* per second (bps), the rate is the highest number of signal elements (bits) that a device is capable of transferring in one second between two devices. Alphabetic characters, for example, being transferred at 300 baud corresponds to about 30 characters per second. Common baud rates are 110, 150, 300, 600, and 1,200 bps.

BAUDOT CODE

An obsolete processing code which uses five separate *bits* to represent a given character. SEE: ASCII, BCD CODE.

BCD CODE

Binary Coded Decimal. A *code* which uses five *bits* for each character. SEE: ASCII, BAUDOT CODE.

BELT PRINTER

A printer which uses a steel belt with character impressions; the belt rotating at high speed. When a desired character is in the correct position, it is struck from behind with a stationary "hammer," thus imprinting the character on the paper. The belt printer forms a solid character. SEE: DAISY WHEEL PRINTER, INK JET PRINTER, MATRIX PRINTER.

BINARY CODE

Code using only zero and one to represent data. SEE: ASCII, BAUDOT CODE, BCD CODE.

BINARY SYSTEM

A number system based on the number 2, just as the decimal system is based on the number 10. The binary system is represented by the digits 0 and 1, and each place in a number represents a power of 2. SEE: HEXADECIMAL SYSTEM, OCTAL SYSTEM.

BIT

Binary Digit. The smallest unit of digital information. It has only two states: zero and one. A bit can be thought of a representing: a yes/no choice, a distinction between true and false, or whether a circuit is on or off.

BOOTSTRAP

A short sequence of *instructions* which, when executed by the *computer*, will automatically allow another longer program to be loaded from an input *peripheral* to the programmable *memory* of the *CPU*.

BPS

Bits Per Second. SEE: BAUD.

BRANCH

A place in a *program* where a choice is made to depart from the normal sequence of program *instructions*. The departure is made by a "branching instruction" in the program. A branching instruction may be one of two types: conditional or unconditional. In *BASIC*, an example of the first type is: IF . . . THEN; of the second type is: GO TO.

BUFFER

A space in a computer system where information is temporarily stored. Usually used to store small sections of data during a transfer process. For example, data may be *read* from a tape cassette in small units, placed in a buffer, then transferred to *main memory* when the *computer* is ready to process the data.

BUFFERED I/O
Input/Output operations using a *buffer* to increase speed. Because of the slowness of I/O devices, information is held in the *buffer* until enough has accumulated to make it worthwhile for the extremely fast *CPU* to act. SEE: BUFFER.

BUG
An error in programming which causes faulty outputs. May also mean a *hardware* malfunction or design error either in the *computer* or in its *peripherals*. SEE: DEBUG.

BULK STORAGE
Synonymous with *mass storage*.

BUS
A physical connection of parallel wires providing a communication line along which data can be sent. Usually shared by several parts of the computer. An S-100 Bus has 100 lines. In a unidirectional bus system, signals from one or more sources, activated one at a time, drive a common load or loads. A bidirectional bus system lets signals go either way on the bus, again activated only one at a time. Most *microprocessor* data buses are bidirectional.

BYTE
The basic unit of information in a computer. Commonly consists of a sequence of eight binary *bits*, usually handled as a unit. One byte usually represents one character. SEE: BINARY SYSTEM, WORD.

CASSETTE RECORDER
A device for preserving internally-stored information. Because most computers lose the information stored in them when they are turned off, a means of keeping the information is necessary. *Binary* information is stored on a *cassette tape* by first converting it to audio signals and recording it on the tape. This method of storage is slower than *discs*. SEE: MEMORY.

CHARACTER
Single items that can be arranged in groups to stand for information. There are two forms: (1) numbers, letters, *graphic* symbols, etc., that can be understood by human beings, and (2) groups of *binary digits* that can be understood by the computer. A character is usually represented by one *byte*.

CHARACTER CHECKING
A procedure for examining each individual character or group of characters to check for accuracy and consistency.

CHARACTER SET
Refers to the characters available to a *computer*, *printer*, or *terminal*. Some devices have only upper case letters plus numbers and a few special characters such as punctuation, #, 1, etc. Others have upper and lower case letters, numbers, and many special characters which may be combined to form designs. SEE: CHARACTER, GRAPHICS.

CHIP
The heart of a *microcomputer*, a piece of silicon smaller than one's fingernail on which thousands of electronic elements are implanted. Called a *microprocessor*, it contains all the circuits one needs to carry out the many computer operations.

CLOCK
A device, inside the computer, that times events and keeps them coordinated. It also controls the rate at which information is processed, a rate sometimes measured in *nanoseconds* or jiffys (1/60 of a second).

CODE
The relationship between *bits* and a set of *characters*. Microcomputers deal only with bits when executing a *program*. Therefore, letters, numbers, and other human understandable characters must be translated into bits. Each character has a bit code representation. The most commonly used code is that known as *ASCII*. Code is sometimes used as a synonym for program. For example: one may say that a programmer generates code. SEE: BAUDOT CODE, BCD CODE.

CODE LEVEL
The number of *bits* used to represent a particular character. SEE: ASCII, BAUDOT CODE, BCD CODE, CODE.

CODING
Preparing a set of computer instructions.

COMMAND
An instruction given to the system through an *input* device or *peripheral*. It is executed as soon as it has been received. SEE: PROGRAM.

COMPACTION
Packing information to make more space in the *memory*.

COMPATIBILITY

There are two types of compatibility: *program* and *hardware*. Program compatibility refers to the ability to run programs on a variety of computers without changing the program *language*. Hardware compatibility means that various components (printers, discs, keyboards, etc.) may be connected directly without intervening electronic devices and that all components use the same *baud* rate, *word length*, and other technical aspects in order to communicate.

COMPILER

A program built into the system that lets the computer translate instructions written in a *high-level language*, understood by a human being, into a *machine-readable (object)* program, meaningful to the computer. SEE: ASSEMBLER, INTERPRETER.

COMPILER LANGUAGE

A computer language more easily understood by a human being than an assembly language. Compiler language instructs a compiler to translate a *source language* into a *machine language*. SEE: ASSEMBLER, COMPILER, INTERPRETER.

COMPUTER

A device that receives and then follows *instructions* to manipulate information. The set of instructions and the information on which the instructions operate are usually varied from one moment to another. If the instructions cannot be changed, the device is not a computer. The difference between a computer and a programmable calculator is that the computer can manipulate text *and* numbers; the calculator can manipulate only numbers. SEE: MICROPROCESSOR.

COMPUTER LANGUAGE

A language used to communicate with a computer. All computer language instructions must be translated by a program in the computer into the machine's internal language in order for the instruction to be implemented. SEE: ASSEMBLER, COMPILER, LANGUAGE.

CONSOLE

The operating portion of a unit. SEE: HARDWARE.

CONTROL PANEL

Type of *I/O* device which allows the user to communicate and *read* computer memory in *binary* form using switches on the front panel. SEE: HARDWARE.

CONTROL UNIT

Portion of a computer which directs the operation of the computer, interprets computer *instructions*, and initiates the proper signals to the other computer circuits to *execute* instructions. SEE: HARDWARE.

COURSEWARE

A combination of content, instructional design, and the *software* which causes a computer to implement instructions. SEE: FIRMWARE, SOFTWARE.

CPS

Cycles Per Second.

CPU

Central Processing Unit. The heart of the computer, controlling what the computer does. It includes three main sections: arithmetic, control, and logic elements. It performs computations and directs functions of the system.

CROSS-ASSEMBLER

Program run on the computer to ''translate'' instructions into a form suitable for running on another computer. SEE: ASSEMBLER.

CRT

Acronym for *Cathode Ray Tube.* Similar in appearance to a television screen. Information in the form of characters and *graphic* designs may be displayed on CRTs at the rate of 9,600 characters per second. A CRT terminal usually comes with a *keyboard* for entering information into the computer. SEE: VIDEO DISPLAY UNIT.

CURSOR

Movable indicator on *CRT* to indicate a specific character or space that is being displayed. The cursor lets the user know where the next character to be typed will appear.

CYLINDER

The *tracks* in a *disc*-storage system that can be recalled without having to move the access device.

DAC

Digital to Analog Converter. SEE: A/D INTERFACE.

DAISY WHEEL PRINTER

A printer which has a wheel mechanism, with characters on the perimeter of the wheel. The wheel rotates to place the appropriate character in print position. A ''hammer'' strikes the character, forcing it against a ribbon, thereby forming an impression on the paper. The daisy wheel printer has the reputation of great reliability, is relatively inexpensive, and forms a solid character on the paper. SEE: BELT PRINTER, INK JET PRINTER, MATRIX PRINTER.

DATA
The information given to or received from a *computer*.

DEBUG
Process of finding, locating, and correcting mistakes or errors in a *program* that might create problems or provide inaccurate information. SEE: BUG.

DIAGNOSTIC ROUTINE
Test program used to detect and identify *hardware* malfunctions in the computer or its associated I/O equipment.

DIGIT
Either a zero or one in the *binary number system*.

DIGITAL COMPUTER
CPU that operates on specific data, performing arithmetic operations. Most computers store information in digital form, that is, as discrete units such as ones and zeros. SEE: A/D INTERFACE, BINARY SYSTEM, HEXADECIMAL SYSTEM, OCTAL SYSTEM.

DIRECT MEMORY ACCESS (DMA)
A technique for rapidly moving data from the *microprocessor* to a *storage device* such as a *disc*. DMA is accomplished at the direction of a *program*. Not all microcomputers permit DMA.

DISC (DISK)
A record-like magnetic-coated piece of material that can store programs, data, or tables of information. The process is similar to storing musical information on a magnetic tape. Commonly found are *floppy* and *hard* disc systems. SEE: HARDWARE, TRACK.

DOCUMENT
A written description of a piece of *software* or *hardware*. It can also be used as a verb which is the process of producing such a description.

DOS
Disc Operating System. A collection of *programs* which are the operating system (*OS*) for a *disc* drive. SEE: DISC, TRACK.

DOT MATRIX
A method of generating characters by converting the *ASCII* code into a suitable group of dots ar-ranged in a 5 × 7, 7 × 9, or other suitable patterned array. SEE: PRINTER.

DRIVER
Small *program* which controls *peripheral* devices and their *interface* with the *CPU*.

DUMP
Copying all or part of a *memory* onto another medium to retain the information yet clearing the memory for other activity.

DUPLEX
Process of establishing two-way communication simultaneously between components of a computer.

DYNAMIC MEMORY
A type of programmable *memory* which requires that the information on tiny capacitors inside *integrated circuits* be refreshed every so often to prevent the data from being lost. Generally uses less power and is cheaper and faster than static memory.

EBCDIC CODE
Eight-bit *code* system: *E*xtended *B*inary *C*ode *D*ecimal *I*nterchange *C*ode.

ECHO CHECK
Error control method in which message is returned to sender for verification.

ECHO-PLEX
Form of error control which displays information given to computer.

EDITOR
A program which allows changing, modification, or movement of programming statements. It allows the programmer to write and modify instructions using the *microprocessor* and a *terminal* as a very sophisticated typewriter. SEE: TEXT EDITOR.

EPROM
*E*lectrically *P*rogrammable *ROM*. A read-only memory which can be erased either by an electrical signal or by ultraviolet light. SEE: RAM, ROM.

ERROR
Difference in value between actual response and desired response in the performance of a controlled machine, system, or process.

ERROR TRANSMISSION
Change in information caused during data transmission.

EXECUTE

The running of a computer program.

EXECUTIVE CONTROL PROGRAM

Main system *program* designed to establish priorities and to process and control other programs; also called a *monitor*.

EXTERNAL STORAGE

Auxiliary storage such as tape or disc. SEE: MEMORY.

FAIL SAFE

System for protecting data against loss in the event of system failure.

FILE

Collection of related data.

FILENAME

Number/letter characters that identify a file.

FIRMWARE

Programs which are permanently stored in *PROM* memory to allow easier understanding of the computer's operation. The programs are loaded in ROM (*ROM* or *PROM*). Firmware is often a fundamental part of the system's *hardware* design, as contrasted to *software*, which is not fundamental to the hardware operation. SEE: EPROM.

FLOPPY DISC (DISK) DRIVE

A device for storing masses of information on a rotating, flexible, metallic-coated plastic disc which is similar to a 45 rpm record. Information can be stored and retrieved extremely fast. Unlike *cassette tape*, on which all information must be scanned, the disc allows the user to go to any area of the disc without searching through intermediate information. Floppy discs typically hold 256,000 *bytes*. SEE: TRACK.

FLOWCHARTING

A programming technique of using shaped blocks to indicate the sequence of operations in a *program*.

FORTRAN

*For*mula *Tran*slater. A science-oriented *high-level language*. SEE: ASSEMBLER, COMPILER.

FREQUENCY

Rate at which anything recurs. Usually measured in cycles or hertz per second.

FULL DUPLEX

Transmission and reception simultaneously. The telephone is a full duplex device. SEE: DUPLEX, HALF DUPLEX.

GIGO

Garbage in, garbage out. Implies that misinformation applied to the *CPU* will result in misinformation *output*.

GRAPHICS

Characters that can be used to form figures, shapes, and forms on the CRT or printer. In addition to letters and numbers, a computer may have a graphic *character set*, so arranged that they can be combined to form almost any desired figure. SEE: CHARACTER.

HALF DUPLEX

System of communication in which either transmission or reception can occur at a given time, but not both simultaneously. SEE: DUPLEX, FULL DUPLEX.

HANDSHAKING OPERATION

Interaction of the *central processor* and *interfaced* devices which requires the device to signal the processor as each command occurs during data transfer. This operation is performed by *modems* or *terminals* to verify that channels are cleared and that operations can proceed.

HARDCOPY

Data or information printed on paper. Used to distinguish between printed information and the temporary image found on the CRT. SEE: PRINTER, TERMINAL.

HARDWARE

Mechanical, magnetic, electrical, and electronic devices which make up a computer. The physical equipment that goes into a computer system, consisting of the *central processing unit* plus all *peripherals*.

HARDWIRED

Physically interconnected and usually intended for a specific purpose. Hardwired logic is essentially unalterable; a *microprocessor*, on the other hand, is programmable and may be adapted to accommodate various requirements.

HEAD

That part of a recorder that does the actual impression on the medium or reads that impression from a prerecorded medium.

HEXADECIMAL SYSTEM

A number system involving 16 characters, using numbers 0-9 and then letters A-F.

Decimal:	0	1	2	3	4	5	6	7	8	9	10	11	12	13	14	15
Hexadecimal:	0	1	2	3	4	5	6	7	8	9	A	B	C	D	E	F

HIGH-LEVEL LANGUAGE

A computer programming language using English words, decimal arithmetic, and common algebraic expressions. Each instruction represents a large number of computer operations. SEE: ASSEMBLER, BASIC, COMPILER, FORTRAN.

HOLLERITH

Coding system which uses combinations of 12 positions on a card to represent characters. SEE: CODE.

IC

*I*ntegrated *C*ircuit. A plastic or ceramic body five cm long, two cm wide, and three mm thick with up to 40 leads extending from it. Inside the body is a *chip*. The body protects the *chip*, and the leads allow electrical connection of the chip to other components. The word "chip" is not to be used to refer to the entire IC.

ICs come in three sizes: SSI (Small Scale Integration—less than 20 gates); MSI (Medium Scale Integration—20-200 gates); and LSI (Large Scale Integration—over 200 gates). Microprocessors use LSI.

INK JET PRINTER

In an ink jet printer, a high-speed stream of electrically charged ink droplets are fired through a magnetic field. The field deflects the droplets to direct them to the proper location on the paper. This type of printer is relatively expensive but extremely fast. SEE: BELT PRINTER, DAISY WHEEL PRINTER, MATRIX PRINTER.

INPUT

Information going into the computer or into a peripheral. The same data may be *output* from one part of the computer and input to some other part of the computer. When using this word, specify what the data are input to or output from.

INSTRUCTION

A set of *bits*, or a command, which will cause a *computer* to perform certain prescribed operations. SEE: PROGRAM.

INSTRUCTION SET

List of commands to which a given computer responds. Instruction sets may vary among computers, even though those computers use the same programming language. SEE: PROGRAM.

INTELLIGENT TERMINAL

Terminal with built-in programmable intelligence enabling it to pre-process information and/or instructions without the aid of a *CPU*.

INTERACTIVE

System capable of two-way communication with a user during operation. A system is interactive if it responds to the user quickly—usually less than a second. All *personal computer* systems are interactive.

INTERFACE

An electronic circuit used to connect one electrical device to another electrical or mechanical device to allow the flow of data between units. It refers to the matching or interconnecting of systems or devices having different functions.

INTERNAL STORAGE

Memory system which is a part of the *computer*, as opposed to external *tape* or *disc* storage. SEE: RAM, ROM.

INTERPRETER

A program used to translate languages at the time of processing. SEE: ASSEMBLER, COMPILER.

I/O

*I*nput/*O*utput of information in a computer system Examples of I/O devices are: *a keyboard*, a *floppy disc* drive, and a *printer*.

JOB

That part of a *program* defined as a task for the computer, complete with all *instructions*, *routines*, *data*, and *addresses*.

KEYBOARD

A device for typing information into a computer. It is similar in design and function to a typewriter keyboard. The computer keyboard has several additional keys for specific computer functions. SEE: CRT, PRINTER, TERMINAL.

K or KILO

Symbol or suffix for 1,000. In dealing with computers, 1 K is used to mean 1,024. A computer with 32 K *bytes* of memory means that it has 32 times 1,024 bytes of memory.

LANGUAGE

A format by which a programmer can communicate more efficiently with a computer where predetermined commands will yield requested actions. *BASIC* is one of the most popular languages.

A language is a defined group of representative characters or symbols, combined with specific rules necessary for their interpretation. The rules enable an *assembler* or *compiler* to translate the characters into forms (such as *digits*) meaningful to a machine, system, or a process. SEE: ASSEMBLER, BASIC, COMPUTER LANGUAGE, COMPILER, FORTRAN, HIGH-LEVEL LANGUAGE, INTERPRETER.

LIBRARY ROUTINES

Collection of standard *routines* that can be used in *programs*.

LINE FEED

The technique of a tele*printer* that advances the paper one line at a time.

LOAD

Process of inserting information in *memory*. Opposite of "*dump.*"

LSI

Large Scale Integration. Technique of making more complex integrated circuits. Refers to a component density of more than 200 transistor gates per chip. SEE: IC.

MACHINE LANGUAGE

A programming language whose instructions are written in *binary, octal,* or *hexadecimal* notation. Programs written in machine language do not need to be translated in order for the computer to execute the instructions. SEE: ASSEMBLER, ASSEMBLY LANGUAGE, COMPILER, INTERPRETER, LANGUAGE, PROGRAM.

MACROINSTRUCTION

An instruction which causes the computer to execute one or more other instructions. These "other instructions" are called *microinstructions.* SEE: INSTRUCTION.

MAGNETIC TAPE

SEE: TAPE.

MAIN MEMORY

That memory which is directly accessible to the computer. It contains the *operating system, programs,* and data being processed. In a microcomputer, main memory is referred to a *RAM* or *ROM.* SEE: MASS STORAGE.

MASS STORAGE

Devices such as *discs* or *tapes* are used to store large quantities of data. These devices are not directly accessible for processing by the computer; therefore the data which are stored must be read into *main memory* before the computer can use it. SEE: STORAGE CAPACITY.

MATRIX PRINTER

The matrix printer is so-called because it forms characters from a matrix of dots. Usually the matrix consists of five dots across and seven dots down or seven dots across and nine dots down. The 5×7 matrix is suitable for upper case letters and numbers; however, for lower case letters and other characters, the resolution provided by the 7×9 matrix is better. Matrix printers have the advantage of being lower in cost than other types but are also slower in print rate. SEE: BELT PRINTER, CHARACTER, DAISY WHEEL PRINTER, INK JET PRINTER, PRINTER.

MEMORY

The *integrated circuits* of a computer which store information. In a microcomputer, these are referred to as *RAM* and *ROM.* SEE: IC, WRITE.

MEMORY CHIP

A *chip* which *stores* data in the form of electrical charges. SEE: MOS CHIP, RAM, ROM.

MICROCOMPUTER

A hardware configuration usually acquired in one of three ways: (1) by constructing several components from individual electronic parts (as in building a stereo system from a kit); (2) by connecting several already-constructed components (as in purchasing a separate amplifier, speaker, and turntable); or (3) by purchasing a unit with built-in components (as in buying a complete stereo system in one package, plugging it in, and using immediately). The end-product of the microcomputer is information. It records this information, processes it, puts it into meaningful terms, communicates it, stores it, and retrieves it when needed. It usually includes the microprocessing unit, a *keyboard* for entering data, a cassette *tape* recorder or a *disc* for storing programs, and a TV-like screen for displaying results. SEE: CPU, CRT, DISK.

MICROPROCESSOR

An *integrated circuit* that can execute *instructions.* It is one component of a *microcomputer.* It is the brains of the central processing unit (*CPU*).

MICROPROCESSOR BOARD

A board (actually made of plastic) to which are attached *integrated circuits*, including microprocessor *chips*, which form the *microprocessor*. SEE: IC.

MICROSECOND

One microsecond equals one millionth of a second. This is the speed at which some computers get and execute *instructions*. SEE: NANOSECOND.

MODEM

An abbreviation of the words "*MO*dulator-*DEM*odulator." It is a device which permits computers to transmit information over regular telephone lines. *Digital electronic signals*, generated by the computer, are converted by the MODEM into high and low tones. This process is known as "Modulation." The tones are a type of *analog signal*. The modem also converts analog signals to digital signals. SEE: HANDSHAKING OPERATION.

MODULATOR

An electronic device that allows a normal television set to be used as the *video display unit*. Frequently referred to as RF Modulator.

MONITOR

1. A *video display unit* which uses a *cathode ray tube* to generate characters. It looks much like a normal TV set; however, the monitor has a much higher degree of resolution, which permits a clear formation of very small characters on the screen.
2. A *program* which oversees the operation of other programs.

MOS CHIP

MOS is an acronym for *metal oxide semiconductor*. A MOS chip is a chip in *integrated circuit* (IC) which can perform a vast number of electrical operations. A MOS chip one-quarter of an inch square can perform operations equivalent to 6,000 discrete electronic devices. A chip this size has the power and ability of a room-sized computer of a few years ago. SEE: IC.

MOTHER BOARD

A *card* in a microcomputer with connections for various components and which is connected to the microprocessor. It forms the *interface* or connecting link between *memory* and *peripheral* devices.

MSI

An abbreviation for *Medium Scale Integration*. Refers to the quantity of circuit components, such as transistors, formed on a single circuit. SEE: IC.

MULTI-PROCESSING

Refers to more than one *microprocessor* executing different *programs* simultaneously. A computer system may contain more than one microprocessor; thus multi-processing may occur within that system.

MULTI-PROGRAMMING

A *microcomputer* can be multi-programmed if two or more *programs* are present in *main memory*. Because the microprocessor operates so rapidly, it appears that each program is *run* simultaneously.

NANOSECOND

One nanosecond equals one thousandth of one millionth of one second or 1×10^{-9} seconds. This is the speed at which many computers get and execute *instructions*. SEE: MICROSECOND.

NOISE

Refers to inaccurate data transmission. This causes typographical errors in *output*. SEE: BUG, DEBUG.

NON-VOLATILE MEMORY

A type of memory which maintains data without requiring *refresh*. *Tape* and *disc* are two media of non-volatile memory. Some types of *ROM* are also able to hold data and are frequently referred to as *static memory*. SEE: DYNAMIC MEMORY, VOLATILE MEMORY.

OBJECT PROGRAM

The form of a program which can be understood by a computer. The object program results from the translation of a human readable program, called *source program*, into a *machine language* program. An object program appears as a series of numbers when printed or displayed. SEE: ASSEMBLER, COMPILER, INTERPRETER.

OCTAL SYSTEM

Refers to a numbering system which has a base of eight compared to the decimal system which has a base of ten. Octal numbering is a compact means of representing *binary* numbers. The following illustration shows the relationship between octal and decimal numbers.

Decimal:	0	1	2	3	4	5	6	7	8	9	10
Octal:	0	1	2	3	4	5	6	7	10	11	12

Octal numbers are identified by a subscript $11_{10} = 13_8$
$$11 \text{ (decimal)} = 13 \text{ (octal)}$$

SEE: CODE, HEXADECIMAL.

OFF-LINE

Refers to data which are stored on devices not immediately accessible to the computer. Data stored on *magnetic tape*, *punched cards*, or *paper tape* must be loaded into *on-line* storage to be available to the computer.

ON-LINE

Refers to the location of data on storage devices which are immediately accessible to the computer. Usually on-line data are stored on *discs*, in *RAM*, or in *ROM*. Data which is *off-line* must be loaded into on-line storage for use.

OPERATING SYSTEMS (OS)

A set of programs that are resident in a computer and facilitate using the attributes of the computer. An operating system typically controls the I/O functions such as managing the keyboard. A *disc-operating system* is referred to as DOS.

OS

SEE: OPERATING SYSTEM.

OUTPUT

Information emanating from a display unit such as a *CRT* or printer. SEE: INPUT.

PAPER TAPE

SEE: TAPE.

PARALLEL CONNECTION

An electronic connector which allows the *microcomputer* to communicate with *peripheral devices (printers, keyboards*, etc.). A parallel connection transmits data in parallel mode, that is, all *bits* of information are sent simultaneously. If the microcomputer is sending in parallel mode then the peripheral device must receive in parallel mode, and vice versa. SEE: SERIAL CONNECTION.

PARALLEL DATA TRANSMISSION

Microcomputers handle data in groups of eight or sometimes 16 *bits*. These groupings are called *words*. Parallel transmission refers to passing words from one component to another as an intact group. An eight-bit word would be transmitted as eight simultaneous bits along eight parallel wires. SEE: PARALLEL CONNECTION. SERIAL CONNECTION, UART.

PERIPHERAL DEVICE

A device, such as a *printer*, *mass storage* unit, or *keyboard*, which is an accessory to a *microprocessor* and which transfers information to and from the microprocessor.

PERSONAL COMPUTER

A microcomputer designed for use by an individual for entertainment, instruction, and bookkeeping chores.

PLOTTER

A *peripheral* device which draws two-dimensional shapes on paper. Some plotters also use colors.

PORT

The two most common types of ports are *RS232* and *20 ma* (read twenty millamps). These ports are frequently referred to as *I/O ports* (input/output ports) and are the connections through which the computer communicates with the outside world. Thus, ports are the "plugs" which connect the computer to *peripheral devices* such as *keyboards* and *printers*. SEE: PARALLEL CONNECTION, SERIAL CONNECTION.

PRINT MECHANISMS

SEE: BELT PRINTER, DAISY WHEEL PRINTER, INK JET PRINTER, MATRIX PRINTER.

PRINTER

A *peripheral device* which accepts *output* data from the *microprocessor* and prints characters on paper. Printers are defined as *impact* or *non-impact* depending on the means by which a character is formed on the paper. Impact printers strike the paper through a ribbon in a manner similar to a typewriter. Non-impact printers form characters by various means such as heat, electrical charges, or spraying ink. SEE: BELT PRINTER, DAISY WHEEL PRINTER, INK JET PRINTER, MATRIX PRINTER.

PROGRAM

A series of *instructions* to a *computer* which cause the computer to solve a problem or perform a task. SEE: ASSEMBLER, BASIC, COMPILER, EXECUTIVE CONTROL PROGRAM, FORTRAN, INTERPRETER, LANGUAGE, MACHINE LANGUAGE, ROUTINE, SUBROUTINE.

PROM

An acronym for *Programmable Read Only Memory*. A type of permanent or *static memory* made of an *integrated circuit* which can be programmed after it has been manufactured. Programming a PROM consists of permanently recording data or instructions on the *chips* which make up the PROM. SEE: EPROM, RAM, ROM.

RAM

An acronym for *Random Access Memory*. Any *memory* which can be written on or read from by a *program* and in which the memory locations can be accessed in a random sequence. RAM can be erased and reprogrammed by the programmer as frequently as necessary. RAM size is expressed as a quantity of *bytes* such as 4K(4,000 bytes). RAM may be expanded by adding *memory chips* or *memory boards*. SEE: EPROM, PROM, ROM.

RANDOM ACCESS MEMORY
SEE: RAM.

READ
The act of retrieving data from *memory* or from an *input/output* device.

REFRESH
The process whereby *volatile memory* is constantly charged with electrical current. This keeps the *bit* pattern of the memory in proper order thereby maintaining the data which are *stored*. Without refresh, the memory would lose electrical charge, consequently losing the stored data. SEE: MEMORY, RAM, ROM.

REGISTER
A temporary *storage device* located in the *microprocessor* which can hold computer *bits* or words.

RESPONSE TIME
The interval of time required for the microprocessor to respond to an instruction or an input from a *peripheral* such as the *keyboard*. In an educational environment, the time interval from the activation of the keyboard to a display on the CRT should be less than three seconds.

REVERSE DISPLAY
Attribute of a *CRT* which permits characters to be displayed either as white on black background or black on white background. SEE: VIDEO DISPLAY UNIT.

RF MODULATOR
SEE: MODULATOR.

ROM
An acronym for *Read Only Memory*. It is made of an *integrated circuit* on which data or *instructions* are programmed at the time of manufacture. It cannot be erased or reprogrammed by computer operations. The size of ROM is expressed as the quantity of *bytes*, for example, 12K(12,000 bytes). SEE: EPROM, PROM, RAM, STORAGE CAPACITY.

ROUTINE
A series of instructions within a *program* which performs a specific subtask of the program. A routine is usually performed only once during the execution of a program. SEE: SUBROUTINE.

RS232
The name of a type of *port* which permits *serial transmission* of data to a *peripheral device*. The RS232 Interface has been standardized by the Electronics Industry Association and is on many *microcomputers*.

RUN
Jargon for *execute*.

SCROLLING
A technique of displaying data on a *CRT* screen. Each line of data appears first at the bottom and moves upward as new lines are displayed. Eventually the line disappears off the top of the screen.

SERIAL CONNECTION
An *input/output port* which allows *serial transmission* of data. In this serial transmission mode, each *bit* of information is sent individually. If a *peripheral device* receives in serial mode, then the microcomputer must send in serial mode, and vice versa. SEE: PARALLEL CONNECTION, SERIAL DATA TRANSMISSION.

SERIAL DATA TRANSMISSION
A means for transmitting computer words by sending *bits* individually in sequence. Whereas in *parallel data transmission*, the bits are carried along parallel wires, in serials transmission only one wire is used; therefore, bits are sent and received singly. SEE: PARALLEL CONNECTION, PARALLEL DATA TRANSMISSION, SERIAL CONNECTION.

SOFTWARE
Refers to *programs* and accompanying *documentation*. Software is stored on *tape* cassettes or *discs* when not being used by the computer. The computer *reads* the software into its *memory* in order to use the programs.

SOURCE PROGRAM
A program written in a language such as *BASIC*, *FORTRAN*, or *COBOL*. The source program must be translated via a *compiler, interpreter*, or *assembler* into a *machine language object program*. The language of a source program is symbolic, that is, the instructions are represented by words or mnemonic devices which are readily understood by humans.

STATIC MEMORY

A type of programmable *memory* which changes only when an electrical charge is applied. It is often found in a *MOS chip*. It does not require *refresh* operations as does *dynamic memory*. SEE: RAM, ROM.

STORAGE CAPACITY

The quantity of *bytes* a *storage device* can hold. It is usually expressed in *kilobytes* which is abbreviated KB. Thus, a disc is said to have a storage capacity of 400KB (400,000 bytes). This can be understood as 400,000 characters such as letters, numbers, spaces, etc. SEE: MAIN MEMORY, MASS STORAGE, MEMORY.

STORAGE DEVICE

A *peripheral* device which holds information. This includes *tapes* and *discs*. SEE: WRITE.

STORE

This term refers to the process of placing data onto some type of *storage device*. Usually the data are to be kept permanently; therefore, they are placed in a *non-volatile memory* such as a *tape, disc,* or *static memory ROM*. SEE: DYNAMIC MEMORY, VOLATILE MEMORY.

SUBROUTINE

A portion of a *program* which performs a specific subtask. A subroutine is usually called upon several times during the execution of the program of which it is a member. SEE: ROUTINE.

TAPE

There are two types of tapes used with microcomputers: (1) paper tape, and (2) magnetic tape. Each is a type of *storage device* which is often used for *mass storage*. Data are stored on paper tape by punching holes into the tape. A character is represented by a certain pattern of holes. In magnetic tape, patterns of electrical charges represent characters. SEE: MEMORY.

TERMINAL

A *peripheral device* which facilitates human communication with a computer. Usually it consists of a *keyboard* with alphabetic and numeric characters coupled with a printing mechanism or a *CRT*. One enters information via the keyboard; the computer responds via the *printer* or *CRT*.

TEXT EDITOR

A system of *programs* which facilitate editing. The functions available usually consist of adding text, deleting text, searching for specified text, paragraphing, and page layout. SEE: EDITOR.

TRACK

The area of a *disc* on which magnetic pulses are recorded. These magnetic pulses are the electrical analog of *bits* or the information which is *stored*. A track is analogous to a groove on a music recording. Information is written onto a track and read off the track by means of a magnetic head in the same way a tone-arm "reads" a musical recording. Instead of a needle, the magnetic head has metallic pads that create (write) or sense (read) magnetic pulses. SEE: MEMORY, PERIPHERAL DEVICE, STORAGE CAPACITY.

UART

Acronym for *Universal Asynchronous Receiver Transmitter*. This device converts *parallel data* transmission to *serial data* transmission, and vice versa. SEE: PARALLEL CONNECTION, SERIAL CONNECTION.

VDU

Abbreviation for *Video Display Unit*.

VERTICAL SCROLLING

A method of displaying text on a video display unit (*VDU*). In the case where more text is stored than can be displayed on a screen, the text is "scrolled," that is, moved up or down on the screen. When scrolled up, the text disappears off the top of the screen; when scrolled downward, the text rolls off the bottom.

VIDEO DISPLAY UNIT

A component of a microcomputer system which displays the output on a screen similar to a TV screen. A television *monitor* is a type of video display unit. SEE: CRT (CATHODE RAY TUBE), MODULATOR.

VIDEO MONITOR

SEE: VIDEO DISPLAY UNIT.

VOLATILE MEMORY

A *memory* device which does not retain information after electrical power is lost. *RAM* is a type of volatile memory. SEE: DYNAMIC MEMORY, REFRESH, ROM.

WINDOW

Refers to partitioning a computer display into independent segments. A *CRT* screen may be divided into segments, one of which may contain explanatory text, another pictures or other graphic symbols, and the third segment representing questions pertaining to the text and pictures. The fourth segment could present responses to the student's answers to the questions. The contents of each segment or window could be varied independently of any other window.

WORD

A grouping of *bits*. Words may consist of eight bits or 16 bits. Computers read, store, and manipulate data in words rather than as individual bits. SEE: WORD LENGTH.

WORD LENGTH

The number of *bits* in a *word*. Most microcomputers have a word length of eight bits, though a 16-bit word length is also available from some manufacturers. SEE: WORD.

WRITE

The act of delivering information to a *memory* device or a *storage* medium. SEE: READ.

Appendix II
Resources Are Macro for Micros

The microprocessor industry is exploding all around us. New makers of hardware (from peripherals to complete systems) and software surface frequently, and some companies soon go under. Computer books and periodicals are flooding the marketplace; some quickly become bibles, while others barely make a ripple.

With this constant flux, the names listed here must necessarily be labeled a sampling rather than an exhaustive compilation of commercial resources available. To keep up-to-date, read the general circulation computer magazines; talk with the operators of computer stores; and get on supplier mailing lists.

MANUFACTURERS

Alpha Microsystems, 17881 Sky Park North, Irvine, CA 92714.

Apple Computer Inc., 10260 Bandley Drive, Cupertino, CA 95014.

Astral Computer Company, 1710 Oldridge Avenue North, Stillwater, MN 55082.

Atari Inc., 75 Rockefeller Plaza, New York, NY 10019.

Bally Manufacturing, 10750 West Grand Avenue, Franklin Park, IL 60131.

Centurion Industries, Inc. 167 Constitution Drive, Menlo Park, CA 94025.

Commodore International, 950 Rittenhouse Road, Norristown, PA 19403.

Compucolor Corporation, 5965 Peachtree Corners East, Norcross, GA 30071.

Cromemco, Inc., 280 Bernardo Avenue, Mountain View, CA 94040.

Digital Equipment Corporation, 146 Main Street, Maynard, MA 01754.

Exidy, 969 West Maude Avenue, Sunnyvale, CA 94086.

Heath, Benton Harbor, MI 49022.

Hewlett-Packard, 1000 Northeast Circle Boulevard, Corvallis, OR 97330.

Imagination Machine, Audio-Visual Accessories and Supplies Corp., 196 Holt Street, Hackensack, NJ 07602.

Interact Electronics, Box 8140, Ann Arbor, MI 48107.

Intertec Data Systems, 2300 Broad River Road, Columbia, SC 29210.

Mattel Electronics, 5150 Rosecrans, Hawthorne, CA 90250.

Midwest Scientific Instruments, 220 West Cedar, Olathe, KS 66061.

Nestar Systems, Inc., 810 Garland Drive, Palo Alto, CA 94303.

North Star, 1440 Fourth Street, Berkeley, CA 94710.

Ohio Scientific, 1333 South Chillicothe Road, Aurora, OH 44202.

Polymorphic, 460 Ward Drive, Santa Barbara, CA 93111.

Processor Technology, 7100 Johnson Industrial Drive, Pleasanton, CA 94566.

RCA VIP Marketing, New Holland Avenue, Lancaster, PA 17604.

Radio Shack, 2617 West Seventh Street, Fort Worth, TX 76107.

Smoke Signal Broadcasting, 31336 Via Colinas, Westlake Village, CA 91361.

Southwest Technical Products Corporation, 219 West Rhapsody, San Antonio, TX 78216.

Technico, 9051 Red Branch Road, Columbia, MD 21045.

Terak Corporation, 14405 North Scottsdale, Scottsdale, AZ 85254.

Texas Instruments, Inc., PO Box 1443, Houston, TX 77001.

Umtech, 2950 Patrick Henry Drive, Santa Clara, CA 95050.

United Microsystems Corporation, 2601 South State Street, Ann Arbor, MI 48104.

Vector Graphics Inc., 790 Hampshire Road, Westlake Village, CA 91361.

Western Digital, Box 2180, Newport Beach, CA 92663.

SOFTWARE

In addition to software available from the major manufacturers for their own microcomputers, other companies create programs compatible with one or more of the popular models. The quality and validity of this commercial software can vary widely. Write for brochures and lists.

Acorn Software Products, Inc., 634 North Carolina Avenue SE, Washington, DC 20003.

Adventure International, PO Box 3435, Longwood, FL 32750.

Apple-Cations, 21650 West Eleven Mile Road, Suite 163, Southfield, MI 48076.

ARESCO, Box 1142, Columbia, MD 21044.

Arkansas Systems, Inc., 8901 Kanis Road, Suite 206, Little Rock, AR 72205.

ATMCO, PO Box 12248H, Gainesville, FL 32604.

Bell & Howell Company, 1700 North McCormick Road, Chicago, IL 60645.

Bits, Inc., 25 Route 101, Peterborough, NH 03458.

Bottom Shelf, Inc., PO Box 49104, Atlanta, GA 30359.

Cavri Systems, 26 Trumbull Street, New Haven, CT 06511.

Charles Mann & Associates, Micro Software Division, 1926 South Veteran Avenue, Los Angeles, CA 90025.

Compu-Quote, 6914 Berquist Avenue, Canoga Park, CA 91307.

Computer Bus, PO Box 397H, Grand River, OH 44045.

Computer Resource Center, Technical Education Research Centers, Inc., 8 Eliot Street, Cambridge, MA 02138.

Conduit, PO Box 388, Iowa City, IA 52244.

Cook's Computer Company, 1905 Bailey Drive, Marshalltown, IA 50158.

Cow Bay Computing, Box 515, Manhasset, NY 11030.

Creative Computing, PO Box 789-M, Morristown, NJ 07960.

Creative Discount Software, PO Box 24B67, Los Angeles, CA 90024.

Data Equipment Supply Corporation, 8315 Firestone Boulevard, Downey, CA 90241.

Educational Activities, Inc., PO Box 392, Freeport, NY 11520.

Edu-Ware Services, Inc., 22035 Burbank Boulevard, Suite 223, Woodland Hills, CA 91367.

Geller Computer Systems, PO Box 350, New York, NY 10040.

Go: Forth Microcomputing, 329-22 St. E., Prince Albert, Saskatchewan, S6V 1N3, Canada.

Hayden Book Co., Inc., 50 Essex Street, Rochelle Park, NJ 07662.

Hebbler Software Services, 7142 Elliott Drive, Dallas, TX 75227.

High Technology, Inc., PO Box 14665, Oklahoma City, OK 73113.

Instant Software, Inc., Peterborough, NH 03458.

Interactive Microware, Inc., PO Box 771, State College, PA 16801.

ISDG Inc., 312 High Gate Avenue, Buffalo, NY 14215.

King, R.W., 3 Nappa Lane, Westport, CT 06880.

Level IV Products Inc., 32238 Schoolcraft, Suite F4, Livonia, MI 48154.

Lifeboat Associates, 2248 Broadway, New York, NY 10024.

Maine Software Library, PO Box 197, Standish, ME 04084 (rentals).

Math Software, 1233 Blackthorn Place, Deerfield, IL 60015.

Med Systems Software, PO Box 2674, Chapel Hill, NC 27514.

Mentor Software, Inc., The Software Factory, PO Box 791, Anoka, MN 55303.

Mercer Systems, Inc., 87 Scooter Lane, Hicksville, NY 11801.

Micro Architect, 96 Dothan Street, Arlington, MA 02174.

Microcomputer Education Applications Network, 1030 Fifteenth Street NW, Suite 800, Washington, DC 20005.

MicroGnome, 5843 Montgomery Road, Elkridge, MD 21227.

Micro Learningware, Box 2134, North Mankato, MN 56001.

Microphys, 2048 Ford Street, Brooklyn, NY 11229.

Micro Power & Light Co., 1108 Keystone, Dept. C, 13773 North Central Expressway, Dallas, TX 75243.

Micro-Pro, 1299 Fourth Street, San Rafael, CA 94901.

Microsoft Consumer Products, 10800 Northeast Eighth, Suite 507, Bellevue, WA 98004.

Millikin, 1100 Research Boulevard, St. Louis, MO 63132.

Minnesota Educational Computing Consortium, Instructional Services Division, 2520 Broadway Drive, Lauderdale, MN 55113.

Muse Software, 330 North Charles Street, Baltimore, MD 21201.

National Coordinating Center for Curriculum Development, State University at Stony Brook, Stony Brook, NY 11794.

Organic Software, 1492 Windsor Way, Livermore, CA 94550.

Percom Data Company, 211 North Kirby, Garland, TX 75042.

Personal Software, Inc., 1330 Bordeaux Drive, Sunnyvale, CA 94086.

Program Design, Inc., 11 Idar Court, Greenwich, CT 06830.

Programma International, 3400 Wilshire Boulevard, Los Angeles, CA 90010.

Programs for Learning, PO Box 954, New Milford, CT 06776.

Program Store, 4200 Wisconsin Avenue NW, Washington, DC 20016.

PRS—Program of the Month, 257 C.P.W., New York, NY 10024.

Quality Software, 10051 Odessa Avenue, Sepulveda, CA 91343.

Queue, 5 Chapel Hill Drive, Fairfield, CT 06432.

Realty Software Co., 2045 Manhattan Avenue, Hermosa Beach, CA 90254.

Scelbi Publications, PO Box 3133, Milford, CT 06460.

Software Exchange, 6 South Street, Milford, NH 03055.

Software Industries, 902 Pinecrest, Richardson, TX 75080.

Solartek, PO Box 298, Guilderland, NY 12084.

Speakeasy Software Ltd., PO Box 1220, Kemptville, Ontario K0G 1J0, Canada.

Supersoft, PO Box 1628, Champaign, IL 61820.

Sybex, 2020 Milvia Street, Berkeley, CA 94709.

Teach Yourself by Computer Software, 40 Stuyvesant Manor, Geneseo, NY 14454.

Technical Products Co., PO Box 12983, Gainesville, FL 32604.

TSA Software, Inc., 39 Williams Drive, Monroe, CT 06468.

Tycom Associates, 68 Velma Avenue, Pittsfield, MA 01201.

GENERAL MAGAZINES

Several of the general magazines have been around long enough to be publishing anthologies of ''best'' articles. Thus:

The Best of Byte. 386 pp.; $11.95. 70 Main Street, Peterborough, NH 03458.

The Best of Creative Computing. Vol. 1, Vol. 2; each $8.95. Box 789-M, Morristown, NJ 07960.

The Best of Micro. Vol. 1, Vol. 2. PO Box 6502, South Chelmsford, MA 01824.

The Best of Personal Computing. $7.50. 1050 Commonwealth Avenue, Boston, MA 02215.

Another anthology, *1979 Periodical Guide for Computerists,* contains 3,000+ articles selected from 24 publications. Subject indexed. $5.95. Also, 1976, 1977, 1978 editions at $5.00 each. E. Berg Publications, 622 East Third, Kimball, NE 69145.

AEDS Journal. Educational Data Systems, 1201 Sixteenth Street NW, Washington, DC 20036. $25/ year.

Byte. 70 Main Street, Peterborough, NH 03458. $18/ year.

Calculators/Computers. Dymax, PO Box 310-F, Menlo Park, CA 94025. $12/year.

*Classroom Computer News by Intentional Educations, PO Box 266, Cambridge, MA 02138 is a new newsprint periodical for students and teachers. One year $9; six issues.

Computers and Education, Computers and the Humanities. Pergamon Press, Maxwell House, Fairview Park, Elmsford, NY 10523. $60 and $35/ year respectively.

*Added by the editor

Computers and People. Berkeley Enterprises, Inc., 815 Washington Street, Newtonville, MA 02160. $14.50/year.

Computer Shopper. The Nationwide Marketplace for Computing Equipment, PO Box F21, Titusville, FL 32780. $10/year.

Computerworld. 797 Washington Street, Newton, MA 02160. $25/year.

Computing Teacher. International Council for Computers in Education, c/o Howard Bailey, Eastern Oregon State College, La Grande, OR 97850. $8/year.

*Courseware Magazine, edited and published by Dan Isaacson, is a new journal of microcomputer software designed and documented for educational use. Each issue features machine-readable programs in a variety of subject areas suitable for grades K-12. Three versions of the magazine are available: Apple II, PET, and TRS-80 Level II. One year $50; five issues.

Creative Computing. Box 789-M, Morristown, NJ 07960. $15/year.

Dr. Dobb's Journal of Computer Calisthenics and Orthodontia. People's Computer Co., 1263 El Camino Real, Menlo Park, CA 94025. $15/year.

Intelligent Machines Journal. 345 Swett Road, Woodside, CA 94062. $18/year.

Interface Age. PO Box 1234, Cerritos, CA 90701. $18/year.

Journal of Computer-Based Instruction. Association for the Development of Computer-Based Instructional Systems, 8120 Penn Avenue South, Bloomington, MN 55431. $20/year (quarterly).

Microcomputing (Kilobaud Microcomputing). PO Box 997, Farmingdale, NY 11737. $25/year.

Minicomputer News. 1050 Commonwealth Avenue, Boston, MA 02215. $9/year.

onComputing. PO Box 307, Martinsville, NJ 08836. $8.50/year (quarterly).

Oregon Computer Teacher. Oregon Council of Computer Education, Computer Center, East Oregon State College, La Grande, OR 97850. $5/year.

Output. Technical Publishing, 666 Fifth Avenue, New York, NY 10103. $18/year.

Personal Computing. 1050 Commonwealth Avenue, Boston, MA 02215. $14/year.

Recreational Computing. People's Computer Co, 1263 El Camino Real, Menlo Park, CA 94025. $10/year.

Robert Purser's Magazine. PO Box 466, El Dorado, CA 95623. $4/issue.

*School Microware is a quarterly software directory which covers instructional microcomputer software available for the three micros most widely used in education: TRS-80 (Model I), the Commodore PET and the Apple II. The periodical is published by Dresden Associates, PO Box 246, Dresden, ME 04342.

SIGCUE Bulletin. Association for Computing Machinery, Special Interest Group on Computer Uses in Education, 1133 Avenue of the Americas, New York, NY 10036. $16.50/year (quarterly).

Software Digest. 7620 Little River Turnpike, Suite 414, Annandale, VA 22003. $88/year (biweekly).

Software Exchange. Box 55056, Valencia, CA 91355.

Technological Horizons in Education (T.H.E. Journal). PO Box 992, Acton, MA 01720. $15/year.

OTHER MAGAZINES, NEWSLETTERS, CLUBS

Periodicals in this listing include magazines specific to the various models of microcomputers and newsletters of user groups.

Aardvark/Journal for OSI. Aardvark Technical Services, 1690 Bolton, Walled Lake, MI 48088.

ADCIS. c/o Joan Lauer Hayes, Computer Center, Western Washington University, Bellingham, WA 98225. $20/year.

Alternate Source. 1806 Ada, Lansing, MI 48910. $9/ six issues.

Apple Cookbook. Apple Orchard, 131 Highland Avenue, Vacaville, CA 95688. $15/year (newsletter).

Apple for the Teacher. c/o Ted Perry, 5848 Riddio Street, Citrus Heights, CA 95610.

Appleseed. Softside Publications, 6 South Street, Milford, NH 03055. $15/year.

Apple Shoppe. PO Box 701, Placentia, CA 92670. $12/eight issues.

Buss. 325 Pennsylvania Avenue SE, Washington, DC 20003. $8.20/year.

Cload. Box 1267, Goleta, CA 93017. $36/year (cassette-based).

Compute. PO Box 5119, Greensboro, NC 27403. $9/ six issues.

Computronics. Box 149, New City, NY 10956. $24/ year.

---

*Added by the editor

Irdis. Box 550, Goleta, CA 93017. $14.95/four issues (cassette-based).

Level I Magazine (on tape). PO Box 8316, Anaheim, CA 92802. $40/year.

MACUL Journal. c/o L. Smith, 33500 Van Born Road, Wayne, MI 48184. $5/year.

Micro: The 6502 Journal. PO Box 6502, South Chelmsford, MA 01824. $15/year.

Mini-Micro Systems. 221 Columbus Avenue, Boston, MA 02116.

Nibble, Box 325, Lincoln, MA 01773. $15/eight issues.

North Star Newsletter. 2547 Ninth, Berkeley, CA 94710.

Peek (65). Unofficial Ohio Scientific Users Journal. 62 Southgate Avenue, Annapolis, MD 21401. $8/year.

PET: Cursor. Box 550, Goleta, CA 93017. $27/six issues (cassette-based).

PET Paper. Aresco, PO Box 43, Audubon, PA 19407. $15/year.

PET User Notes. PET User Group, PO Box 371, Montgomeryville, PA 18936. $5/year.

Prog-80. Softside publications, 6 South Street, Milford, NH 03055. $15/year.

Rainbow. PO Box 43, Audubon, PA 19407. $15/year.

Softside: Apple; Softside: Atari; Softside: S-80. Softside Publications, 6 South Street, Milford, NH 03055. Apple and Atari, each $15/year; S-80, $18/year.

TRS-80 Computing. Computer Information Exchange, Box 158, San Luis Rey, CA 92068. $15/year.

TRS-80 Monthly Newsletter. Mathematical Applications Service, Box 149 RS, New City, NY 10956. $24/year.

TRS-80 Notebook. Route 3, Nazareth, PA 18064. $14/year.

TRS-80 Software Exchange. Softside Publications, PO Box 68, Milford, NH 03055. $15/year.

TRS-80 User Group Newsletter. Microcomputer Consultants, 629 Dixie Lane, South Daytona, FL 32019. $24/year.

TRS-80 User Notes. Econo-Computer, PO Box 157, Springfield, PA 19064. $6/year.

User Notes: 6502. Eric C. Rehnke, Publisher, PO Box 33093, North Royalton, OR 44133. $13/year.

'68' Micro Journal. 3018 Hamill Road, Hixson, TN 37343. $14.50/year.

80 Microcomputing. Pine Street, Peterborough, NH 03458. $15/12 issues.

80 Software Critique. PO Box 134, Waukegan, IL 60085. $24/year.

80-US Journal. 3838 South Warner Street, Tacoma, WA 98409. $16/year.

5100 User Notes. Computer Information Exchange, Box 158, San Luis Rey, CA 92068. $5/year.

USER GROUPS

User groups and local computer clubs are good sources of information, mutual assistance, and software exchange. Computer stores generally can put you in touch with such groups in your area.

SOFTWARE BOOK PUBLISHERS

Adam Osborne & Associates Inc. (Osborne/McGraw-Hill), PO Box 2036, Berkeley, CA 94702.

Addison-Wesley Publishing Co., Jacob Way, Reading, MA 01867.

Byte Book Division, 70 Main Street, Peterborough, NH 03458.

Camelot Publishing, Box 1357, Ormond Beach, FL 32074.

Creative Computing Press, PO Box 789-M, Morristown, NJ 07960.

Dilithium Press, PO Box 92, Forest Grove, OR 97116.

E&L Instruments (Bugbooks), 61 First Street, Derby, CT 06418.

Elcomp Publishing Co., 3873-L Schaefer Avenue, Chino, CA 91710.

Entelek, Ward-Whidden House/The Hill, PO Box 1303, Portsmouth, NH 03801.

Essex Publishing Co., 285 Bloomfield Avenue, Caldwell, NJ 07006.

Hayden Book Co., 50 Essex Street, Rochelle Park, NJ 07662.

Howard W. Sams & Co., Inc., 4300 West 62nd Street, Indianapolis, IN 46206.

Kilobaud Microcomputing, Book Dept., Peterborough, NH 03458.

Scelbi Publications, PO Box 2036, Berkeley, CA 94702.

Sybex Inc., 2020 Milvia Street, Berkeley, CA 94704.

Tab Books, Blue Ridge Summit, PA 17214.

Wiley & Sons, Inc., 605 Third Avenue, New York, NY 10016.

Appendix III
Funding Sources for Microcomputers*

by Frederick W. Michael, Jr.

Finding funds to purchase microcomputers and software for instruction has become a challenging—and, for many, an ultimately rewarding—task.

For nonprofit institutions, a variety of federal programs and innovative local administrators have proven good sources of money and information for microcomputer purchases. In addition, such traditional sources of "extra" financial support for equipment as business/civic groups and PTAs have quickly realized the importance of teaching today's students about computers.

Those instructional programs that are ineligible for federal or state money may qualify for outside funding from some of these business, civic, and service organizations as well as from a number of private foundations.

The information in this article (which reflects conditions as of June 1980) was compiled by contacting federal agencies and all state departments of education in the continental United States.

FEDERAL FUNDING

These federal programs permit, but do not guarantee, funding of programs that are educationally sound and justified. If the use of microcomputers is integral to the education plan, the equipment's purchase may be funded. Requests for outright purchase of microcomputer equipment, without an accompanying education plan, probably will not be funded.

From the large number of federal education-related programs, the 19 listed here are the ones educators have used most frequently for buying microcomputer equipment. Each item gives appropriate federal titles, the authorizing legislation, a brief description of the program, and a contact.

Adult Education—Grants to States. (Adult Education Act, PL 91-230 as amended.) To expand educational opportunities and encourage establishment of programs for adults. Special emphasis on instructional programs in computational skills, reading and writing of English. *Contact*: Paul Delker, Division of Adult Education, Department of Education, Washington, DC 20202; phone (202) 245-2278.

Bilingual Education—Title VII. (Bilingual Education Act, Title VII of ESEA of 1965, PL 89-10 as amended by PL 95-561.) To demonstrate effective ways of providing children (3-18 years of age) of limited English proficiency with instruction to enable them, while using their native language, to achieve competence in English. Funds may be used for a variety of instructional activities including curriculum and materials development. *Contact*: Josue Gonzalez, Office of Bilingual Education and Minority Languages Affairs, Department of Education, Washington, DC 20202; phone (202) 245-2600.

Teacher Centers. (Higher Education Act of 1965, Title V-B, Section 532 as amended by PL 94-482 and PL 95-561.) To provide grants for operating teacher centers to improve inservice training for teachers and to develop improved curriculums for the schools. State agencies screen applications, provide technical assistance, and disseminate services. Each center is controlled, within the limits of state and local law, by a Teacher Center Policy Board with a majority of classroom teachers. *Contact:* Allen A. Schmieder, Division of Teacher Centers, Assistant Secretariat for Elementary and Secondary Education, Department of Education, Washington, DC 20202; phone (202) 653-5839.

---

*As this book goes to press, the possibility of new block grant programs going into effect may invalidate some of the information in this article.

Educationally Deprived Children—Local Educational Agencies. (Elementary and Secondary Education Act of 1965, Title I, PL 89-10 as amended—Title I ESEA part A, Subpart 1.) To expand and improve educational programs to meet the needs of educationally disadvantaged children in low-income areas, whether they are enrolled in public or private elementary and secondary schools. These formula grants are to provide instructional activities to supplement existing programs. *Contact:* Paul Miller, Division of Program Development, Office of Compensatory Education, Department of Education, Washington, DC 20202; phone (202) 245-2266.

Handicapped—Research and Demonstration. (Education of the Handicapped Act, Title VI, Part E, PL 91-230 as amended by PL 95-49.) To improve the education of handicapped children through research and development projects and model programs (demonstrations). *For research, contact:* Max Mueller, Research Projects Branch, Division of Innovation and Development, Office of Special Education, Office of Special Education and Rehabilitative Services, Department of Education, Washington, DC 20202; phone (202) 245-2275. *For model programs, contact:* Jane Case Williams, Program Development Branch (same address); phone (202) 245-9722.

Handicapped Media Services and Captioned Films. (Education of the Handicapped Act, Title VI, Part F, PL 91-230, PL 94-142 as amended.) To provide for acquisition and distribution of media materials and equipment and to provide for research into the use of media. *Contact:* Malcolm Norwood, Captioned Films and Telecommunications Branch, Division of Media Services, Office of Special Education and Rehabilitative Services, Department of Education, Washington, DC 20202; phone (202) 472-4640.

Vocational Education—Program Improvement and Supportive Services. (Vocational Education Amendments of 1963 as amended by Education Amendments of 1976, PL 94-482.) To assist states in improving their programs of vocational education and supportive services for those programs through research, innovation, curriculum development, sex equity, personnel development, and guidance. *Contact:* LeRoy A. Cornelson, Division of State Vocational Program Operations, Office of Vocational and Adult Education, Department of Education, Washington, DC 20202; phone (202) 472-3440.

Vocational Education—Program Improvement Projects. (Vocational Education Act of 1963, Title I-B as amended by Education Amendments of 1976, PL 94-482.) To provide support for projects for research,

currciulum development, and demonstration in vocational education. It must be demonstrated that an improved teaching technique or curriculum material is likely to be used in a substantial number of classrooms within five years. *Contact:* Howard Hjelm, Division of Research and Demonstration, Office of Vocational and Adult Education, Department of Education, Washington, DC 20202; phone (202) 245-9634.

Emergency School Aid Act. (Education Amendments of 1972; Title VII—Emergency School Aid Act, PL 93-318 as amended by PL 93-380 and PL 95-961.) To provide financial assistance to help a school district solve educational problems arising from a plan to eliminate minority group segregation and discrimination among students and faculty; and to encourage the voluntary elimination, reduction, or prevention of minority group isolation. *Contact:* Jesse Jordan, Division of Equal Educational Opportunity Program Operation, Office of Elementary and Secondary Education, Department of Education, Washington, DC 20202; phone (202) 245-7965.

Education for Gifted and Talented Children & Youth. (Gifted and Talented Children's Education Act of 1978; Part A of Title IX of the Elementary and Secondary Education Act of 1965 as amended by Section 802 of the Education Amendments of 1978, PL 95-561.) To meet the educational needs of gifted and talented children and thereby promote the development of their special potential, this program awards grants and contracts to eligible state and local education agencies, institutions of higher education, and other public and private agencies and organizations. Used to plan, develop, operate, and improve programs to enhance the education of gifted and talented children at the preschool, elementary, and secondary school levels. *Contact:* Harold C. Lyon, Jr., Office of Gifted and Talented, Office for Special Education and Rehabilitative Services, Department of Education, Washington, DC 20202; phone (202) 245-2482.

Libraries and Learning Resources. (Elementary and Secondary Education Act of 1965, Title IV-B, PL 89-10 as amended by Section 401 of PL 93-380.) To acquire school library resources, instructional materials, and instructional equipment for use by children and teachers in public and private elementary and secondary schools for instructional purposes only. Local education agencies have complete discretion in dividing funds among program purposes. *Contact:* Milbrey L. Jones, Office of Libraries and Learning Technologies, Office of Research and Improvement, Department of Education, Washington, DC 20202; phone (202) 245-2592.

Improvement in Local Educational Practices. (Elementary and Secondary Education Act, Title IV, Part C as amended by PL 95-561.) To assist local education agencies in improving their educational practices through development of activities addressing educational deprivation, gifted, talented, handicapped, improvements in basic skills, and improvements in compensatory education efforts. *Contact:* Alpheus White, Office of Elementary and Secondary Education, Division of State Educational Assistance, Department of Education, Washington, DC 20202; phone (202) 245-2592.

Fund for the Improvement of Postsecondary Education. (Education Amendments of 1972, Title III, Section 301, PL 92-318.) To increase the effectiveness of postsecondary education, with priority given to learner-centered change, increased cost-effectiveness, and far-reaching impact. *Contact:* Arturo Madrid, Fund for the Improvement of Postsecondary Education, Office of Educational Research and Improvement, Department of Education, Washington, DC 20202; phone (202) 245-8091.

Educational Research and Development. (Education Amendments of 1976, PL 94-482.) To improve student achievement in the basic education skills, including reading and mathematics, through educational research and development. *Contact:* Olive Covington, Office of Public Affairs, National Institute of Education, Department of Education, 1200 Nineteenth Street NW, Washington, DC 20208; phone (202) 254-7150.

Science Education Research and Development and Resource Improvement. (National Science Foundation Act of 1950, as amended.) To improve science instruction at all grade levels, with grant money used for paying costs necessary to conduct research or development studies. *Contact:* Marjorie Gardner, Division of Science Education Resources Improvement, National Science Foundation, 1800 G Street NW, Washington, DC 20550; phone (202) 282-7786. *Also:* Joseph Lipson, Division of Science Education Development and Research (same address); phone (202) 282-7900.

Appalachian Vocational and Other Education Facilities and Operations. (Appalachian Regional Development Act of 1965, Sections 211 and 214, PL 89-4 as amended.) To provide the region's residents with basic facilities, equipment, and operating funds for training and education necessary to obtain employment. *Contact:* Henry Krevor, Appalachian Regional Commission, 1666 Connecticut Avenue NW, Washington, DC 20235; phone (202) 673-7874.

Coastal Plains Education Demonstration Projects. (Public Works and Economic Development Act of 1965, Title V, Section 517 of PL 879-136 as amended by PL 94-188.) To expand opportunities for residents in North Carolina, South Carolina, Georgia, Florida, and Virginia to obtain vocational and technical training through the planning, equipping, and operation of vocational and technical education projects. *Contact:* James W. Butler, Coastal Plains Regional Commission, 215 East Bay Street, Charleston, SC 29401; phone (803) 724-4250.

Upper Great Lakes Education Demonstration Projects. (Public Works and Economic Development Act of 1965, Title V, Section 517, PL 89-131.) To assist residents of the region to obtain vocational and technical training. *Contact:* Oscar Lund, Upper Great Lakes Regional Commission, Hawkes Hall, 2231 Catlin Avenue, Superior, WI 54880; phone (715) 392-7111.

Pacific Northwest Education Demonstration Projects. (Public Works and Economic Development Act of 1965, Title V, Section 517 of Pl 89-136 as amended by PL 94-188.) To expand the opportunities for residents in Idaho, Oregon, and Washington to obtain vocational and technical training. *Contact:* John McCullen, Pacific Northwest Regional Commission, 700 East Evergreen Boulevard, Vancouver, WA 98660; phone (206) 696-7771.

STATE/LOCAL FUNDING

The states operate virtually no programs similarly useful in financing microcomputer purchases. Instead, most existing state funds are apportioned, under a strict formula, to local school districts. The strength of this system is the discretion each local district has to spend the funds on local priorities.

Competition for these local dollars can be tough, but innovation and ingenuity can secure funding for microcomputers. As with applications for federal money, educators who develop a sound instructional plan incorporating microcomputers have the most success.

Activities showing initiative and involving students and the community also have helped to persuade local districts to spend money on microcomputers. Successful activities include:

- Demonstrating the equipment's capabilities to administrators, school board members, PTA groups, and taxpayer organizations, to show why it is needed.
- Developing a presentation on the importance of computer literacy in today's world.

- Sponsoring a "computer fair," with students and educators demonstrating the technology and its capabilities.
- Conducting inservice training programs to acquaint other educators with the utility of microcomputers.
- Implementing a public information program, by providing the local media with feature stories and press releases about microcomputers and how they can be used.

OTHER SOURCES OF FUNDING

Educators searching for funds should not overlook local groups, such as the PTA and civic/business organizations. Some of the activities already suggested can be instrumental in securing funds from these sources. Many local organizations also may be able to aid nonpublic instructional programs to obtain microcomputers for worthwhile projects.

Foundations can be a source of funding for public and nonpublic programs alike. Most people are familiar with a few major foundations, which constantly receive requests for support of all types of projects; but many overlook the numerous smaller foundations, where the chances of success may be greater. Proposals should be tailored to the special interests of the individual foundation, however.

The most important single reference work on grant-awarding foundations is *The Foundation Directory*, now in its seventh edition. The directory, which lists foundations arranged by states as well as by subject, is available in many libraries or may be ordered from Columbia University Press (136 South Broadway, Irvington, NY 10533).

Those seeking foundation funds can also consult The Foundation Center, a nationwide network of foundation reference collections for free public use. The headquarters office of The Foundation Center (888 Seventh Avenue, New York, NY 10019) can provide the location of the nearest regional collection.

INFORMATION SOURCES

The funding situation changes quickly, but a number of publications provide up-to-date information.

About federal funding: *Catalog of Federal Domestic Assistance, Federal Register,* and *Commerce Business Daily.* All three may be purchased on a subscription basis from the Superintendent of Documents, U.S. Government Printing Office, Publications Department, Washington, DC 20402.

About foundations: *The Foundation Directory* (described earlier); *The Foundation Grants Index* (included as a separate section in *Foundation News,* which is available by subscription from The Council on Foundations, Inc., Box 783, Old Chelsea Station, NY 10011); and *About Foundations: How To Find the Facts You Need To Get a Grant* (a paperback guide that can be purchased from The Foundation Center).

Bell & Howell has published a more comprehensive examination of funding sources for microcomputers, with recommendations for successful proposal writing. *Funding Report for Microcomputers,* a 44-page booklet, is free from local Bell & Howell microcomputer dealers or from Bell & Howell, Audio-Visual Products Division, 7100 North McCormick Road, Chicago, IL 60645.

Note: Special acknowledgment is due the staff of the Office of Public Affairs of the Department of Education for their help in verifying personnel and office titles in that recently reorganized agency.

Editor's note: Copies of Apple's educational foundation guidelines and brochures are available upon request from: Foundation for Advancement of Computer Aided Education, 20863 Stevens Creek Blvd., Building B2, Suite A1, Cupertino, CA 95014; telephone (408) 225-3295.

Appendix IV
Student Use of Computers in Schools

Prepared by National Center for Education Statistics, US Department of Education, Jeanette Goor, Project Director

About one-half of the Nation's school districts provide students with access to at least one microcomputer or computer terminal, according to a recent survey of school districts conducted by the National Center for Education Statistics (NCES), U.S. Department of Education.*

The newly available low-cost microcomputers, sometimes called personal computers, have created renewed interest in student use of computers in schools. Reportedly, school districts are providing students with access to these computers for a variety of learning and instructional purposes. However, no national information on the extent or nature of interactive use of computers by students has been available to assist planners among concerned public education authorities and among interested segments of the private sector. The NCES survey was intended to help fill this gap in planning information.

School districts make available almost 52,000 computers to students for educational purposes. This estimated total represents a mix of microcomputers and the more traditional terminals connected to a central processor.** In the short time they have been available for purchase, microcomputers have come to outnumber terminals, proportionately 3 to 2.

More than twice as many districts provide microcomputers as terminals (Table 1). These districts put three-fourths of their available microcomputers, and a

slightly smaller proportion of their terminals, to use at the secondary school level.

Approximately 1 of every 4 public schools (about 22,000) currently has at least one microcomputer or computer terminal for instructional use by students. These schools represent one-half of all secondary schools, 14 percent of all elementary schools, and 19 percent of all other types of schools, such as vocational, special education, and combined elementary and secondary schools.

The most frequently reported educational use is to provide students with an understanding of computer concepts (computer literacy). Other major uses are to improve student learning in selected subject areas and to challenge high achievers. Fewer than half of the districts with computers use them for remedial and compensatory education. Most districts rely upon their computers for more than one of these educational purposes.

Computer availability within districts generally is limited, both in number of computers and location of computers (Table 2). Students in about three-fourths of the districts with microcomputers, and in a similar proportion of those with terminals, have fewer than five computers available for their use. In the majority of districts having computers, only one elementary school and/or one secondary school has computer access.

About 18 percent of the districts that provide no current access plan to initiate student use of computers within 3 years. Most of these districts are small—fewer than 2,500 students. Potential growth in usage could be greater, however, since many districts reported that they were uncertain about future plans.

All districts in the survey reported on operational and planning needs considered critical to the initiation or expansion of the interactive use of computers. More

*School districts were requested to report only interactive use of computers, use that results in immediate computer response to direct student contact.

**Microcomputers were described in the survey as including a TV-like screen for display, a typewriter keyboard, logic and internal memory, some means of secondary storage for programs, and costing up to $5,000 each.

than 40 percent identified each of two such needs: teacher training and a greater range of instructional computer programs. About one-third of the districts felt that assistance in planning an educational computer program and technical assistance in support of the program were needed. Additionally, almost one-third specified financial assistance as an "other" need.

The survey was requested by the Department of Education's Task Force on Educational Technology. It was conducted by NCES's contractor, Westat, a research firm in Rockville, Maryland, using NCES's Fast Response Survey System (FRSS). In late October 1980, questionnaires were sent to a national sample of 579 districts, representing the 15,834 districts in the Nation. A response rate of 97 percent was achieved.

To obtain additional copies of this preliminary report, information about the survey or FRSS, or be placed on the mailing list to receive the forthcoming final report, contact the FRSS Project Officer, Jeanette Goor, National Center for Education Statistics, Room 620, Presidential Building, 6525 Belcrest Road, Hyattsville, Maryland 20782.

Table 1
Public school districts providing students access to at least one computer for educational purposes: United States, 1980

(Table entries are school districts providing access.)

| Type of access | Type of school, by grade level | | | | More than one level |
| | Total (at least one level) | Elementary level | Secondary level | Combined elem/sec schools and special schools | |
	(1)	(2)	(3)	(4)	(5)
At least one microcomputer or one terminal	7,606	2,196	6,616	678	1,884
	(in percents of column 1)				
At least one microcomputer or one terminal	7,606	29	87	9	25
At least one microcomputer	6,631	29	84	9	22
At least one terminal	2,973	21	99	5	25
At least one microcomputer *and* one terminal	1,998	17	95	3	15

Note: Column 1 represents the unduplicated number of districts providing access to computers at any level. Since some districts make computers available at more than one type of school, the percents in columns 2 - 4 include duplicated counts of districts. The difference between the total duplicated counts (col. 2 - 4) and the unduplicated count (col. 1) represents the percent of districts providing computer access at more than one level (col. 5).

Table 2
Availability of computers within districts: United States, fall 1980

a. By number of computers per district

Number of available computers per district	Districts providing access	
	To microcomputers	To terminals
At least one	6,631	2,973
	(in percents)	
At least one	<u>100</u>	<u>100</u>
One	40	35
2-4	37	37
5-10	13	14
11-20	6	6
More than 20	3	8

b. By number of schools with access, per district

Number of schools with access, per district	Districts providing access	
	At elementary schools	At secondary schools
At least one	2,196	6,616
	(in percents)	
At least one	<u>100</u>	<u>100</u>
One	56	68
2-4	24	25
5-10	13	6
11-20	4	†*
More than 20	3	*

†Fewer than 1 percent.
*Note: Percents may not sum to 100 because of rounding.

Appendix V
Organizations

The following organizations are sources for a variety of information on microcomputers and computer literacy:

American Association of School Administrators (AASA), 1801 N Moore St, Arlington, VA 22209.

American Educational Research Association (AERA), 1126 16th St, NW, Washington, DC 20046.

Association for Computing Machinery, 1133 Avenue of the Americas, New York, NY 10036.

Association for Educational Communications and Technology (AECT), 1126 16th St, NW, Washington, DC 20036.

Association for Educational Data Systems (AEDS), 1201 16th St, NW, Washington, DC 20036.

Association for the Development of Computer-Based Instructional Systems (ADCIS), Bond Hall, Western Washington University Computer Center, Bellingham, WA 98225.

Computer-Using Educators, c/o Don McKell, Independence High School, 1776 Education Park Dr, San Jose, CA 95133.

Human Resources Organization, 300 N Washington St, Alexandria, VA 22314.

International Council for Computers in Education (ICCE), Department of Computer and Information Science, University of Oregon, Eugene, OR 97403.

Library and Information Technology Association (LITA), American Library Association, 50 E Huron St, Chicago, IL 60611.

Microcomputer Education Application Network, Suite 800, 1030 15th St, NW, Washington, DC 20036.

Minnesota Educational Computing Consortium (MECC), 2520 Broadway Dr, St Paul, MN 55113.

National Association of Secondary School Principals (NASSP), 1904 Association Dr, Reston, VA 22091.

National Council of Social Studies (NCSS), 3615 Wisconsin Ave, NW, Washington, DC 20016.

National Council of Teachers of English (NCTE), 1111 Kenyon Rd, Urbana, IL 61801.

National Council of Teachers of Mathematics, 1906 Association Dr, Reston, VA 22091.

National Science Teachers Association (NSTA), 1742 Connecticut Ave, NW, Washington, DC 20009.

National Videodisc/Microcomputer Institute, Utah State University, Logan, UT 84322.

Northwest Regional Education Laboratory, 710 SW 2nd St, Portland, OR 98204.

Region IV Education Service Center, Office 863, Houston, TX 77001.

SMUGAL (School Micro-computer Users Group of Alameda County), c/o Glenn Fisher, Alameda County Office of Education, 685 A St, Hayward, CA 94541.

Society for Applied Learning Technology (SALT), 50 Culpeper St, Warrenton, VA 22186.

Society of Data Educators, 983 Fairmeadow Rd, Memphis, TN 38117.

Bibliographies

Computer Literacy Bibliography

by Susan Friel and Nancy Roberts

Code: E—Elementary Grades
J—Junior High School
H—Senior High School
R—Reference

A. COMPUTER APPLICATIONS/SOCIETAL ISSUES

Adams, J. Mack and Douglas H. Haden. *Social Effects of Computer Use and Misuse*. New York: John Wiley & Sons, 1976. (H+,R) Includes introductory chapter on computers, chapters on history, applications, artificial intelligence, misuses of computers, privacy, and the social, economic and philosophical implications.

Ahl, David H. ed. *The Best of Creative Computing*. Vol. 1, Morristown, N.J.: Creative Computing Press, 1976. (R) The best on a variety of topics from *Creative Computing Magazine*.

The Best of Creative Computing, Vol. 2, Morristown, N.J.: Creative Computing Press, 1977. (R) The best on a variety of topics from *Creative Computing Magazine*.

Arbib, Michael. *Computers in the Cybernetic Society*. New York: Academic Press, 1977. (R) Contains some valuable information. Topics covered include information about computers, simulation of complex systems, data banks, artificial intelligence and networks.

Bailey, Richard. *Computer Poems*. Drummond Island, Michigan: Potagannissing Press, 1973. (R) Collection of poems either computer-generated or inspired from random computer-generated "thoughts."

Ball, Marion and Sylvia Chase. *Be a Computer Literate*. Morristown, N.J.: Creative Computing Press, 1977. (E) An introduction to computers and to writing simple programs in BASIC.

Benquai, August. *Computer Crime*. Lexington, VA: D.C. Heath & Co., 1978. (R) Explores strengths and weaknesses of existing legal structure in investigating and prosecuting crimes that involve the use of computers.

Billings, Karen and David Moursund. *Are You Computer Literate?* Forest Grove, OR: Dilithium Press, P.O. Box 92, Dept. CT, 1979. (J,H) Well done book. Covers a variety of computer literacy topics and offers many activities to develop student awareness and understanding of computers.

Davis, William and Allison McCormack. *The Information Age*. Reading, Mass: Addison-Wesley, 1979. (H) Sections include an overview of the computer impact, the basic technology, uses of computers (primarily in data processing), problems and future views.

Dorf, Richard. *Computers and Man: Second Edition*. San Francisco: Boyd and Fraser Publishing Co., 1977. (H+) Beyond the usual computer-literacy topics, includes valuable information in such areas as simulation and games, computers in government systems, in the arts and artificial intelligence and cybernetics.

Graham, Neill. *The Mind Tool: Computers and Their Impact on Society. 2nd Edition*. St. Paul, Minnesota: West Publishing Co., 1980. (J,H) Excellent overview, with short and informative chapters on computer applications in many different areas, as well as introductory programming using BASIC.

Holorien, Martin O. *Computers and Their Societal Impact*. New York: John Wiley & Sons., 1977. (J,H) Includes applications in education, business, government, crime and health. Has a chapter introducing BASIC and a chapter on flowcharting.

Leavitt, Ruth ed. *Artist and Computer*. Morristown, N.J.: Creative Computing Press, 1976. (R) Good discussion (with many pictures) of the computer's role in the artistic process.

McCauley, Carole Spearin. *Computers and Creativity*. New York: Praeger Pub., 1974. Focus is on the creative process and the use of computers in such areas as poetry, graphics, art, music, and dance.

Microcomputer Site Directory: Applications in Educational Settings. Cambridge, MA: Gutman Library, Harvard Graduate School of Education, 1981. (R) The 40-page directory lists more than 250 educational sites across the country where microcomputers are being used for instructional and administrative purposes. Sites are listed by state and a detailed subject index is provided.

Mowskowitz, Abbe. *Inside Information: Computers in Fiction*. Reading, Mass.: Addison-Wesley, 1977. (R) Contains several short science fiction stories.

*Nazzaro, Jean N. ed. *Computer Connections for Gifted Children and Youth*. Reston, VA: The Council for Exceptional Children, 1981. (R) Collection of original and reprint articles arguing that gifted children need computer education as part of their basic education. The text demonstrates programs already in use in schools and homes. Provides basic information and resources for starting and developing computer projects for the gifted.

Nelson, Ted. *Computer Lib/Dream Machines*. Swarthmore, PA: Ted Nelson, Publisher (distributed by The Distributors, 702 S. Michigan, South Bend, IN 46618). (R) Interesting and fun to read. Covers all kinds of thoughts about and uses of computers.

*Papert, Seymour. *Mindstorms: Children, Computers, and Powerful Ideas*. New York: Basic Books, 1980. (R) Reports on the author's work with very young children over the past ten years at the Artificial Intelligence Lab at MIT. Focus is twofold: a discussion of Papert's use of LOGO, a computer language, and Turtle, "an object to think with." Whereas most computer languages are intended for learning content with specific subject areas or for programming, LOGO focuses on the thinking process. The intent of the language is to facilitate both children's thinking and thinking about thinking. The "Turtle" is a device controlled by even elementary children to perform child-developed feats, a result of their powerful thinking—or "mindstorms."

Parker, Donn B. *Crime By Computer*. New York: Charles Schribner's Sons, 1976. (R) Information on the variety of ways computers have been used as tools to aid in committing crimes.

Rothman, Stanley and Charles Mosmann. *Computers and Society*. Chicago: Science Research Associates, 1976. (H) Sections include what computers are, the computer influence in society, how computers are controlled, and a look at the future.

Sanders, Donald H. *Computers and Society*. New York: McGraw-Hill, 1973. (J,H) Includes sections on computers, computer influence in society, selected uses of computers, and a look at the future.

Scientific American. *Computers and Computation*. San Francisco: W. H. Freeman & Co., 1971. (R) Somewhat of a classic, containing readings in such areas as fundamentals of artificial intelligence and computer models.

Silver, Gerald. *The Social Impact of Computers*. New York: Harcourt Brace Jovanovich, 1979. (H) Very good book. Consists of four parts: the beginnings; what computers are; how computers are used; and how computers relate to people. Has good chapter introducing some of the more common privacy and credit laws in effect.

Smith, Robert Ellis. *Privacy, How to Protect What's Left of It*. Garden City, New York: Anchor Press/Doubleday, 1979. (R) Good overview of many of the issues concerning privacy and computerization.

Spencer, Donald D. *Computers in Society: Wheres, Whys and Hows of Computer Use*. Rochelle Park, N.J.: Hayden Book Co., Inc., 1974. (J,H) Chapters focusing on different applications of computers.

*Taylor, Robert P. ed. *The Computer in the School: Tutor, Tool, Tutee*. New York: Teachers College Press, 1981. (R) Brings together nineteen essays by five pioneers in the field of computers in educa-

---

*Added by the editor

tion: Alfred Bork, Thomas Dwyer, Arthur Luehrmann, Seymour Papert, and Patrick Suppes. Discusses the computer's potential and its limitations; defines the role of the teacher and student in discovering new microworlds of learning; and analyzes the probable impact of the new technology on education in the years ahead.

Van Tassel, Dennie L. *The Compleat Computer*. Santa Cruz, CA, University of California: Science Research Associates, Inc., 1976. (R) Collection of readings on a variety of areas related to computers.

Computers, Computers, Computers. New York: Thomas Nelson, Inc., 1977. (R) Variety of short science fiction selections.

Weizenbaum, Joseph. *Computer Power and Human Reason*. San Francisco, CA: W. H. Freeman, 1976. (R) Philosophical discussion of the computer as a metaphor to help better understand our world. Arguments for appropriate uses of computers are presented. Attacks the ethos of The Artificial Intelligence community.

Wessel, Milton R. *Freedom's Edge: The Computer Threat to Society*. Reading, MA: Addison-Wesley Pub. Co., Inc., 1974. (R) Good discussion of a variety of issues involving the use and misuse of computers. Still timely.

B. PROGRAMMING; COMPUTER SCIENCE; WHAT IS A COMPUTER?

Albrecht, Robert. *My Computer Likes Me When I Speak in BASIC*. Menlo Park, CA: Dymax, 1972. (E,J) Intended for beginners. Presents all aspects of BASIC in an elementary way.

Ball, Marion J. *What is a Computer?* Boston: Houghton Mifflin Co, 1972. (E) Short book which clearly describes the development of computers, their operation, how they function and the fundamentals of flowcharting.

Brainerd, Walter S., Charles Goldberg, and Jonathan Gross. *Introduction to Computer Programming*. New York: Harper and Row, 1979. (R) Designed for college students. Excellent reference for providing an introduction to what computers can be programmed to do. Explanations rely on knowledge of general purpose algorithm language that is developed in the text. Transfer of concepts can be made to specific computer languages.

Braude, Michael. *Larry Learns About Computers*. Minneapolis, Minnesota: T.S. Denison Co., Inc., 1972. (E)

Brown, Jerrald R. *INSTANT (Freeze-Dried Computer Programming in) BASIC*. Forest Grove, OR: Dilithium Press, P.O. Box 92, Dept. CT, 1977. (E,J,H) Book for microcomputer programming or DEC BASIC PLUS.

DeRossi, Claude. *Computers: Tools for Today*. Chicago: Children's Press, 1972. (E)

Dwyer, Thomas and Margot Critchfield. *BASIC and the Personal Computer*. Reading, MA: Addison-Wesley, 1978. (H,R) Excellent introductory text to BASIC on the personal computer, with demonstrated computer applications in several areas, including games, art, business and simulation.

Dwyer, Thomas and Michael Kaufman. *A Guided Tour to Computer Programming in BASIC*. Boston: Houghton Mifflin, 1973. (J,H) Consists of three parts: about computers, writing computer programs, and professional computer applications. While written primarily for high school, the style is such that it could be used for upper elementary school.

Finkel, Leroy and Gerald Brown. *BASIC (2nd ed): A Self-Teaching Guide*. New York: John Wiley and Sons, 1978 (H,R) Very good self-teaching text geared to use while sitting at a computer/computer terminal. Can be used, however, without having direct access to a computer.

Foley, Jacobs, Bower and Basten. *Discovery and Structure: Individualizing Mathematics—Flowchart I, II, III*. Reading Mass.: Addison-Wesley Publishing Co., 1970. (E) Each book introduces flowcharting and then applies the use of flowcharts to mathematics.

*Frederick, Franz J. *Guide to Microcomputers*. Washington, DC: AECT Publication Sales, 1980. (R) An "everything you wanted to know about . . ." guide to microcomputers, including computer languages, operating systems, compatible systems, special accessories, timesharing, service and maintenance, potential instructional and media center applications, and an extensive list of resources.

Graham, Neill. *Introduction to Computer Science*. St. Paul, Minn: West Publishing Company, 1979. (R) Designed for college students, this book pro-

*Added by the editor

vides an excellent reference. It covers the topics of algorithms and programs, data structures, file organization and processing and introduction to numerical methods using an informal algorithmic language or pseudocode. Transfer of concepts can be made to specific computer languages.

Matt, Fred C. *Instructo Paper Computer*. Paoli, Penn: Instructo/McGraw-Hill, 1979. (J,H) Designed to provide experience in operating, and understanding the operation of a computer.

McQuigg, James D. and Alta M. Harness. *Flowcharting*. Boston: Houghton Mifflin, 1970. (J,H) Short workbook on flowcharting that provides a good introduction.

Moursund, David. *Basic Programming for Computer Literacy*. New York: McGraw-Hill, Inc., 1978. (H) Designed for the computer programming component of Computer Literacy Instruction (BASIC). It begins with an introduction to problem solving and focuses on reading programs and modifying programs before program writing.

Scharff, Robert. *The How and Why Wonder Book of Robots and Electronic Brains*. New York: Wonder Books, Division of Grosset and Dunlap. (E)

Spencer, Donald. *Computers in Action: How Computers Work*. Rochelle Park, N.J.: Hayden Book Co, 1974. (J)

The Story of Computers. Ormond Beach, CA: Abacus Computer Corporation, 1975. (J)

Srivastana, Jane Jonas. *Computers*. New York: Thomas Crowell Co., 1972. (E)

Stern, Nancy. *Flowcharting—A Self-Teaching Guide*. New York: John Wiley, 1975. (J,H) A clearly written introductory presentation of the use of flowcharting as a step in organizing a computer program.

Walter, Russ. *The Secret Guide to Computers*. Vol 1: *BASIC;* Vol. 2: *Applications;* Vol. 3: *Languages;* Vol. 4: *Systems;* Vol. C1: *Hassles In Basic;* Vol. C2: "*. . . Tough Questions.*" Boston, MA: Russ Walter, 92 St. Botolph Street, 02116. (J,H,R) Worth the reasonable investment. Contain much information on several areas.

Weissman, Kenneth. *School Basic*. Hanover, N.H.: Kiewit Computer Center. Dartmouth College, 1970. (J,H) Simply written. Geared to secondary mathematics curricula.

C. TEACHING RESOURCES

Ahl, David. *Basic Computer Games*. Morristown, N.J.: Creative Computing Press. (E,J,S,R)
More Basic Computer Games. Morristown, N.J.: Creative Computing press. (E,J,S,R) Sequel to the first book, *Basic Computer Games*.

Apple Personal Computer Magazine. "Computers in Education," Vol. 1, No. 1. (E) A well written description of several different examples of computer uses in education along with a look to the future.

*"Computers and the Handicapped." *Computer 14* (January 1981): 9–54. (R) The January 1981 issue of *Computer* magazines is devoted to the topic "Computers and the Handicapped." Articles and authors included are: "Computing and the Handicapped: A Promising Alliance" by Margaret Giannini; "Computing and the Handicapped: The Challenge in Education" by Henry Blaszczyk; "Intelligent Prosthetic Devices" by M. A. Rahimi; "Communication Devices for the Nonvocal Disabled" by Andrew Thomas; "The Impact of Microcomputers on Devices to Aid the Handicapped" by Aylor, Johnson, and Ramey; and "Practical Application of Microcomputers to Aid the Handicapped" by Gregg Vanderheiden.

Computers in Education Resource Handbook. Eugene, OR: University of Oregon, Dept of Computer Science, 1976. (R)

Edwards, J. B., Ellis, A. S., Richardson, D. E., Holznagel, D. and D. Klassen. *Computer Applications in Instruction: A Teacher's Guide to Selection and Use*. Hanover, N.H.: Time Share Corporation, 1978. (R) Very good general introduction to uses of computers in education. Includes four sections: the essentials of hardware; instructional uses of computers; selecting computerbased instructional units; readings on computers in the curriculum.

Ellis, Allan B. *The Use and Misuse of Computers in Education*. San Francisco, CA: McGraw-Hill, 1974. (R) Good thoughtful overview of computers and the role they should have in education.

Harris, Diana ed. *Proceedings of the National Educational Computing Conference*. Iowa City: University of Iowa, Weeg Computing Center, 1979. (R) A collection of 69 papers presented at the first

*Added by the editor

NECC. Topics range across all educational levels and disciplines.

Illinois Series on Educational Applications of Computers: Computing-Teacher Education Papers. Urbana, Ill: University of Illinois, Dept of Secondary Education, 396 Education Building, 1979. An excellent collection of 22 booklets discussing all aspects of computers in education. A must for anyone's library. Can be ordered for the amazing cost of 50¢ each.

Kosel, Marge and Geraldine Carlstrom. *Elementary, My Dear Computer*. Lauderdale, MI: Minnesota Educational Computing Consortium, 2520 Broadway Dr., 1978. (E) Guide designed as a reference for use in teaching students the basic idea of what a computer is and how it operates. It also shows teachers how to incorporate use of computers into daily classroom experiences.

Kurshan, Barbara. *Computer Literacy: Practical Ways to Teach the Basic Mathematical Skills*. Richmond, Virginia: Virginia Council of Teachers of Mathematics, 1978. (E,J,H) Summary of what to do and how to do it in teaching computer literacy for Elementary, Junior High and High School.

Lidtke, Doris. *Computers and Computer Applications: A Film Bibliography*. Portland, Oregon: Oregon Council for Computer Education, 1977. (R)

Minnesota Educational Computing Consortium. 2520 Broadway Dr., Lauderdale, MN 55113. (E) Programs available for purchase specifically designed for elementary students. Very valuable resource for software.

Molnar, Andrew. "The Next Great Crisis in American Education—Computer Literacy." *EDUCOM Bulletin*. Spring, 1979. (R) A strong argument, by the program Director of the Division of Science Education Development and Research of The National Science Foundation for the importance of making our population computer literate.

Papert, Seymour. "Computers and Learning" in *The Computer Age: A Twenty-Year View*. Michael L. Dertouzos and Joel Moses eds. Cambridge, MA: The MIT Press, 1979. (R) Excellent summary of Papert's views as result of years of work with children and LOGO.
"Teaching Children Thinking" *Logo Memo No. 2*. Cambridge, MA: MIT, Artificial Intelligence Laboratory. (R) Exciting discussion of the potential power of creative use of computers with children.

People's Computer Company. *What to do After You Hit Return*. Menlo Park, CA: 1263 El Camino Real, Box E. (E,J,H,R) Collection of games, to be played using a computer. Each game is explained and listings are provided in the back of the book.

Rice, Jean. *My Friend—The Computer: Teacher's Guide and Activity Book to Accompany "My Friend—The Computer."* Minneapolis: T. S. Dennison & company, 1976. (E) The student book and teacher's guide together focus on seven topics: what is a computer, how it works, how it is used, the history of computers, input/output devices, flow charts and writing simple BASIC programs. The teacher's guide also provides transparencies, lists of objectives, resources and suggestions for planning.

Ricketts, Dick, project director. *Course Goals in Computer Education K-12*. Portland, Oregon: Commercial Educational Distributing Services, P.O. Box 8723, 1979. (R) Contains goals for use in planning and evaluating Elementary and Secondary school curricula in computer education (which includes such topics as computer literacy computer science, computers and society, data processing, and computer programming).

Documents and Reports*

Academic Computing Directory: A Search for Exemplary Institutions Using Computers for Learning and Teaching. Alexandria, VA: Human Resources Research Organization, 1977. (ED 148 396, not available from EDRS.)

Identifies some of the schools, colleges, and universities successfully using computers for learning and teaching in the United States. Compiled to help teachers, administrators, computer center workers, and other educators exchange information, ideas, programs, and courses, it lists contacts who are willing to share their knowledge with others. Ninety-four elementary and secondary schools, 71 public school districts, 37 community colleges, 158 private and public colleges and universities, and 7 public access institutions are listed. Arranged geographically by state for each type of institution, entries include information on reasons for inclusion, enrollment, users, illustrative applications, computers, terminal, public information, and contact. A list of exemplary institutions in academic computing is attached.

Allenbrand, Bob, and others eds. *Course Goals in Computer Education, K-12.* Portland, OR: Commercial-Educational Distributing Services, 1979. 217p. (ED 194 074, order from Commercial Educational Distributing Services, PO Box 8723, Portland, OR 97208; publication #617, $13.50, or EDRS.)

Intended as guidelines for planning and evaluating elementary and secondary school curricula in computer education, the program and course goals presented address only general program outcomes and specific course outcomes, leaving behavioral and planning objectives to be determined at the classroom teacher level. Two taxonomies are provided: the first describes the three types of goals in this collection—knowledge (information), process (skills and abilities), and values (attitudes and opinions); the second classifies the components of a specific subject.

Baker, Justine. *Computers in the Curriculum. Fastback 82.* Bloomington, IN: Phi Delta Kappa Educational Foundation, 1976. 45p. (ED 133 166, EDRS.)

Discusses computer education for teachers, reports the results of a nationwide survey on what teacher training institutions are doing about computer education, and looks into computer education trends in American school districts. Additionally, briefly discusses results of a national survey of superintendents' attitudes concerning the role of the computer in the classroom and the training of teachers using computers for instruction. An annotated bibliography on the use of computers in education is included.

"Choosing a Classroom Microcomputer." Herstein, E. May 1979. 2p. Paper presented at the Association for Educational Data Systems 17th Annual Conference, 14–18 May 1979, Detroit, MI. (Reprint: AEDS, 1201 16th St, NW, Washington, DC 20036.)

Suggests several criteria: ease of use, variety of input and display devices, expandability, and others.

Dennis, J. Richard. *Teacher Education in Use of Computers.* The Illinois Series on Educational Application of Computers, No. 1e. Urbana, IL: University of Illinois, Department of Secondary Education, 1979. (ED 183 181, not available from EDRS.)

Two model programs have been developed for preservice and inservice training of teachers in the instructional applications of computers. The preservice model features a background in computer science, foundations of instructional computing using a total school view and content specific view, a task-centered practicum in instructional computing, and practice teaching. The inservice trianing model consists of three stages: (1) initial literacy, (2) implementation, and (3) maintenance or growth. Curriculum maps are provided for both programs and three references are listed.

"Elementary Computers; L'Anse Creuse Public Schools, Atwood Elementary." Hollingsworth, J. May 1979. 2p. Paper presented at the Association for Educa-

---

*The entries in this section were taken from searches of ERIC and ECER. Some of the annotations have been edited or abbreviated.

tional Data Systems 17th Annual Conference, 14–18 May 1979, Detroit, MI. (Reprint: AEDS, 1201 16th St, NW, Washington, DC 20036.

The use of microcomputers reinforces and enriches the learning experiences of elementary students.

"Implementation of the Apple II Microcomputer in Minnesota." Borry L., and Arneson, J. May 1979. 3p. Paper presented at the Association for Educational Data Systems 17th Annual Conference, 14–18 May 1979, Detroit, MI. (Reprint: AEDS, 1201 16th St, NW, Washington, DC 20036.)

Describes Minnesota's efforts to implement the Apple II microcomputer into schools throughout the state. Points addressed include: status of microcomputers; the microcomputer study; the bid for a state contract for microcomputers; teacher inservice training; applications software development, acquisition, and distribution; and demonstration of selected courseware.

"Hardware Developments; Microcomputers and Processors; Grade School/High School Instructional and Computer-Aided Design." Papers presented at the Association for Educational Data Systems Annual Convention, 3–7 May 1976, Phoenix, AZ. Some parts may be marginally legible due to print quality of original. (Reprint: AEDS, 1201 16th St, NW, Washington, DC 20036; ED 125 662, EDRS.)

Compiled are ten papers describing computer hardware and computer use in elementary and secondary school instruction. An oral/aural terminal is described, followed by two papers about the use of minicomputers and microprocessors. Seven papers discuss various uses of the computer in elementary and high school instruction: to plot and display conic sections and environmental designs, to help teach reading skills, and to generate tests or homework exercises. One paper recommends the use of games in computerized drills, and another explains computerized demonstration of some mathematics principles. The importance of the school computer coordinator is outlined by the Minnesota Educational Computing Consortium.

"Micro in a Macro World: Curriculum Development for the Microcomputer." Rose, S. Y. May 1979. 4p. Paper presented at the Association for Educational Data Systems 17th Annual Conference, 14–18 May 1979, Detroit, MI. (Reprint: AEDS, 1201 16th St, NW, Washington, DC 20036.)

The Dallas Independent School District is adapting concepts from its existing baseline curriculum for microcomputer CAI use. Elementary level math and reading strands are being developed and peripheral hardware (video disks and computer controlled audio) is being tested for possible inclusion. The major limiting factor

encountered thus far is the microcomputer's restricted memory. CAI curriculum must be appropriately adapted to the characteristics of both the microcomputers and the learner population. Includes seven references.

"Micros in the Classroom." Gerhold, G., and Kheriaty, L. April 1980. 3p. Paper presented at the "Computer-Based Instruction: A New Decade" 1980 Conference, 31 March–3 April 1980, Washington, DC. (Reprint: Association for the Development of Computer-Based Instructional Systems, Bellingham, WA.)

Any system worthy of serious consideration for the classroom must combine the virtues of good mini-based and maxi-based systems (e.g., good author language, disk storage, full computational power) with the advantage of micro-based systems (e.g., graphics, flexibility). This paper describes such a system, which also offers the advantage of economy. Includes two references.

"The Microcomputer as a Communication Device for Nonvocal Children with Limited Manual Dexterity." Shirriff, W. April 1980. 6p. Paper presented at the "Computer-Based Instruction: A New Decade" 1980 Conference, 31 March–3 April 1980, Washington, DC. (Reprint: Association for the Development of Computer-Based Instructional Systems, Bellingham, WA.)

Cerebral palsy frequently limits speech capability as well as manual dexterity. In some cases the operation of an electric typewriter is impossible, even with the use of a keyboard mask. This paper discusses the use of the Radio Shack Level II TRS-80 and the 16K Commodore PET (two of the microcomputers most commonly available to school systems) as communication devices for nonvocal children who have limited manual dexterity.

"Microcomputers in the Elementary School: What Experience Has Taught Us So Far." Jokela, W. April 1980. 2p. Paper presented at the AEDS 18th Annual Convention. "A Gateway to the Use of Computers in Education," 13–16 April 1980, St. Louis, MO. (Reprint: AEDS, 1201 16th St, NW, Washington, DC 20036.)

Through a bid process in October 1978, the Apple II microcomputer was specifically selected for support and software development. A little more than a year later, over 850 Apple microcomputers were purchased by educational institutions in Minnesota. This paper presents tips on the caretaking and use of equipment, which the author has learned from viewing the use of microcomputers in elementary schools in Minnesota.

Milner, S. D. *The Practitioner: A Newsletter for the On-Line Administrator*. October 6, 1979. 12p. (Available from: Research Department of the National Association of Secondary School Principals, 1904 Association Dr, Reston, VA 22091.)

> Entitled ''Microcomputers . . . The Future Is Now,'' the newsletter describes a typical system, applications, how to select a system, sources of information, and some examples of the variety of purposes for which microcomputers are currently being used in schools.

Muiznieks, V. *A General Introduction to Microcomputers*. The Illinois Series on Educational Application of Computers, No. 26. Urbana, IL: University of Illinois, November 1978. (ED 178 054, EDRS.)

> Includes a description of microcomputers, the basic concepts of their operation, how bits are used, the computer memory and control and advanced concepts.

''Renaissance Man: The Key Components.'' Association for Educational Data Systems Proceedings: 17th Annual Convention, 14–18 May 1979. (Reprint AEDS, 1201 16th St, NW, Washington, DC 20036; ED 175 446, EDRS.)

> The 86 papers presented cover educational applications of computers in CAI, instructional and learning processes, computer-related curriculum, educational administration, computer resources, and data-center administration.

Rosen, Elizabeth, and Hicks, Bruce. *Computer Literacy*. Urbana, IL: University of Illinois Department of Secondary Education, June 1977. 10p. (ED 142 200, EDRS.)

> Briefly reviews books dealing with simple concepts and terminology related to computers, and recommends those which are better for children and high school students. A bibliography lists all books considered.

Sledge, D. comp. *Microcomputers in Education: A Selection of Introductory Articles*. London: Council for Educational Technology, 1979. (Available from CET, 3 Devonshire St, London W1N 2BA, England.)

> The 14 articles included in this publication give a general introduction and provide background reading on microcomputers in education. Aspects covered include the nature of the microcomputer, its management, and potential uses; types and capability of equipment; purchase and running costs; various languages; and available software.

Index

Compiled by Linda Schexnaydre